"When students don't 'get it,' teachers (and parents) need a better answer than 'try harder!' This book gets teachers pointed in the right direction by asking and answering the questions: What is the underlying brain process that needs to be strengthened to help a particular student progress? And how can I do that?"

—**Bill Jackson,** president, Great Schools

"The notion that educational administrators should first and foremost think of themselves as *learning leaders* is reason enough to explore this book. In the fast-moving world of educational reform, this work stresses the importance of putting the science of learning front and center in the current debate about how to improve schools. I highly recommend it to a wide audience of those committed to the maxim that effective teaching results in higher student learning."

—**Michael Spagna,** Ph.D., dean, Michael D. Eisner College of Education, California State University, Northridge

"*Schools for All Kinds of Minds* is for all kinds of teachers. There's more than one way to learn and more than one way to teach, but only one way to have high expectations for the students in our schools. This book helps teachers with high expectations turn that thought into action."

—**Mike Feinberg,** co-founder of KIPP (Knowledge is Power Program)

"This book provides school leaders with a framework and strategies that will help them move beyond an ever-growing list of accountability mandates to a focus on all students as learners that can reach their true potential."

—**Eric Hirsch,** director of special projects, New Teacher Center

"*Schools for All Kinds of Minds* is a book for the present and the future. In the present, it provides tangible steps to better understand how different students learn and what to do about it. As we seek to transform our education system into a student-centric one for the future, this book should be a vital part of the conversation around what that system should look like and how we get there."

—**Michael B. Horn,** executive director of education, Innosight Institute, coauthor of *Disrupting Class*

"This book shows educators that there is a way to make schools work for the benefit of *all* students. It inspires teachers to think about learning in a way that successfully supports and accommodates the wide variety of learners in today's classrooms."

—**Mary Mannix,** learning specialist, Indian Creek School (Crownsville, MD)

"All educators who are genuinely interested in improving student success, and their own knowledge about learning, will benefit from the research and practical suggestions in this book."

—**Ian Adamson,** retired superintendent of Alternative Programs, Curriculum, Instruction and Special Education Support Services, Peel District School Board, Ontario, Canada

"The perfect book for dedicated and committed leaders who struggle in a woefully imperfect educational system."

—**William Broderick,** head of school, Fort Worth Academy, U.S. Department of Education National Distinguished Principal

"For more than a decade, All Kinds of Minds has led the way in translating neuroscience into educational practice. Codifying this impressive body of work, this book is a must-read for any educational leader who is truly committed to helping every child become a successful learner."

—**Paul Yellin,** director, The Yellin Center for Student Success, associate professor of pediatrics, NYU School of Medicine

"A book for any school or district leader who believes data-driven decision making involves more than end-of-year test scores, *Schools for All Kinds of Minds* is a very accessible review of using the science of how children learn to support and spur dramatic learning gains."

—**JB Buxton,** principal consultant, The Education Innovations Group, Former Deputy State Superintendent, N.C. Department of Public Instruction

"Students everywhere deserve principals, district leaders, and teacher leaders who have not only read this book, but who have taken the ideas in it to heart—and who have worked in partnership with students and their families to create schools and classrooms that teach to all kinds of minds."

—**Gene Thompson-Grove,** director, Professional Development and Special Initiatives Public Schools of Brookline, national facilitator, The School Reform Initiative, Inc.

"This essential book puts the customization of school-based learning opportunities front and center with accessible descriptions of how our brains work and concrete tools for maximizing their full potential. A must-read for educational leaders at all levels."

—**Sandra J. Stein,** chief executive officer, NYC Leadership Academy

"This book is valuable for educators, policymakers, and parents who wish to implement an improvement-oriented learning culture in our schools. If the recommendations in the book are implemented, there will be a breakdown of barriers between special and regular education and an acceleration of the transformation of analog schooling into new, evidence-based digital learning systems."

—**Susan Tave Zelman,** former superintendent, Ohio Department of Public Instruction, senior vice president, chief advisor and system consultant for education policy, Corporation for Public Broadcasting

"If you are looking for practical, researched ways to improve student attitudes or increase student achievement, this is a great book to read. It is clear, comprehensive, and compelling."

—**Joe Nathan,** director, Center for School Change, Macalester College, St. Paul, Minnesota

Schools for All Kinds of Minds

BOOSTING STUDENT SUCCESS BY
EMBRACING LEARNING VARIATION

Mary-Dean Barringer
Craig Pohlman
Michele Robinson

Foreword by Paul Orfalea

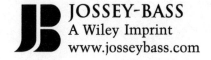 JOSSEY-BASS
A Wiley Imprint
www.josseybass.com

Library of Congress Cataloging-in-Publication Data

Barringer, Mary-Dean, 1953-
    Schools for all kinds of minds: boosting student success by embracing learning variation / Mary-Dean Barringer, Craig Pohlman, Michele Robinson; Foreword by Paul Orfalea.—1st ed.
      p. cm.
    Includes bibliographical references and index.
    ISBN 978-0-470-50515-1 (cloth)
      1. Educational psychology. 2. Learning, Psychology of. 3. Educational technology—Study and teaching. I. Pohlman, Craig. II. Robinson, Michele, 1968- III. Title.
    LB1051.B2494 2010
    370.15—dc22

2009046310

Printed in the United States of America
FIRST EDITION
HB Printing   10 9 8 7 6 5 4 3 2

CONTENTS

FOREWORD: AMERICA NEEDS ALL
KINDS OF MINDS

In May 2002, I found myself staring at the cover of *Fortune* magazine. The lead article was "Overcoming Dyslexia" and inside was my story. The author noticed a strange and common theme as she talked to the world's most successful CEOs and other high achievers. Many of us seemed pretty hopeless as kids, labeled dyslexic or "learning disabled." Yet, all of us have been enormously successful in our careers. Our different ways of learning, thinking, and seeing the world have energized America's entertainment industry, launched successful companies and brands, won Nobel Prizes and Olympic medals, and designed diverse creations from famous works of art to Nerf balls. As Dr. Sally Shaywitz of Yale University said in that article, "Dyslexics are overrepresented in the top ranks of people who are unusually insightful, who bring a new perspective, who think out of the box" (Morris, 2002, p. 56).

The recognition of my learning differences came early. I failed second grade and spent part of my third grade year in a class of children regarded as "mentally retarded," which goes to show how little was known of individual learning differences at that time. My school years were distinguished by invitations to leave practically every high school in Los Angeles. My parents painfully watched their child struggle to learn and tried everything they could think of to help me read, hoping my self-confidence would not completely disappear. My teachers were also frustrated. They worked hard, but too few people understood dyslexia or ADD in those days. A well-meaning educator told my mother to enroll me in trade school so I could become a carpet layer.

Learning differences are far more prevalent than most people think. About one in seven kids struggle in school because of known "disabilities," and that translates into *millions* of kids. Without help, the outlook is often grim. Many of these kids will be branded as intellectually inferior, and never get close to realizing their full capabilities—a major loss to themselves, their families, and our country.

I was fortunate to have parents who knew I was capable of so much more and convinced me that once I was out of school, I would succeed. I got through college because my dyslexia and ADHD fostered risk taking, problem solving, and resilience. I somehow figured out my own strategies to deal with my learning difference. I also learned that I saw things others didn't. Working on a collaborative project with fellow students at USC's Marshall School of Business gave me the idea that led to Kinko's. As the group's "gopher," I had to make copies in the library's reserved book room. The long lines and inconvenience triggered my entrepreneurial instincts.

For over a decade, the Orfalea Foundations have encouraged parents and schools to see all children as distinct learners with unique profiles of strengths and weaknesses. We've also worked tirelessly to change the public perception of specific learning conditions like dyslexia and ADD. We know that a struggle with learning does not mean you're disabled; it means you learn differently. The goal of my autobiography, *Copy This* (Workman Publishing, 2005), was to provide hope and optimism to kids and their families who are feeling as frustrated in their classrooms as I did in mine.

My wife, Natalie, and I hold this fundamental belief: When faced with a child who learns in very different ways, you first work to discover and emphasize strengths. As I've learned firsthand, it is your strengths that are the foundation of a successful adult life. I've learned to love how my mind works and firmly believe it is the reason for the success I've enjoyed.

This book describes an approach that will help school leaders transform our schools into learning centers for all kinds of students. The key to this approach is helping educators really understand how to prevent students from needless struggle, while building on their strengths and assets. Science and brain research are helping us all understand how people vary in their learning. All Kinds of Minds has put this knowledge into programs and resources for teachers, parents, and students. The result is a better understanding of how each of us learns and an approach to teaching that provides hope and optimism for *all* students, building confidence that they *can* learn and faith that their schools can help them.

Our world faces increasingly complex challenges every day. Yes, we need our students to graduate with the twenty-first-century skills and knowledge that will keep our economies sound, our democracies stable, and our communities thriving. But more than ever, America needs the kinds of minds that generate new perspectives, seek solutions, and discover emerging opportunities. Those are the minds of many of the students in your schools today who, at first glance, look a lot like the struggling student I was in school. I invite you to take a second look at the individuals who walk through your school doors. Join us in helping as many kids as possible become more aware of their unique talents and more confident in their learning abilities—and help us rescue the wonderful potential that may otherwise be lost.

January 2010   Paul Orfalea

References

Morris, B. "Overcoming Dyslexia." *Fortune*, 2002, *145*(10), 54–70.

Orfalea, P., and Marsh, A. *Copy This: Lessons from a Hyperactive Dyslexic Who Turned a Bright Idea into One of America's Best Companies.* New York: Workman, 2005.

To Roch Hillenbrand
Chair, Board of Trustees
All Kinds of Minds Institute

Your support and leadership enables us to continue the work
to ensure that all kinds of minds find all kinds of success.

ACKNOWLEDGMENTS

Our first thank you goes to you, the reader. Purchasing this book helps our not-for-profit organization in two ways. You are willing to consider how our approach to helping all students who struggle with some aspect of learning might work in your school. With the proceeds from this book going to All Kinds of Minds, you are also supporting our organization as we continue our efforts to equip educators with a science of learning so that all students are ensured success in school and life.

If we could have five authors on the title page, you would see the names of two of our colleagues who made major contributions to this book. Dr. Cynthia Crenshaw designed professional development exercises for learning leaders as well as brought greater texture and depth to our school case studies. Susan Gallagher is the most amazing project manager a team could have. Her depth of knowledge of our work combined with her extraordinary editing and management skills were truly the backbone of this effort. Susan brings a spirit of adventure and a disposition for tolerance to any task.

We are blessed to have dozens of "All Kinds of Minds" family contributing to this work. Within our organization, Melanie Mason and Julie Schmidt helped with the visual support for the book, from the cover design to graphics. They also lent their critical guidance to earlier drafts of the book. Darla Iuliucci, Adrianne Gilbert, Andrea O'Neal, Lisa Fox, Mary Jo Dunnington, Katie O'Neal, and Sharon Kepley all contributed research, insights, writing, and helping hands at critical junctures. As the three main authors, we wish that every collaborative project we engage in could embody the attributes of this writing effort: respect, critical friends, skillful organization and time management, flexibility, humor, and high energy. Any author will tell you it takes a village to produce a book—and the "villagers" at All Kinds of Minds certainly picked up a great deal of work for us while we embarked on this endeavor. Thank you all for juggling myriad things that we might have let slip through the cracks.

Over the years, we've worked with many schools, organizations, and institutions that have helped to bring our programs to nearly 50,000 educators. We owe a debt of gratitude to those who have served as professional development providers and lent the talents of their staff to this work: Bank Street College (New York), Cattaraugus-Allegany BOCES (New York), Children's Health Council (California), Christian Learning Center (Michigan), Dunn Institute (Rhode Island), Etta Israel Center and California State University at Northridge (California), Forsyth Country Day School (North Carolina), Holland Hall (Oklahoma), Houston Independent School District (Texas), Learning Center of North Texas, New York City Board of Education, Peel District School Board (Canada), Oak Hill School (Switzerland), and Old Trail School (Ohio), along with our state contracts with the departments of education in North Carolina, Oklahoma, and South Carolina. The stories and vignettes in this book all spring from the efforts of these organizations to bring All Kinds of Minds programs to schools and educators.

An all-star cast of professionals provided feedback and guidance at different stages of this book. We are grateful for their wisdom on so many fronts: Ian Adamson, Sara Ankrapp, Barnett Berry, Janet Boucher, Julie Brothers, Ann Byrd, Bill Broderick, JB Buxton, Barbara Freeman, Eric Hirsch, Michael Horn, Kathi Howard, Mary Mannix, Arlene Mullin, Shari Nickle, Michael O'Brien, Stacy Parker-Fisher,

Marshall Raskind, Marcey Regan, Max Roach, Pat Sinelli, Michael Spagna, Sandra Stein, Liz Swearingen, Gene Thompson-Grove, Glenda Walker, and Claire Wurtzel. A special "shout out" to Margie McAneny at Jossey-Bass, who first conceived the idea that this book was an important contribution to helping all children learn.

Nonprofits don't survive over a decade without extraordinary guidance and support from trustees and donors. All Kinds of Minds is no exception, and we are indebted to the dozens of individuals who have served in these roles since 1995. In particular, Sally Bowles has supported this organization at key junctures in its evolution.

Last, we must thank our cofounders. Working with AKOM's first CEO, Mark Grayson, Charles Schwab led the charge to build and fund a world class organization. The genius of learning expert Dr. Mel Levine provided the neurodevelopmental framework and philosophy that is the foundation of the work at the All Kinds of Minds Institute.

Since 1995, hundreds of employees have contributed to building this organization from the initial groundbreaking efforts of a few visionaries, including pioneering learning specialists Ann Hobgood and Martha Reed. We hope that this book honors the many contributions of these individuals to our knowledge base, programs and outreach, and advocacy to ensure that no child has to struggle needlessly to learn.

ABOUT THE AUTHORS

Mary-Dean Barringer is the Chief Executive Officer of All Kinds of Minds, a nonprofit Institute that translates ground-breaking research from neuroscience and other disciplines on how children learn—and vary in their learning—into a powerful framework that educators can use in their schools.

Throughout her path in education, Mary-Dean has dedicated herself to keeping America focused on learning—making sure schools are the most effective learning environments for all children. She was a founding board member of the National Board for Professional Teaching Standards and then served as Vice President of Outreach and Mobilization from 1990–2000. Her core responsibilities and achievements involved working with state policymakers and national organizations to develop financial and other incentives to encourage teachers to seek National Board Certification. By 2000, 38 states and 200 districts had embraced the program that grew in volume from 200 in the first year to 14,000 six years later.

Mary-Dean started her career as teacher of exceptional needs students in Michigan. As a special education teacher for 13 years, Mary-Dean received numerous awards and recognition for her innovation and advocacy, including the 1985 Council for Exceptional Children's

National Teacher of the Year award and induction in 2008 into the Eastern Michigan University College of Education Hall of Fame.

Craig Pohlman, Ph.D., is the Director of Mind Matters at Southeast Psych, a learning assessment and consultation program in Charlotte, North Carolina. The mission of Southeast Psych (www.southeast psych.com) is to put psychology into the hands of as many people as possible to enhance their lives. Craig began his career teaching science to elementary and middle school students in New York City. He later earned his doctorate in school psychology at the University of North Carolina at Chapel Hill (UNC-CH), where he trained at The Clinical Center for the Study of Development and Learning, University of North Carolina School of Medicine. After an internship in the Dallas Public Schools, he returned to UNC-CH for a fellowship, later earning appointments as Clinical Assistant Professor and as Clinical Scientist. Prior to joining Southeast Psych, he was Senior Clinical Scholar at All Kinds of Minds and Senior Neurodevelopmentalist at the Success in Mind clinic in Durham, North Carolina.

A licensed psychologist, Craig has conducted or supervised thousands of assessments of struggling learners and has trained thousands of professionals on assessment techniques. He also has designed systems and tools to help others integrate neurodevelopmental assessment into their work with students. His previous books are *Revealing Minds*, a hands-on guide for professionals who assess students facing learning challenges, and *How Can My Kid Succeed in School?*, which describes a process for parents and teachers to better understand a child's strengths and weaknesses.

Michele Robinson has dedicated the past decade to the work of All Kinds of Minds, serving in a variety of roles to support and advance the mission of the Institute. She has developed program curricula, trained facilitators, supported research, translated the knowledge base, and personally taught thousands of educators the All Kinds of Minds approach. Her recent work has been focused on schoolwide application of this model. Michele's use of the AKOM approach transformed her own teaching practice and inspired her to join the revolution led by this visionary organization. Prior to her work at All Kinds of Minds, Michele earned her master of education degree in elementary education from the University of North Carolina at Charlotte and taught students in grades 1–5 for nine years.

INTRODUCTION: AN ENDURING DILEMMA

Millions of students will struggle in school today. Just as they do every day.

In classrooms in your school, these students will feel discouraged, misunderstood, and alone. Not because they can't learn, but because the way they learn doesn't align with the way they are taught.

Thousands of teachers will struggle today. Just as they do every day.

In your school and district, these teachers will feel discouraged, inadequate, and alone. Not because they can't teach, but because they have not been able to target their teaching strategies to the varied learning profiles of their students.

Too many of our schools are unequipped for the diversity in learning that unfolds in classrooms. District policies are hampered by traditional notions of ability and unvarying approaches to meeting the high standards of curriculum, instruction, and required annual standardized testing. Educators often lack the know-how that's emerging from the latest research on the mind, brain, and learning to adequately respond to individual student needs.

When students are taught in a way that is incompatible with how they learn, the natural strengths of their minds are neglected. This failure to reach a student's abilities is too often portrayed as a deficiency of the individual, resulting in low self-esteem, high levels of anxiety, and disengagement with learning and school. Or we point to the inadequacy of the teacher and local schools, driving many promising educators from a profession that needs their dedication and commitment at this unprecedented time for education in our nation.

Without effective and nurturing intervention, both student and teacher may give up on school—and learning—altogether. The resulting loss of productive individuals who contribute to our society is unfathomable.

One Educator's Story

My career in education began in 1975 as a teacher of "exceptional needs" students. These were individuals who had struggled mightily in their previous classrooms or had been considered to have handicaps to such an extent that new special education classrooms were the first stop for their free and appropriate education.

Every year, children and adolescents came through my door accompanied by data and numerous other descriptors designed to help them obtain an array of special support and to help me figure out the kind of instruction they needed. Gregory, at age twelve, had not spoken words, leading me to begin to design alternative communication strategies. This provided a starting point, but our journey together as teacher and student progressed successfully when I concentrated on finding answers to one simple question: I wonder how he learns?

What I loved about that challenging period of my teaching career was that this simple question drove everything I did in the classroom. I became an astute observer of each of my students, looking for clues as to what made them tick when they were successful at something and how they were different at home than in a school environment. Paula never spoke in the classroom and led me to believe that she was nonverbal, but she answered the phone when I had to call her home. James understood humor—from the physical play of clowns to the more sophisticated wordplay of jokes—revealing a level of conceptual understanding I may have missed by simply looking at his work or relying on his expressive language weakness. Shack could not do simple mathematical procedures in a workbook but could point out recurring mathematical patterns found with numbers and shapes in the physical world.

I sought a variety of perspectives, always hoping someone might see something that I missed. I thought of myself as a combination ethnographer and archeologist. I was pulling pieces from my "dig" into a child's life and trying to understand a new culture of learning so I could create the right script for very unique roles that each student and I as teacher would play in our educational journey. The only way I knew to approach this unfamiliar range of learning differences was to think about using science in its richest sense—embracing wonder, a culture of inquiry, the quest for rich data and evidence-based practice. It worked. Searches yielded observable phenomena leading to patterns that led to insights into how students' minds worked.

I was not to become an expert in a subject matter area during my education career (although I have developed a strong background in literature and social sciences). But I did become a "learner" expert, developing the know-how and tools to figure out how to successfully reach some of the most complex and puzzling students who attended the schools where I worked.

One Organization's Mission

I lead All Kinds of Minds to continue this work on a large scale. I am driven by a belief that our nation will not achieve the results we desire in stopping the persistent and chronic underperformance and disengagement of so many students unless we build expertise in our education workforce to better understand the variety of ways students learn. Currently this knowledge about learning and its normal variation is primarily the domain of the clinical and scientific communities. While there have been recent efforts to broadly communicate the benefits brain research can bring to learning,[1] it is unacceptable that we have not figured out how to move this body of knowledge into the world of education.

That is what All Kinds of Minds does. Since 1995, this organization, working with renowned learning expert Dr. Mel Levine, has translated the latest research from multiple disciplines into a framework to understand learning and its variations. We have shared that knowledge and how to use it to target specific teaching strategies to learners with thousands of educators through our programs and resources. With twenty-three independent studies to date that have investigated what happens when educators use this approach, we've gathered evidence that more students, teachers, and schools are finding success in the core business of education: learning for all kinds of minds (see Appendix C: The Effects of the Schools Attuned Program: A Snapshot of Research Results).

All Kinds of Minds seeks to work with others who realize that by harnessing these new insights from the sciences on how people learn to the tools, processes, and strategies used by expert practitioners, we can make two critical contributions to education. First, we will prevent needless struggles in school for thousands of students hoping to find success at learning and life. Second, we will be the leaders who seize the opportunity to do what many national voices are suggesting America must do: create the future of learning. There is a growing and powerful argument that we must transform the educational landscape from a world of schooling to a world of learning. Educators in today's schools need to have learning expertise in addition to content knowledge. They need this expertise not only to reach the students slipping through the cracks in schools today but to transition into the new roles that will emerge as the *teaching* profession becomes a *learning* profession in this twenty-first century.

Getting from here to there requires that those of us in current education leadership positions—principals, district administrators, coaches, mentors, and teacher leaders—reshape our role to that of a "learning leader." It is a role that requires a dual focus of school leadership, nurturing the student and teacher struggling within today's classroom while laying the building blocks for a new way of education that creates the personalized, customized learning journeys students and parents are beginning to demand. Learning leaders model the characteristics of this role for their faculty and make creating the conditions for teacher learning on behalf of student learning a high priority.

This book introduces an approach that today's school leaders, in a new role as learning leader, can use to help greater numbers of students find success while shifting education to a learner-centric enterprise. I refer to it as the All Kinds of Minds model, which involves these components:

- *Expertise in the science of learning*, based on the understanding of eight constructs that form the mind's ingredients for learning and the belief that differences are *variation*, not deviation
- *Evidence gathered from multiple sources*, including using a phenomenological approach as part of the data necessary to understand how specific students learn
- A *problem-solving model* that uncovers the complexity and richness of how a child learns, identifying learning assets as well as weaknesses and discovering passions and affinities that can drive scholarship, careers, and other life choices
- A *set of five core beliefs* about how *all* students are treated
- A *commitment* to align school and educational practices and policies to the way students learn and vary in their learning

How do you get started? The first step is to continue reading. Chapter One provides a larger context supporting the need for the approach presented throughout this book. Chapters Two and Three will help you introduce your faculty to an overview of the science of learning developed from findings from neuroscience, cognitive science, and behavioral science. The research has been translated into insights to help generate understanding about how the adults and students in your school are wired to learn. These findings are synthesized into neurodevelopmental knowledge that creates an overarching framework for diagnosis and informing instruction. The strategies, tactics, and examples described in Chapters Four through Seven demonstrate how to apply these insights so that the adults in your school have a better understanding of themselves as learners and can then use the approach to make personalized and successful learning plans a reality for those students that your school and district have always had trouble reaching.

We've designed this book to help you at the very beginning stage of implementing this approach. Specifically, you'll find ideas throughout the book for the following:

- *Acquiring and processing new information.* Boxes are included throughout each chapter, and professional development activities conclude each of the chapters. These items are intended to help learning leaders process the concepts presented, reflect on their own practice, and discover alignment with the All Kinds of Minds philosophy and approach. Once you become familiar with the questions and activities, you can consider how to utilize them in your educational setting.

- *Embedding this approach to learning practices into your existing professional development structures.* We assume you have existing professional learning communities, Critical Friends or Lesson Study groups, and other well-established processes around professional development in your school. (If not, that is a critical success factor to put into place before any school-level professional development can start.) The content of this book can easily be part of a formal book study, particularly when supplemented by other resources that provide deeper engagement with the neurodevelopmental constructs. Or, specific activities could be selected to assist faculty in reflecting on their own learning profiles as well as educational practices and school. By using these tools, you will assess the alignment of your current environment with the All Kinds of Minds approach.

- *Testing strategies with selected students who are struggling to learn.* Help teachers try applying strategies with students in your school who are struggling. Consider using the ideas in Chapters Four and Five as an additional component to your Response to Intervention program. Chapters include real-life stories of how this approach has been used by educators as well as a detailed look at how the learning framework and assessment approach is used to improve writing instruction and evaluation. With this basic foundation, faculty can acquire a deeper insight about individual learning needs and become more adept at understanding and managing learning challenges and opportunities. The result? Over time, with continued pursuit, you will have a school filled with both learning experts and subject matter scholars.

- *Continued learning and advocacy.* As you read through this book, make a personal commitment to embrace the "small wins" approach by identifying your first few actions. Share what you learn with colleagues. Go to the All Kinds of Minds Web site, www.allkindsofminds.org (see Appendix E for a list of resources available on the Web site). In addition to a multitude of resources, you'll find ways to stay abreast of our growing knowledge base and to connect to other people who are energized by using this approach to support teachers as they help students who learn differently find success.

An Invitation

We hope that because you are reading this book, you are willing to be part of this powerful movement to bring the science of learning to the art of teaching, rescuing those students who are struggling to learn right now while transforming education for generations to come. Leaders know that what matters in learning is what happens in class, in those moments when teacher meets students. Such leaders—like you—find themselves waiting for the larger transformation to learning-driven schools while pursuing the many daily small wins that address the urgency of the struggling student.

Arthur Levine, former president of Teachers College in New York City, stated this eloquently when he wrote that "today's reformers have one foot in the old world and one in the new, inchoate world of education. Experimenting and pushing, they must sustain our schools until they can be replaced by the ones we need for the future."² While the large, systemic change desired may be beyond our immediate grasp, learning leaders who embrace a science of learning to show that it is indeed possible to match pedagogy to a student's learning profile will achieve something equally important for our times. They will save the lives of the far too many children we continue to lose in the industrial era, factory-inspired model in many of today's schools.

Today's school leaders, willing to work with a foot in each world, are in the best position to harness bring the energy of these pioneering new ideas from the science of learning to the realities of classrooms. They can better meet the needs of today's students so vulnerable to school failure while accelerating this transformation. We're inspired by the exciting visions for student learning that so many of you are generating. All Kinds of Minds hopes to harness your genius and enthusiasm and share your stories through our Web site to spark a much larger dialogue that can move the nation from an education agenda to a learning agenda.

We are well aware of the enormously challenging work of changing school culture and practices and are not so naïve to think that picking up a new book is sufficient support for leaders engaged in these efforts. This book is not about leadership nor is it a detailed approach for a school improvement effort. Rather, it is a framework to help all learners—teachers and students—understand how they learn and how they can learn better. It's a critical first step to discovering how to personalize learning. To that end, this book is intended to provide some starting points for this dialogue for the future, as well as some immediate actions you can take to use this knowledge about learning with some of the different kinds of minds in your school.

We invite you to use the information and strategies in this book to bring success to all the learners in your school—teachers and students—and add to the growing portraits of possibility for educational change.

Mary-Dean Barringer, CEO,
All Kinds of Minds

Understanding Learning as the Core Business of Schools

If you think our future will require better schools, you're wrong.
The future of education calls for entirely new learning environments.
If you think we will need better teachers, you're wrong.
Tomorrow's learners will need guides who take on fundamentally
different roles.[1]
—KnowledgeWorks Foundation and Institute for the Future
2020 Forecast: Creating the Future of Learning

Jan Stewart was attending an introductory networking dinner with some colleagues, a cohort of principals who had joined a professional network of school leaders that had agreed to work in targeted district schools to increase student achievement. They were enjoying this time to get to know each other and learn about their individual school cultures and challenges. Jan had been the principal of Eastville Middle School for several years and smiled as she listened to the spirited talk. The conversation began with broad ideas about new theories and ways of addressing individual needs and learning diversity through approaches like differentiated instruction, universal design for learning, curriculum mapping, and the like. The principals talked about needing new ways to deliver instruction and debated online learning, smaller classes, looping, and modifying use of time.

Typically conversations drifted toward district policies that the principals were unhappy with, but tonight was different. Jan's friend Brian Thomas, the new principal at Marshall Junior High, began sharing a story about an individual student he was concerned about. Darren, a bright eighth grader, was generally a strong student, although he'd had some recent difficulties. In particular, he'd received poor grades on writing assignments, especially on essays and research papers. His state writing test had just come back, and he had barely scored a 2 within the 1 through 4 ranking, putting him at below grade level.

Darren did well on multiple choice tests and his handwriting was fine, but his papers, reports, and essays were returned to him with the same messages: "Highly disorganized," "Needs more elaboration" and "Incomplete." The continued negative feedback on writing assignments frustrated Darren and he felt humiliated about it. "I don't get it," he had said when Brian asked what was going on. "I rewrote that essay twice and it still came back with marks all over it."

His teachers thought highly of Darren, noting that he participated in class discussions and was well liked by his peers, but they had exhausted their ideas for strategies to help him. Darren's language arts teacher said she'd taught him the 6+1-trait writing process and showed him the state writing test rubrics that described the difference between a score of a 2 and the acceptable 3. His social studies teacher had introduced a writer's workshop as part of her class. These hadn't produced a change in Darren's writing. His teachers shrugged and said Darren might be going through a rebellious period and not putting effort into his assignments, or he was just lazy. One teacher firmly believed that Darren had learning disabilities that should be addressed in a resource room and not her classroom, pushing to send Darren through the referral process.

Brian worried that he likely had dozens of Darrens in his new school and wondered how he would be able to help the teachers reach those students while also trying to inspire them to transform education for all the students that attended—and would attend—Marshall in the future. Darren was a particular risk, but Brian asked, "Won't we let down all of our students if we keep doing business the same old way?"

This chapter will explore
- A model of education centered around learners and learning
- The rationale for embracing the science of learning
- The role of learning leader versus school leader
- Use of a "small wins" strategy to support change in school practices

What's Today's School Leader to Do?

Anticipating the future while attending to the here and now is the work of all school leaders who are devoted to educating all learners. At its core, education is a future-oriented enterprise, charged with preparing the next generation of workers, citizens, and leaders. For decades, political and policy conversations about education have been centered on the knowledge competencies determined to be essential for students to compete in a twenty-first-century work environment and to thrive in a democracy. The ultimate measure of success is documentation that students have acquired skills and competencies at acceptable levels and graduated from high school ready for postsecondary life. Every May, communities celebrate milestones of graduation: kindergarten, fifth grade, eighth grade, and high school.

And every May and June, teachers and principals are haunted by the faces that have disappeared. Was there something else that could have been done to increase engagement and stem the dropout rate of students who struggle to learn and find success in our schools? Communities of educators across the country engage in such debates. They hope and plan for grand educational change and reform to address the systemic issues that are part of the chronic problem of poor school performance for so many children. Individually, principals and teachers aspire to save as many of these children as they can.

> " The reality of schools is that the tyranny of the urgent drives what happens in classrooms every day. "

The reality of schools is that the tyranny of the urgent drives what happens in classrooms every day. School leaders live in the moment, addressing the immediate demands of learners encountered, day after day. Getting second graders reading fluently, preventing a fourth-grade slump, getting all ninth graders to pass algebra, helping students make it to senior year, and navigating the annual ritual of high-stakes testing is the world of school leaders. It's also preventing cruelty from bullying or the humiliation when a student is not learning at a predetermined pace, or the disengagement when students feel no adult knows or cares who they really are. For every student claimed as a success story, the ones who missed the mark haunt all of us. How do we—as individuals who lead—bring new thinking to solve this enduring dilemma?

Lead with a Bifocal Lens to Transform Learning

Many school leaders view their work through a "bifocal lens" that permits them to lead with clarity of a future vision of success for all students and a focus on the current demands in the school environment. A bifocal lens permits a learner-centric view of education by which a leader can shift effortlessly between the future and present. It allows a leader to define the tactical steps to move toward a learner-centric school environment that serves both teachers and students. While engaging in the daily hard work of creating this culture, such a lens incorporates a compelling scenario for the school that fits with new, inspiring goals of education and learning. Such leaders have found they can address the immediacy of specific learner needs using the findings from a new science of learning such as the All Kinds of Minds approach; this is fueling the transformation of schooling better suited to the learner-centric world described by many education futurists.

A bifocal lens also helps school leaders address learning at three levels: their own, their colleagues and faculty, and their students. Addressing learning at these levels by working to understand *how* people learn reshapes our perspective when we—or those individuals in our charge—aren't succeeding. Typically we view those who aren't succeeding as lacking something internal (motivation, intelligence) or external (opportunity, social well-being, and so on). We focus on interventions to make up for those things. And while this has value, those interventions don't come close to solving the problems of why many teachers and students still don't succeed. Stepping back, helping all understand how they are wired to learn so that they can take ownership for their learning profile (and the strategies that can enable greater success) is a new dimension to bring to the table.

School leaders who are determined to help teachers inspire all students to bold accomplishments while identifying the right strategies for their most complex and struggling learners know one thing to be true: what makes this bifocal lens work is making learning the core business of school. This isn't the same as emphasizing assessment data, standards, and instruction. Rather, it means focusing on the foundation upon which all newer initiatives and drivers for change rest: an understanding of *how* people are wired to learn and the implications for bolder notions of schooling and instruction. Making learning the core business of schooling is a cornerstone of the All Kinds of Minds approach.

> "Researchers have made remarkable progress in developing learning principles from neuroscience. This new research offers a very solid framework for developing curriculum by subject matter in a way that respects principles of learning . . . (and) helps confront learning challenges by providing scientifically valid, neurodevelopmental profiles of students' strengths and weaknesses from kindergarten through high school. The neuroscience message is an asset-oriented, student-centered strategy that is research based, upbeat and positive."[2]
>
> —Harvey and Housman, *Crisis or Possibility: Conversations About the American High School*

Brian Thomas's concerns about inspiring a vision of powerful education for all students while zeroing in on the "Darrens" and the teachers who are struggling in Marshall Junior High are both the right concerns. The National Association of Secondary School Principals (NASSP) supports this as well and urges its members to take part in large-scale school reform by "breaking ranks" and implementing the report's thirty-one action steps, which are focused on a learner-centric model of education. One of the three key recommendations and subsequent set of actions stressed the "development of personalized learning, where students see their learning as meaningful and relevant, as well as rigorous and challenging."[3] NASSP believes that if principals act on the recommendations, they will ultimately see the success of every student, not only those typically served well by current middle and high schools.

This transformational work is one of the hardest and most challenging tasks one can undertake. But reframing conversations about why we need changes in education from a discourse of crisis to a discourse of possibility is energizing. The leaders in these discussions about school transformation see the power of new technologies to make curriculum and instruction accessible to students with differences in how they approach learning. Like the authors of the 2004 report, *Crisis or Possibility: Conversations About the American High School*, they know that the explosion of findings from neuroscience provides an overarching framework to better understand learning and thus help them make better decisions about the right curriculum, instruction, and resources to help the learners in their schools become more engaged and invested in finding academic success.[4]

Despite the efforts of many educators, scientists, and academics, the science of learning does not typically appear as a component of preparation programs and continuing education efforts for teachers and administrators.[5] The focus of learning for educational professionals is acquisition of content and pedagogy knowledge, with only superficial coverage of knowledge of learning and learners. The science supporting learning and learners tends to remain within the domains of knowledge in the clinical and medical professions. For educators to acquire and use this new knowledge for today's struggling learners—and to create new instructional scenarios for *all* learners—we have to recognize the quicksand of our educational past and how it unintentionally creates barriers.

Resist the Pull of the Past

"Advances in neuroscience are creating new notions of performance and cognition and reshaping discussions of social justice in learning."[6]

—KnowledgeWorks Foundation and Institute for the Future
2020 Forecast: Creating the Future of Learning

This past decade has seen an explosion of findings from neuroscience and studies on cognition suggesting how we can all improve our cognitive and mental performance. Baby boomers flock to new technologies and games to enhance active working memory. They read publications like *Scientific Mind*. The U.S. government provides funding for national labs like the Institute for the Brain and Learning at University of Washington. Neuroscientists and cognitive psychologists are the new management gurus, with the *Harvard Business Review* publishing the implications of John Medina's *Brain Rules* on business management[7] and Gregory Bern's *Iconoclast: A Neuroscientist Reveals How to Think Differently*[8] hitting the best-seller list of business books.

So why is it that the science of learning has not penetrated the one sector—education—in which the core business is learning?

Daniel Pink, provocative author of the best seller *A Whole New Mind*, posed a key question as he pondered why efforts to really transform schools and education are stymied. Do our current schools bring a comforting wave of nostalgia or a rush of an exciting new future of learning?[9]

Most schools are the rare institutions we enter in which the environment—classrooms, hallways, furniture, and rituals—have largely remained the same for more than forty years. And this familiarity typically evokes a wave of comfort rather than a sense of concern. If we were to enter a business and see mainframe computers and punch cards, visit a hospital without ultrasounds or magnetic imaging for diagnosis, or work in an office with Selectric typewriters and rotary phones, we'd think we'd stepped back in time.

Elementary classroom practice is sometimes a replica of our own experience of long ago. Children gather for circle time on the rug and do the daily calendar, recite the days of the week, copy the "news of the day" in print or cursive from the chalkboard. We laugh at the teacher in the movie *Ferris Bueller's Day Off* who drones on in a lecture, pausing only for a fill-in-the-verbal-blank answer by asking, "Anyone, anyone?" It's funny because it is familiar.

It may be the power of nostalgia that is associated with the common yet positive shared experience of school that pulls so many of our most dedicated and creative reformers to refashion golden moments of education rather than imagining bold new ways of learning. We *can* in the twenty-first century create another breathtaking democratic achievement for our diverse learners, but it will not be like the successes America achieved in the industrial era.

Nostalgia constrains creative thinking. Listen to local and national conversations about how to fix our schools and system. There is talk about accountability, charters, low-performing schools, data-driven decision making, nationally benchmarked standards and tests, twenty-first century skills, extended school time, pay for performance, teacher quality, community schools, strategic management of human capital, graduation rates. We now have shared acronyms—NCLB, NAEP, AYP, IEP, RTI, EOG, SAT, the list goes on. But we're missing a key word in our shared educational vocabulary, or even an acronym that includes it: LEARNING.

> " We're missing a key word in our shared educational vocabulary, or even an acronym that includes it: LEARNING. "

A hypothesis is that most people who lead the national efforts to improve education were, by and large, successful students in the education system. Therefore, current efforts to improve education for all learners largely follow the strategy of our past reform achievements—using legislation and policy levers to ensure access for all children to the best education. Solutions tend to be focused on expanded access to those inputs believed to have enabled the achievements they have made: high-quality teachers steeped in content knowledge, tough standards and assessments like the New York Regents exam, more schools with this kind of rigor at their core, more time to learn, parental involvement, enrichment opportunities, and so on.

Leaders working on education reform recognize that many factors have created a new global, technology-driven world, but solutions offered to prepare students for this are largely a return to variations of this golden era of education. Reformers want more children to have access to the experiences and resources that enabled their success, yet they haven't considered the possibility that their success might have resulted because their minds were wired to succeed at the specific tasks that counted as academic achievement and overall school success—those relying largely on memory, linguistic, and attention strengths.

Curtis Johnson, one of the authors of *Disrupting Class,* states, "It is a mistake to confuse either the permission to create new schools or setting rigorous standards with learning. What matters is what happens in class, whether physical or virtual."[10] Many educators, school leaders, and policymakers—working on new standards, new schools, and new systems—talk *around* learning but not *about* learning. Some might argue this is merely a semantic assertion—we know that the reason we have been so focused on education reform for decades is that we want our students to learn in more relevant, rigorous, and engaging ways than ever before.

> " Educators, school leaders, and policymakers—working on new standards, new schools, and new systems—talk *around* learning but not *about* learning. "

It's plausible, yet without a specific focus on learning we have missed solutions from the science of learning research that are essential to bringing about the transformation in education we hope to achieve. We have new insights into the way students are wired to learn and how they vary that can help us address the persistent challenge of so many kids missing the mark in today's schools. We have innovative programs and tools to personalize and customize learning, demonstrating how we might accelerate how we transform the ways we educate all learners for a complex, changing world. Yet when *learning* is not one of our top education vocabulary words, ideas from scientific learning research do not find their way into our discussions.

The new role of schools and education that many thought leaders are urging won't go anywhere if we don't talk about the new kind of learning we need. Tom Friedman, in his best-selling book *The World Is Flat*, contends that the most important function of school is to teach students *how* to learn in order to prepare them for the future; the majority of students are being educated for jobs and roles that don't exist today.[11] Chester Finn, former deputy secretary in the U.S. Department of Education, concurs with the need for fresh ideas stemming from real experiences with student learning in our education reform discussions; he challenges readers in a commentary in *Education Week* that "people are good at different things—and plenty of traits matter besides academics."[12]

Shift from a School Leader to a Learning Leader

The term "learning leader" is widely associated with Douglas Reeves[13] and his framework for school leadership development. The construct compatible with the All Kinds of Minds approach is one articulated by Hargreaves and Fink based on a report about learning issued in 1996 by the United Nations Educational, Scientific and Cultural Organization (UNESCO).[14] They argue that "being a leader of learning means more than poring over and perseverating on achievement results or finding quick ways to boost the figures or narrow the gaps."[15]

It requires the consistent work summarized in the following box in building a deep learning foundation in today's school and developing the expertise for leading learning into the future.[16]

Learning leaders must

- Be passionate advocates for and defenders of deep and broad learning for all students. . . .
- Put learning before testing while promoting assessment for learning. . . .
- Become more knowledgeable about learning. . . .
- Commit to improving old basics of literacy and math but not to the exclusion of everything else, while emphasizing the new basics of creativity. . . .
- Engage students in discussion and decisions about their own learning. . . .
- Create the emotional conditions for learning . . . by personalizing learning for every student.
- Become omnipresent witnesses to learning by (analyzing and discussing) responses to student work.[17]

—Hargreaves and Fink, *Sustainable Leadership*

Many of the organizations that support and represent today's school leaders have acknowledged the necessity of a shift to a learner-centric purpose of education. The National Policy Board for Educational Administration updated its standards in 2008 to reflect the recent lessons learned about education leadership that enable student success.[18] To drive the point home that standards of professional practice in leadership must link to this learner-centric focus, each of the redesigned six core standards begins with "An education leader promotes the success of every student by. . . ."

The National Association of Independent Schools (NAIS) conducted a survey in 2005 among leaders in education, business, and media to predict the key trends that will affect independent education for the next two decades and the actions schools should take now. The NAIS noted both the challenges and opportunities that arise when science and technology move at warp speed and predicted that, each year, new findings from cognitive psychology and neuroscience will need to be infused into all aspects of education. The recommended action step from NAIS? Provide high-quality, research-based, professional development opportunities for faculty, staff, and parents to learn about "brain-based" teaching and other applications of the science of learning to gain an understanding of how each student learns.[19]

> "The opportunities to implement major changes in education based on what we know today about how the brain works places educators in the position to venture into ways of learning only imagined a generation ago."[20]
>
> —Kenneth Wesson, Educational Consultant in Neuroscience
> NAIS Opinion Leaders Survey

Arthur Levine, Clayton Christensen, and colleagues along with KnowledgeWorks Foundation are part of an emerging group of "futurists" all describing this shift, aided by technology, to an individualized and time-variable system of education. In this system, the teacher serves as a diagnostician of how each student learns and what the student needs to learn. The teacher helps select and guide the program each student should follow and assess the student's progress. Pedagogy is reinvented continuously in such systems as it is geared to particular learning profiles and includes myriad instructional possibilities such as classes, tutorials, mentoring, apprenticeships—both in real and virtual learning spaces called schools.[21] KnowledgeWorks Foundation, in the *2020 Forecast: Creating the Future of Learning*, imagines many of the new roles adults may play in this exciting world of learning, some of which are described in the following box.

As school leaders become learning leaders using the approach described in this book, they not only build the capacity of their faculty to reach today's students with learning differences; they also develop

2020 Forecast: Creating the Future of Learning predicts that "learning agents" will shape this future by redefining the roles of the profession. With a solid grounding in the "science of learning" and a student-centric focus, the roles we'll see include

- *Learning partners:* Students with compatible personalities but different learning profiles are matched to support each other.
- *Personal education advisors:* Local education agencies assign these professionals to help families create, nurture, and maintain learning plans.
- *Learning fitness instructors:* These individuals help learners build and strengthen the basic cognitive, social, and emotional abilities essential to learning.
- *Assessment designers:* Using social networks and insights into cognitive functioning, they create more appropriate methods for evaluating literacy, learning journeys, and other innovative forms of instruction.
- *Learning journey mentors:* Mentors work with the other roles, creating and navigating learning itineraries for groups of students.[22]

—KnowledgeWorks Foundation and Institute for the Future
2020 Forecast: Creating the Future of Learning

the experts to fill these new kinds of roles that will emerge when the teaching profession makes the transition to a learning profession.

Create a Series of "Small Wins" for "Big Change"

"Small wins" is a strategy cited in social science research—best described by and credited to psychologist Karl Weick in the 1980s— of redefining the scale of social problems to actionable, significant tasks.[23] The idea of the small wins strategy involves reframing large-scale, social sector challenges—like the failure of public education to teach all children successfully—into smaller actionable tactics.

Small wins (sometimes referred to in education reform solutions as "rapid prototypes") are characterized as concrete, significant tasks that produce a visible result while moving one step closer to a new vision or one step away from an unacceptable condition. Using this approach, school leaders—and the faculty—gain some experience to figure out how the knowledge and shift to learning expertise and leadership at the classroom level can begin to reshape some of the larger school and district practices. Small wins build confidence and provide proof of concept.

> " Small wins (sometimes referred to in education reform solutions as "rapid prototypes") are characterized as concrete, significant tasks that produce a visible result while moving one step closer to a new vision or one step away from an unacceptable condition. "

One example of using the small wins strategy is to apply the knowledge and approach in this book with the most complex and challenging learners in a school—those individuals targeted for gains in student achievement. Former astronaut George "Pinky" Nelson now works with schools to improve science education for students targeted as "at risk." He relays a story from his work with an elementary school in the state of Washington that illustrates how the small wins approach could be used with the All Kinds of Minds approach by starting with a faculty-identified cohort of students.

At the start of the school year, the principal asked her faculty members if they thought they had any students that might fail. Each teacher named two or three. After taking all the names, collecting their school photos and compiling their smiling faces into a composite picture of a cohort, the principal reconvened the staff, presented the class portrait, and asked, "Now that we've identified these students as a high risk for failure, what should we do about it?"

From then on, that group of students—and their progress—became the focus of the entire faculty and biweekly meetings. Much like the grand rounds in medical practice, teachers brought examples to meetings of how they were teaching and assessing science instruction in innovative ways. When they were stumped, they presented their student "case" for others to question, offer advice, share strategies and suggestions. The progress of each student was noted every other week on cards attached to their photos; as students met and maintained grade-level performance, their photo and cards were removed from the cohort portrait and the focus continued on those who remained and struggled. During the year, as part of this process, teachers gradually enhanced their role as learning diagnosticians and experts.

The principal then reported the most astonishing finding at the end of the year. Not only did 90 percent of the students they targeted achieve grade-level performance on end-of-year tests, but the focus on improving instruction for the most challenging students benefited all students, with the majority of the students achieving among the highest scores in the state.[24]

All Kinds of Minds wants educators to use the science of learning and the accompanying processes in the approach to advance success and achievement for a greater number of students. We need learning leaders who will help bring this knowledge and these tools to teaching faculty to build the capacity and confidence to reach those students about whom they so worry. And more important, America needs these learning leaders to spark a new, energized national conversation about the future of learning by sharing what can be done with the most challenging students to illuminate what is possible for all.

Key Ideas

• Bringing about the shift to learner-centric system of education requires that school leaders adopt the practices of learning leaders, establishing both a focus and new research on learning to teachers and students at the school level.

• Leading with a bifocal lens ensures that the needs of today's struggling learners are being met and that progress toward a learner-centric model of education is being made.

• Research about the mind, brain, neuroscience, and learning is expanding, but to date, this body of knowledge hasn't penetrated the education industry or schools.

• Education hasn't embraced the science of learning or the ideas of "futurists" because of the pull of strong traditions and related nostalgia of a golden era of our education system.

• Transformation can occur if there is a shift toward making personalized learning our vision of the future and helping teachers build the capacity to adopt a greater role as diagnosticians and learning specialists.

2

Bringing the Science of Learning into the Classroom

Jan Stewart was in her office, at the end of a long day, mulling over how to organize the professional development for the Eastville Middle School faculty in the coming year. She knew this was an essential element to her charge of increasing student achievement in her school, and she had to present a draft of a plan to her principals' cohort next week. She shuddered as she recalled the pedagogical wars that had resulted from past initiatives. There were still scars from the "whole language versus phonics" instruction battles when her elementary school was focused on reading. The math initiative didn't fare much better; faculty spent most sessions arguing about the merits of direct instruction of facts and procedures over the more conceptual approach of teaching mathematics for understanding.

What Jan wanted was a way to build the confidence and competencies of her staff so that more students could learn effectively and experience greater achievement at Eastville. Jan also needed to instill her staff with a "can do" attitude and wanted strategies and an approach that would unify staff, not cause further divisions. She leaned back in her chair and thought, "I want professional conversations that generate energy and an inspiring vision."

She wondered if a focus on learning instead of the typical focus on some aspect of teaching methodology would work. She picked up the phone and called Brian to discuss the merits of this idea. He agreed that it should unify a staff of teachers. After all, don't all teachers want the students in their classrooms *to learn? Both Jan and Brian felt like a focus on learning was right for the Professional Learning Communities at Eastville. Brian even recommended an article that he'd read in USA Today about "a new science of learning."*[1]

As Jan hung up the phone, she quickly located the online version of the article. It would be a great place to start with her staff. She was feeling better about her professional development plan for the upcoming year. There was still a lot to figure out, but having Brian and the principals' cohort to support her through this change made her feel confident that this initiative would be different than past ones.

This chapter will explore
- The importance of viewing learners as individuals with unique profiles of strengths and weaknesses
- The value of a neurodevelopmental framework for describing learners
- The rationale for focusing on strengths and affinities
- The benefits of promoting the self-insight of students
- The need to forge alliances with struggling learners
- Beliefs about teaching all kinds of minds

UNDERSTANDING LEARNING AND LEARNERS HELPS EDUCATORS MAKE GOOD decisions about instruction and strategies. In recent years the science of learning has produced several models for understanding and appreciating the unique qualities of individual learners. For example, Gardner's "theory of multiple intelligences"[2] includes several categories of ability, such as linguistic and logical-mathematical, in which individuals can differ. Sternberg proposed thinking about intelligence in terms of three components: analytic (used to solve problems with reasoning), synthetic/creative (generating new insights and innovations), and practical/contextual (dealing with one's immediate context, or "street smarts").[3] The Cattell-Horn-Carroll (CHC) model of intelligence includes a single measure of overall ability, but it also contains numerous broad cognitive abilities that are subdivided into more narrow abilities,[4] which allows for an even wider range of individual differences. The Center for Applied Special Technology (CAST) proposes that individual differences in learning exist in three neural networks: recognition (enabling the identification of patterns), strategic (planning, executing, and monitoring self-generated mental and motor patterns), and affective (attaching emotional significance to actions and encountered objects).[5]

In addition, recent neuroscience has injected a new form of optimism into the learning field, stemming from the concept of *plasticity*. Specifically, research has shown that the functional organization of the brain and mind is altered by experience, meaning that positive experiences can "rewire" the brain in beneficial ways. Also, development has been shown to be an active process derived from experiences as well as biology.[6] So the seventh grader who struggles mightily with comprehending science concepts can begin to "get it" if he gets the instruction best suited for his brain (as can the second grader with reading problems, and the eleventh grader with writing weaknesses, and so on).

> A neurodevelopmental profile is like a balance sheet of learning strengths and weaknesses.

The emerging "mind, brain, and education" movement calls for more dynamic interchanges between research and educational practice.[7] This includes appreciating the complexities of academic tasks and how instructional strategies may vary in effectiveness as a result of the numerous factors that can account for skill weaknesses.[8] Put simply, knowing what's going on with a student helps with picking the right strategies. In *Disrupting Class*, Christensen, Horn, and Johnson assert that "every student learns in a different way," and that "a key step toward making school intrinsically motivating is to customize an education to match the way each child learns best."[9]

All Kinds of Minds has developed a neurodevelopmental approach to help educators more deeply understand the complexities of individual learners and for learning processes in general. The approach uses a framework consisting of *constructs* (such as memory and language) and component *functions* (such as long-term memory and phonological processing).[10] These constructs and functions are the currency of the balance sheets of strengths and weaknesses that all learners possess. The All Kinds of Minds approach is based on core principles that help educators navigate their decision-making process. It is not necessarily a stand-alone program in a school or district. It complements and even enhances other initiatives (such as positive behavior supports, writer's workshop, and formative assessment) by elevating educators' capacities to observe learners and to interpret learning patterns. This chapter describes the core principles and some research from the science of learning that supports the All Kinds of Minds approach.

The Science Behind Using a Neurodevelopmental Lens

All Kinds of Minds defines *neurodevelopment* as the ever-changing set of mental operations that allow people to learn from and interact with their environments. Neurodevelopmental constructs include concepts with which most everyone is familiar: memory, language, attention. Some constructs, such as higher-order cognition, have direct applicability with schoolwork, like solving a math word problem or understanding a scientific principle. Other constructs, like social cognition, are important to school performance in more indirect ways (such as getting along with cooperative learning teammates) but are undoubtedly important for lifelong success.

> " All Kinds of Minds defines *neurodevelopment* as the ever-changing set of mental operations that allow people to learn from and interact with their environments. "

Definitions and background for neurodevelopmental functions
are provided in Chapter Three.

When educators understand brain function, they are in a better position to make sound decisions about instruction and strategies. For the most part, a detailed understanding of brain *anatomy* is
not relevant to teacher practice. An eighth-grade literature teacher,
for instance, does not need to know that language is associated with
the temporal lobes. But that eighth-grade teacher *should* know about
language as a construct: its components, how they manifest in adolescents, how they affect reading and writing performance (positively
and negatively), and what strategies should be employed if language
functions are not operating appropriately. In essence, neuroscience's
real value to educators is how it illuminates the links between learning
functions and academic skills.

The science of learning provides educators with the knowledge
and skills to differentiate their instruction so that more students
gain greater access to information and skills. Differentiating instruction according to learner needs is at the heart of the CAST approach.
Unreliable function in any of three neural networks can be addressed
by providing learners multiple means of taking in information (for the
recognition network), expressing ideas and knowledge (for the strategic network), and engaging with content (for the affective network).[11]
Christensen, Horn, and Johnson argue for more customization in
learning, contending that "schools need to move . . . toward a modular,
student-centric approach."[12]

Describing learners in terms of neurodevelopmental functions, or
viewing learners through a neurodevelopmental lens, can pave the way
to such customization. For example, math is a subject that contains
a large amount of visual information, and students who can readily make meaning out of images are at an advantage. Educators who
appreciate this can boost math comprehension by helping students
to use schematic or conceptual imagery, such as visualizing how an

operation like subtraction can change quantities. Reading achievement can be improved through focused training on the meaningful components of words, which research has shown to be important for language development. Looking beyond traditional academic skills, this kind of lens can help teachers support positive socialization. Regular conversations can guide children's development by helping them to negotiate emotional understandings and by exposing them to culturally relevant ways of interpreting emotional experiences. Table 2.1 presents examples of research studies related to using a neurodevelopmental lens in the classroom.

> Performance data can reveal *who* isn't learning and *what* isn't being learned but not *why* students are struggling or *how* to address their needs.

Table 2.1 Examples of Research on Using a Neurodevelopmental Lens

Nature of Reading Decoding Problems

Educators can better understand the nature of reading decoding problems by appreciating how such difficulties can stem from sources such as
- Poor short-term memory
- Trouble processing word sounds
- Difficulty interpreting visual symbols and letter patterns[13]

Active Working Memory and Math

Fourth, fifth, and sixth graders solved addition problems while indicating on a keyboard whether an auditory tone was high or low (to occupy working memory)
Increased demands on working memory resulted in poorer arithmetic performance and less efficient use of strategies
The negative effect of overloading working memory decreased with age, indicating that more working memory resources are needed during the initial phases of skill acquisition[14]

Active Working Memory and Reading Fluency

Improving timing and rhythm boosted phonics and reading fluency in elementary school students, apparently due to efficiency gains in working memory[15]

Development of Semantics and Syntax

Brain imaging demonstrated that by age six, children have not yet developed maturity in specific aspects of language, namely semantics and syntax, meaning that reading and writing tasks need to be gauged accordingly[16]

Table 2.1　(Continued)

Semantics and Reading Efficiency

Focused training on the semantic characteristics of words led to improvements in reading efficiency in seven- and eight-year-olds who had experienced difficulty with reading [17]

Schematic Math Imagery and Spatial Thinking

Use of schematic math imagery (or visuals that depict values and relationships between values) is characteristic of students who have strong higher spatial thinking [18]

Social Thinking of Bullying Victims

Students who associated themselves with the victim role used more defensive, preemptive processing of threatening cues and had more frequent experiences of victimization

Such children also showed distress in conflict situations, which may serve as further reward to aggressors

Students can be taught to control their own emotional arousal, attend nondefensively to threats, and receive cognitive retraining to reduce self-perceptions as victims [19]

Improving Emotional Understanding

Exploring the feelings of a story character (when narrating a wordless book and answering questions about characters' feelings) resulted in an increase in emotional understanding [20]

PICTURE THIS!

Schools that use RTI have a great opportunity to implement a learning framework at a systemic level. Learning leaders can work to institute a neurodevelopmental vocabulary within the conversations about which tier of services students should receive and what strategies they should get within those tiers. Descriptions of learners' strengths and weaknesses enhance the quantitative data gathered through progress monitoring of skill development.

Thinking in terms of students' learning profiles lends itself well to differentiating instruction and to triage models like response to intervention (RTI). Frequent or regular progress monitoring alone is not enough to improve achievement; teachers need to tailor instruction to student needs.[21] Students have individual characteristics that facilitate the degree of success they have with particular intervention programs.[22] Positive outcomes result when teachers analyze information, form hypotheses about causes of reading problems, and then use those hypotheses to guide decision-making in the intervention process.[23] In short, a neurodevelopmental lens helps teachers see the unique qualities of learners, and how to make better instructional decisions to meet their needs.

The Science Behind Focusing on Strengths and Affinities

Strengths are learning functions that are operating reliably or with a high level of efficiency or sophistication. Strengths include solid or advanced academic skills, as well as talents and abilities that fall outside of traditional school areas (such as music). In some instances, strengths are noteworthy only in comparison to the learner's weaknesses. Affinities are activities or topics that are strongly appealing to the student, even to the point of passionate interest. Examples include Civil War history, gardening, model shipbuilding, debate, ballet, sports statistics, horses, marine biology, and working with multimedia.

> Strengths and affinities may overlap, but not always; a person may love to cook and be good at it, but the world has more than a few capable but begrudging cooks, as well as cooks who love to prepare food but need a cookbook to boil water.

Research has shown that one of the ingredients for long-term life success for those with learning problems is awareness of strengths and talents, both academic and nonacademic.[24] Also, a feature of resilient children is having an interest or hobby that brings comfort when aspects of their lives are in disarray.[25] Brooks and Goldstein describe mastery experiences as "islands of competence" that can bolster resiliency by leveraging assets.[26] Finally, nurturing strengths is consistent with tenets of positive psychology, which emphasizes and promotes happiness, subjective well-being, and character assets.[27]

The Science Behind Promoting Self-Insight

Educators can do more with detailed descriptions of students than customize instruction and strengthen strengths. They also can share descriptions, in developmentally appropriate ways, so that that learners gain self-insight. *Metacognition* refers to this kind of insight into one's own learning strengths and weaknesses as well as more general knowledge about the learning process.[28] A large body of research supports the idea that learners benefit from improved metacognition.

Children are better equipped to cope with challenges when they are aware of their weaknesses and vulnerabilities as well as their assets and talents.[29] Self-insight can lead to self-advocacy when tackling challenges in optimal ways and selecting life paths best suited to one's strengths and affinities. Table 2.2 includes examples of research on self-insight and the benefits of metacognition.

The Science Behind Empowering Students Through Alliances

By deeply understanding students, illuminating and developing their strengths, and promoting their self-insight, teachers will inherently

Table 2.2 Examples of Research on Self-Insight

Strategy Selection and Reading Comprehension

Feedback that students in grades 5–8 got from using strategies (such as asking, "Did I understand that passage?") enhanced metacognition, led to revised strategy selection, and improved reading comprehension[30]

Self-Appraisal and Math

Second, third, and fourth graders were asked which math problems they could solve correctly, to solve the same math problems, and then evaluate their accuracy on another set of problems

Students with math difficulty showed poor metacognition; they were overconfident about the number of problems they could accurately solve and were less accurate in evaluating the accuracy of their answers[31]

Self-Awareness and Long-Term Success

Self-awareness has been found to be associated with long-term success of individuals with learning problems, particularly when they know the specifics of their problems[32]

forge alliances with students that can help them succeed in the face of learning challenges. Teachers who invest the time and effort to "get" students are more likely to develop trusting relationships. Such teachers understand the nature of learning struggles, avoid attributing failure to "character flaws," and work to help students address specific breakdown points in academic work.

Researchers and experts in resilience theory have touted the benefits of alliances for at-risk students. Successful adults with learning problems have identified the importance of support and guidance from "significant others," including mentors and teachers.[33] Brooks and Goldstein defined the "charismatic adult," who is not necessarily a parent, as one who fosters resilience by helping kids feel special and appreciated.[34] In short, a supportive adult can be a protective factor for a student.[35]

Beliefs About Teaching All Kinds of Minds

The science of learning, sampled in the previous sections, provides the foundation for a set of beliefs about teaching all kinds of minds:

- Inspire optimism in the face of learning challenges
- Discover and treasure learning profiles
- Eliminate humiliation, blaming, and labeling of students
- Leverage strengths and affinities
- Empower students to find success

These beliefs provide a roadmap for instructional decision making, ranging from the selection of strategies for an individual learner, to developing instructional approaches for a whole group, to building a positive classroom climate, and so on. In addition, these beliefs can be used by school leaders to establish policy and affect climate at the building level or even the district level.

Inspire Optimism

All students deserve and need to see a future filled with hopeful possibilities and excitement. The adult world accommodates, needs, and values all kinds of minds to fill all kinds of roles. Therefore, every student, especially those students who face learning challenges, should be helped to see the special possibilities for a fulfilling and gratifying life. Many struggling learners hear so many negative messages that they assume the worst about their futures. But some of the most successful adults experienced learning difficulties as children or adolescents. A learning problem is not a life sentence to strife and mediocrity.

> **PICTURE THIS!**
>
> Downplaying labels in descriptions of learners, emphasizing thorough descriptions, and promoting the empowerment of learners through improved self-insight can all contribute to the development of a positive school culture. Consider how your school reflects and promotes this kind of culture.

Discover and Treasure Learning Profiles

Every person has a set of strengths and weaknesses that make up a learning profile. Teachers have direct access to many clues about learning that can be used to reveal profiles. Understanding and appreciating learners' individual differences not only respects students but also guides instructional decision making. A learner's profile might serve him or her well at some ages and under certain circumstances, but not as well at other times or places. For example, a student may be well equipped to perform in literature class but not in algebra, or in art but not biology, or in third-grade math but not fourth-grade math. Students continually move through different grades, lessons, classrooms, and tasks. Illuminating a profile helps teachers support students in these various settings and ultimately paves the way for students to be self-advocates.

Eliminate Humiliation, Blaming, and Labeling

Students' strengths and weaknesses vary widely. No one can be good at everything. Many students possess highly specialized minds and deserve to be recognized for their abilities rather than being declared defective for their shortcomings. Educators should find ways to go beyond labels (like "deficit," "disorder," and "disability"), which are too often simplistic and unhelpful for educational planning. Labels can be self-fulfilling prophecies—students who think of themselves as disabled may start acting that way. The more specific we are in our descriptions of a student's profile, the more effective we can be in helping him or her find success. Therefore we strive to label *learning phenomena* rather than students. Examples include describing a learner's attention strengths and weaknesses rather than simply referring to him as "ADHD," determining that long-term memory is causing a reading difficulty instead of identifying a learner as "dyslexic," and exploring the possibility that a student's behavior problems might be rooted in a neurodevelopmental weakness (such as in language or social cognition) as opposed to describing her as "oppositional" or "conduct disordered." Later chapters provide more specific examples of how to eliminate humiliation, blaming, and labeling.

> Labels can be self-fulfilling prophecies—students who think of themselves as disabled may start acting that way. The more specific we are in our descriptions of a student's profile, the more effective we can be in helping him or her find success.

Leverage Strengths and Affinities

In the long run, strengths matter much more than weaknesses. How many adults choose fields of study or occupations that expose their weaknesses? Adults naturally gravitate toward their strengths. So, a priority for schools should be helping kids discover and then develop their talents and strong abilities. Similarly, affinities, or passionate interests, can be used to motivate students and to make material more engaging. For example, reading about something that stirs excitement can enhance reading skills. Strengths and affinities form the foundation for life-long success. Chapter Five includes several real-life examples of how educators uncovered and leveraged strengths and affinities.

Empower Students

Teachers can empower students to find success in many ways. They can help students better understand their learning profiles and how their minds work. They can show students how to leverage their strengths and affinities. By being transparent about the rationale behind strategies and instructional approaches, they can promote self-advocacy as well as metacognition. Through strong alliances educators can lead struggling students on the path to becoming successful life-long learners.

Key Ideas

- Deeply understanding learning and learners helps instructional decision making.
- A neurodevelopmental framework can help educators understand individual learners as well as the complexity of the learning process.
- In addition to being an intuitively positive approach, the efficacy of focusing on learner's strengths and affinities has been supported by research.
- Boosting learners' self-insight about learning, or metacognition, is beneficial.
- The science of learning supports the notion of empowering students through alliances with supportive adults.
- Beliefs about teaching all kinds of minds include
  - Inspiring optimism in the face of learning challenges
  - Discovering and treasuring learning profiles
  - Eliminating humiliation, blaming, and labeling of students
  - Leveraging strengths and affinities
  - Empowering students to find success

Learning Leadership in Action

Consider the learning environment to be the classroom, team, or school, whichever is the most pertinent to your educational practice. Then select one, several, or all of the statements about the All Kinds of Minds approach to reflect on or discuss.

Example: *An individual teacher uses her planning period to reflect on how she approaches learning differences in her classroom.*

All Kinds of Minds Approach: The science of learning and core principles	How does your learning environment reflect this statement?	What would a learning environment that embodies this statement look like?	What are some small wins you could use to get started?
Use a neurodevelopmental lens	I present instructions to the class by stating the directions and writing them on the board.	I would understand the learning profiles of the students who struggle with directions. I would use additional strategies to help all students understand the directions.	Identify 3–5 students who may struggle with directions.
Promote self-insight	Students expect to see and hear directions, but they may/may not be aware of what works best for them.	I would engage students in conversations about their learning profiles, and students would know what approaches/strategies are most effective for them.	Talk to each of those students about their preferences for directions.

(See blank template on next page.)

All Kinds of Minds Approach: The science of learning and core principles	How does your learning environment reflect this statement?	What would a learning environment that embodies this statement look like?	What are some small wins you could use to get started?
Use a neurodevelopmental lens			
Promote self-insight			
Empower students through alliances			
Inspire optimism in the face of learning challenges			
Discover and treasure unique learning profiles			
Eliminate humiliation, blaming, and labeling of students			
Leverage strengths and affinities			
Empower students to find success			

3

Key Ingredients of Learning

For Eastville Middle School's first professional development event of the year, Jan decided to facilitate a quick text-based discussion using the USA Today article that Brian had suggested. It provided a frame for an initial discussion on learning. The staff conversations were lively, and there was a positive energy of possibility in the room. As she circulated through the room, Jan was especially intrigued with how knowledgeable and passionate Mr. Chapman, one of the science teachers, was about the topic. Jan had noted early in her first year of working with Mr. Chapman that he often had insightful ideas to share during staff meetings and professional development activities. He was well respected among his peers and viewed as an innovator and natural leader. Jan made a mental note to schedule a meeting with him later that week to find out more about what he was doing in his classroom.

Jan began the meeting by asking Mr. Chapman about a student he had mentioned who was struggling in science and some other subjects. As he started discussing Paul, she was amazed at what she heard. Mr. Chapman did not once use anything resembling a label like "ADHD" or "LD," and he never even hinted at referring Paul for special education services so that he would be out of his classroom. Instead, he talked about Paul's strengths—memory, higher-order cognition, receptive language, spatial ordering, and several other terms Jan knew she had to learn more about. Mr. Chapman also mentioned a few examples of how he had adjusted his teaching approach because he felt he had been "overloading" particular "neurodevelopmental functions," like active working memory. "I've become very interested in neuroscience and what it means for learning," he said. "It really seems to make a difference for the students in my science classroom."

After the conversation, Jan sat back in her chair. She was impressed by how well Mr. Chapman seemed to understand Paul as a learner. Although she had introduced the idea of the science of learning to her staff through the USA Today *article, she had really only scratched the surface. She realized that she was incredibly fortunate to have a well-respected teacher on staff who was already using this approach to help students achieve success in his classroom. She wanted to share this conversation with Brian, so she sent him a quick e-mail asking if they could meet for an hour before the next principals' cohort meeting. Then she pulled out her partially completed professional development plan and began to pencil in some new ideas.*

This chapter will explore
- The neurodevelopmental framework of All Kinds of Minds:
  - Attention
  - Higher-order cognition
  - Language
  - Memory
  - Neuromotor function
  - Social cognition
  - Spatial ordering
  - Temporal-sequential ordering
- Comparisons of the All Kinds of Minds framework to other learning frameworks, such as Gardner's theory of multiple intelligences

---

TEACHERS HAVE DIRECT ACCESS TO AN INCREDIBLE WEALTH OF INFORMATION about students' learning. Work samples, behavior, oral comments and questions, and so on, are all clues about learning strengths and weaknesses. Gathering and then making sense of these clues is made easier with a conceptual framework for sorting and organizing them.

A framework is like a set of file folders. All of the related clues (such as math fact fluency or knowledge of the periodic table) are filed in a particular folder (like long-term memory). Some clues (like trouble following directions) may be sorted into multiple files (such as attention or language) until enough clues have been gathered to better determine what they indicate for that particular learner (and some clues actually stem from multiple causes).

All Kinds of Minds proposes a neurodevelopmental framework for organizing evidence about learners' profiles. The categories in this framework are described later in this chapter; many (such as memory) are familiar to most everyone. Some categories are subdivided for more specificity. Using a framework creates a shared vocabulary and promotes communication. When teachers, students, and parents use similar terms to describe learners, collaboration is made much easier. Learning plans are more readily handed off to different teachers. Also, using a common vocabulary facilitates teachers supporting each others' thinking and problem solving.

The framework used by All Kinds of Minds is an organizing structure through which all learners, including those who struggle, can be understood. It was developed by Dr. Mel Levine and colleagues at the All Kinds of Minds Institute. The framework is similar to neuropsychological frameworks but also draws from child and adolescent development and cognitive science as well as disciplines such as linguistics and occupational therapy. Since it is used to describe learners in terms of profiles of strengths and weaknesses, it does not include a general intelligence factor such as an IQ, a number that too often becomes a way to label learners. Finally, this framework was developed to link with academic skills such as reading and writing, so one criterion for inclusion of components was relevance to such skills (Chapter Seven explores the linkages between this framework and writing).

The framework consists of several constructs, which are listed in Table 3.1 along with brief descriptions.[1] The constructs, in turn, consist of several neurodevelopmental functions (or functions, for short). (See Figure 3.1.) For example, the construct of memory contains functions

Table 3.1 Neurodevelopmental Constructs in the All Kinds of Minds Framework

Construct	Brief Description
Attention	Maintaining mental energy for learning and work Absorbing and filtering incoming information Overseeing the quality of academic output and behavior
Higher-Order Cognition	Understanding concepts Evaluating products, ideas, and opinions Generating original ideas Applying logical approaches to complex problems
Language	Understanding incoming oral and written information Communicating ideas orally and in writing
Memory	Briefly recording new information Mentally juggling information while using it to complete a task Storing and then recalling information at a later time
Neuromotor Function	Using large muscles in a coordinated manner Using finger and hand movements Coordinating muscles needed for handwriting
Social Cognition	Knowing what to talk about, when, with whom, and for how long Working and playing with others in a cooperative manner Nurturing positive relationships with influential people
Spatial Ordering	Understanding information that is presented visually (such as maps, graphs, and symbols) Generating products that are visual Organizing materials and spaces
Temporal-Sequential Ordering	Understanding the order of steps, events, or other sequences Generating products arranged in a meaningful order Organizing time and schedules

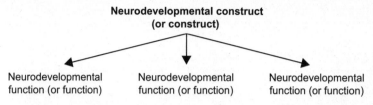

Figure 3.1 Neurodevelopmental Constructs and Functions

Additional information about the neurodevelopmental framework, including supporting research, can be found at www.allkindsofminds.org.

such as active working and long-term memory. Though functions within the same construct are related and have some overlapping features, they are distinct enough to be considered separate entities. The next sections of the chapter provide overviews of the constructs in this framework.

Attention

Attention is not a single entity, but rather three different systems that maintain alertness, orient to sensory events and process incoming information, and regulate output and behavior.[2] Everyone has a profile of attention, regardless of whether they meet the diagnostic criteria for ADHD. For a given learner, some aspects of attention may work well, and other aspects may function less reliably. Attention is susceptible to mismatches with the environment or task demands. For example, even someone with good attention could have trouble staying focused for a three-hour lecture delivered with no visual aids and few breaks. Having a handle on a learner's attention profile, including how well it meets current demands, goes a long way toward having a deep understanding of that learner.

The Russian neuropsychologist Alexander Luria was a pioneer in describing how the brain and mind are organized. He divided attention into three units: Unit 1 regulates levels of alertness, Unit 2 analyzes newly received information, and Unit 3 programs and regulates activity.[3]

In the All Kinds of Minds framework, the three attention systems are the mental energy controls, processing controls, and production controls,[4] which collectively can be conceptualized as a car's dashboard that both directs and monitors the functioning of the engine (or brain) as illustrated in Figure 3.2. The mental energy controls regulate the initiation and maintenance of cognitive energy flow for learning, work, and behavioral control. They represent the brain's fuel tank and are represented as a fuel gauge on the attention dashboard. Everyone experiences low mental energy at times and knows how difficult staying alert and vigilant can be at the end of a long day, late at night, very early in the morning, and so on. Unfortunately, some learners experience this kind of "brain drain" frequently, especially when faced with academic tasks that require sustained effort, such as composing a book report or term paper. For such learners, most work is too much work. While their peers continue to plug away at academic tasks, they get excessively fatigued. Learners with limited mental energy often have trouble initiating tasks, as if they cannot establish inertia at the

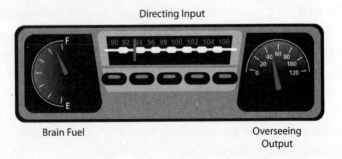

Figure 3.2 *Attention as a Dashboard*

outset. Sometimes learners with low energy resort to fidgeting and other body movement in order to keep their minds vigilant and maintain alertness—physical activity can stimulate mental activity.

Consider all the sensations you're currently experiencing. What are you hearing? Smelling? Sensing with your skin? Tasting? Seeing? Which have been suppressed while reading? Which may have drawn your focus? Processing controls sort this sensory information. Similar to how a radio receiver sets on a particular signal, the processing controls determine the relative importance of available inputs. A problem with this is often labeled *distractibility* or *inattention*. The processing controls also absorb information with appropriate intensity and maintain focus for sufficient stretches of time, sometimes referred to as *sustained attention*. All learners have to grapple with a huge amount of detail; those with weak processing controls often have difficulty picking up details, leading to little mistakes that are often easily corrected when pointed out to the learner. Whenever information seems to "go in one ear and out the other," the processing controls could be to blame. Problems with the processing controls can affect other constructs, including language and memory—understanding and remembering something is difficult, if not impossible, without first sufficiently attending to it.

> The production controls are similar in definition to so-called executive functions, which regulate thought and mental output. But the concept of executive functions has evolved and expanded to include what processing controls do, as well as aspects of higher-order cognition, such as using logic to solve problems. All Kinds of Minds makes a cleaner break within attention (production versus processing) and across constructs, allowing for more specific descriptions of learners.

Akin to a dashboard's speedometer, the production controls oversee academic and behavioral output, including impulse and rate control, previewing and planning, and self-monitoring. Students who routinely leap before thinking, work in haphazard ways, and have trouble detecting how well they are doing are showing signs of weak production controls. Writing is an academic task that places huge demands on the production controls, which makes written output a good place to look for evidence of this kind of attention difficulty: little to no planning or outlining, rushed and messy work, limited editing, and numerous mistakes.

Although variations exist, the development of the three attention control systems are reflected in the major segments of a child's life. The mental energy controls come on line during early childhood (think about babies and toddlers gradually settling into sleep patterns). The processing controls surge during the elementary school years (when learners have to cope with the bombardment of all sorts of academic and nonacademic information). The production controls gain prominence in adolescence (when youngsters meet so many kinds of behavioral temptations and challenges to their self-regulation). Of course, weaknesses with any of these aspects of attention can arise at different times. Table 3.2 lists some positive signs and trouble signs related to attention.

Table 3.2 Attention: Positive Signs and Trouble Signs

Positive Signs	Trouble Signs
Readily starts working and maintains effort level	Has trouble initiating and sticking with tasks
Appears to have sufficient energy when working	Appears excessively fatigued when working
Maintains focus for adequate stretches of time	Loses focus relatively quickly; susceptible to distractions
Notices key details	Misses key details
Resists impulses	Susceptible to impulses
Plans before starting a task	Jumps into tasks without sufficient planning
Works at an appropriate pace	Rushes through work
Notices and corrects mistakes	Misses mistakes and opportunities to improve work quality

Higher-Order Cognition

Perhaps the most critical construct for lifelong success is higher-order cognition, which refers to complex and sophisticated thinking. As with attention, higher-order cognition is multifaceted, which is why it is represented as a set of rotating cogs rather than a single entity. (See Figure 3.3.) Its components include

- *Applied reasoning:* Thinking in a systematic way in order to solve problems that do not have a readily apparent solution
- *Evaluative* (or *critical*) *thinking:* Appraising ideas, products, points of view, and opportunities
- *Complex decision making:* Applying stepwise approaches to resolving complicated questions or challenges
- *Brainstorming and creative thinking:* Generating original ideas or perspectives; thinking in innovative ways concerning expression, resolving dilemmas, and overcoming obstacles
- *Conceptualization:* Integrating sets of features that form categories of ideas (such as "cooperation" and "social activism") or things (such as "fruits" and "invertebrates")

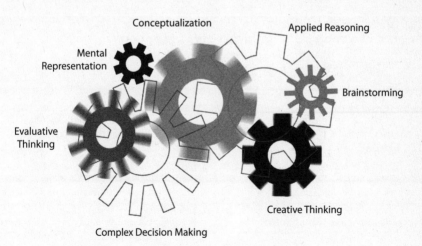

Figure 3.3 Higher-Order Cognition's Turning Cogs

Contemplate how you are formulating an understanding of the neurodevelopmental framework. Are you thinking about how the constructs relate to each other? Are you connecting with prior knowledge? Are you drawing from your experience with learners to find examples of the constructs in action? Higher-order cognition uses many mechanisms to build concepts.

PICTURE THIS!

Higher-order cognition is a critical element of quality teaching. Consider facilitating professional development activities on strengthening specific aspects of higher-order cognition such as applied reasoning, conceptualization, and creative thinking. Our schools need as many teachers as possible who are adept at thinking systematically to solve problems, comprehending concepts, and generating original ideas and perspectives.

Higher-order cognition is important for understanding the wide range of ideas and processes students encounter in school. Students make use of higher-order cognition when they use logic to solve math problems, make complex decisions when setting up a science experiment, come up with innovative ways to express ideas in writing or other media, use evidence to support their opinions or to critique the opinions of others, and so on. In essence, higher-order cognition is about deeply understanding things, not merely memorizing or regurgitating them. Table 3.3 lists potential positive signs and trouble signs for higher-order cognition.

Table 3.3 Higher-Order Cognition: Positive Signs and Trouble Signs

Positive Signs	Trouble Signs
Sees connections among material from different sources (such as history and science)	Struggles with making connections among material from different sources
Shows a good imagination for creative writing and artwork	Draws heavily from existing sources for ideas, or needs helps from others
Takes risks with new ideas	Conservative with ideas and proposals
Solves problems in systematic ways	Haphazardly tries to solve problems
Draws inferences from limited information	Struggles with inferencing or "reading between the lines"
Develops an understanding of an idea by considering its components or connections to other ideas	Has trouble understanding new things without considerable support

Language

Being able to understand and utilize language is central to success in school. This is good news for students whose brains are wired for language, but decidedly bad news for the rest. Language is among the most multifaceted of the constructs because it includes so many abilities related to communication, such as being aware of word sounds, pronouncing words, comprehending written symbols, understanding syntax, building sentences, telling stories, extending thinking through discussion or writing, and so on.[5] The hierarchical structure of language can be visualized as a series of nesting boxes, each with a side that receives input and another that generates output. (See Figure 3.4.) The sized boxes correspond to the different sizes of language chunks:

- *Word sounds:* Also known as phonemes
- *Meaningful word parts:* Also known as morphemes; examples include prefixes and suffixes
- *Whole words:* Vocabulary or lexicon
- *Sentences:* Syntax and grammar
- *Multiple sentences:* Lengthier pieces of language, such as a paragraph, story, chapter, speech, or book

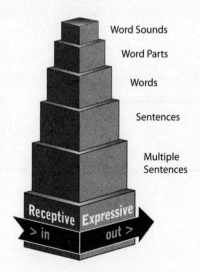

Figure 3.4 Language's Nesting Boxes

Receptive language is the input side and encompasses the processing and understanding of oral and written information. Contemplate the complexity of reading and understanding the text on this page. Did you encounter words that you didn't know? Did you have to reread any sentences? Receptive language is critical for reading comprehension as well as the decoding of printed words (processing word sounds, understanding meaningful word parts—such as prefixes—and having a rich vocabulary).

Expressive language represents the output side and includes communicating and producing ideas orally and in writing. We utilize expressive language when we converse, compose e-mails, and even send text messages. The most tangible application of expressive language in school is writing, though students are expected to communicate orally all the time, such as during class discussions and collaborative projects. Table 3.4 lists some of the positive signs and trouble signs of language.

Table 3.4 Language: Positive Signs and Trouble Signs

Positive Signs	Trouble Signs
Performs accurate decoding and spelling	Makes decoding and spelling errors that don't make sense phonetically (like "widdend" for "wooden")
Understands words encountered in reading and discussion	Misinterprets word meanings
Follows extended explanations, even if complex sentence structures are used	Is confused by explanations, especially with complex sentence structures
Comprehends abstract and figurative language	Struggles to get past literal interpretations of abstract and figurative language
Makes good choices about words and can alter words with prefixes and suffixes	Uses words inaccurately and has trouble altering words with prefixes and suffixes
Constructs grammatically correct sentences	Makes grammatical errors
Crafts extended pieces of language (like reports or presentations) to express thinking	Produces extended pieces of language that are not sufficiently organized or coherent or that do not elaborate on ideas

Memory

Memory has multiple components, including long-term memory and active working memory. Long-term memory comprises two processes—storage of information and retrieval of information—that can vary in effectiveness for a learner. For instance, a learner might be able to store information (allowing her to perform well with recognition questions like multiple-choice items) but struggle with retrieval (which would manifest as difficulty with free recall questions like open-ended items). Long-term memory may be symbolized as a file cabinet: information is both filed (stored or consolidated) and pulled (retrieved or accessed), as illustrated in Figure 3.5. Also, the more organized the information is for storage, the more efficient the retrieval. This is one explanation for the limitations of rote memory. Learners more readily access information that is categorized—such as in themes—and that is cross-referenced with connections to other topics illuminated.

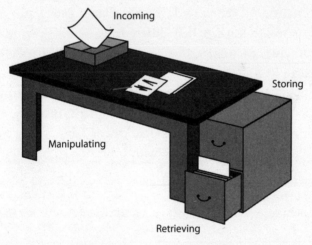

Figure 3.5 Memory as a File Cabinet and Desktop

The Cattell-Horn-Carroll framework includes long-term retrieval, defining it as both storing and retrieving information.[6]

Long-term memory is important for many aspects of school, such as learning math facts, U.S. presidents, capitalization rules, procedures for factoring an equation, and so on. The more efficiently students can access information, the more effort and thought they can direct toward other tasks, such as comprehending or generating new ideas. Though technological developments of the digital age (such as search engines and handheld devices) give individuals quick and easy access to huge quantities of information, learners will still be expected to commit a great deal to long-term memory, at least for the foreseeable future.

Without writing anything down, rank order the most important three facts you've so far encountered in this chapter. You're using your active working memory to sort this information in your mind (you would also use active working memory if you were to recite your telephone number in reverse order, without paper or pencil). Active working memory is the brain's workspace that processes[7] both auditory and visual information.[8] It is where we mentally juggle information while using it. Active working memory may also be visualized as desk space where information is temporarily stored while organizing it or using it (refer to Figure 3.5); learners have different sizes of desk spaces and vary in their capacities to organize material on their desk spaces. Some have likened active working memory to a computer's RAM (where software runs), and long-term memory to a hard drive (to which information can be uploaded and downloaded). As with long-term memory, a learner's active working memory could operate better with certain modalities (such as spatial information) than with others (such as language-based material); an important task for educators is often to identify the information formats that are most effective for a particular student's memory. Table 3.5 includes several positive signs and trouble signs for memory.

Neuromotor Function

Neuromotor function describes control over the movement of large muscles, hands, and fingers. Exerting such control requires signals that travel in two directions: from the brain to the muscles (to direct motions, such as throwing a ball or controlling a pencil) and from

Table 3.5 Memory: Positive Signs and Trouble Signs

Positive Signs	Trouble Signs
Holds on to beginning of reading passage when reaching the end	Forgets information from beginning of reading passage when reaching the end
Completes multistep tasks and executes multistep math procedures	Loses track of multiple steps
Performs mental math calculations	Struggles with mental math calculations
Handles the many tasks involved in writing (like spelling, punctuation, ideation)	Has trouble juggling the many tasks involved in writing
Easily learns new terminology, facts, and procedures	Slow to recall facts
Recognizes previously encountered patterns	Studies by rote rather than strategically
	Has particular trouble with cumulative subjects
Retrieves one half of a pair when given the other half (such as definitions with terms, names with faces)	Struggles to recall information, even when given recognition cues (like multiple-choice options)
Recalls proper procedure for the problem or situation	Uses incorrect procedure for a problem or situation

muscles to the brain (to convey where the body is in the middle of a motion). Contemplate how you are using your neuromotor functions right now. Are you hand-writing notes and using graphomotor function? Are you using fine motor function to highlight text? (See Figure 3.6.)

The most important neuromotor function for schoolwork has historically been graphomotor function, or motor abilities for hand-writing. But control over small movements, or fine motor function, and large movements, or gross motor function, also are utilized in school. Fine motor function is used for a variety of academic tasks, including keyboarding and drawing. Graphomotor function and fine motor function are discrete, even though both relate to small hand movements—a student could be an excellent artist but still struggle with handwriting legibility.

Neuromotor functions can vary, and educators should be prepared to encounter students who exhibit excellent fine motor function (for example, they can play a woodwind instrument with ease), and yet struggle with graphomotor function. Besides athletics, gross motor function is used for dance, play, and any activity requiring body control (including the planning of movements). Success with such activities can bolster confidence, while failure can cause negative self-esteem and even social problems. Table 3.6 includes a sampling of positive signs and trouble signs related to neuromotor functions.

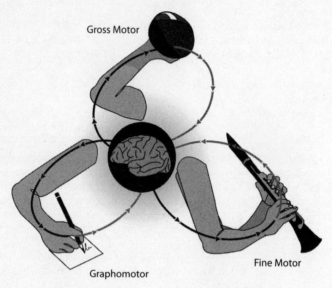

Figure 3.6 Neuromotor's Two-Way Connections

Table 3.6 Neuromotor Function: Positive Signs and Trouble Signs

Positive Signs	Trouble Signs
Writes letters and numbers smoothly and with consistent formation	Shows hesitancy when forming some letters, which may have inconsistent appearance
Handwriting is legible	Handwriting has limited legibility
Has appropriate endurance for handwriting	Hand fatigues quickly when writing
	Needs to watch hand and pencil closely when writing
Uses a comfortable handwriting grip	Uses an awkward handwriting grip
Is skilled at activities requiring manual dexterity, such as typing and playing woodwind instruments or the piano	Slow to learn new skills requiring manual dexterity
Moves finger and hands with smooth coordination	Is clumsy with hand and finger movements
Readily learns new athletic skills	Has trouble learning new athletic skills
Shows good balance and body coordination	Struggles to balance and coordinate body movements

Social Cognition

Along with higher-order cognition, social cognition is especially important for success in adulthood. Shortcomings with memory and neuromotor function, for example, can be addressed with strategies or by selecting a career or field of study that deemphasizes those weaknesses. But the capacity to navigate interactions with others (including verbal and nonverbal tactics), to perceive and monitor social information, and to respond appropriately within social settings is essential for a wide array of careers and life activities. At its essence, social cognition is thinking about social interactions, which is why it is represented as a person contemplating how to interact with others in a group in Figure 3.7. Social information can be extremely complicated to decipher because of the subtlety of many of the signals, the speed with which they come at a person, and the huge amount of information to absorb.

Social cognition and language are related, as good verbal communication makes relating to others easier. Contemplate your social cognition by recalling a recent conversation with a colleague, parent, or student. What verbal or nonverbal signals did you detect? How did you use that information to make decisions during your interaction? How effective were the choices you made and how did you know?

Figure 3.7 Social Cognition

Researchers have identified several specific aspects of so-called verbal pragmatics (or social language "rules of the road"), including

- Selecting appropriate conversation topics[9]
- Transitioning to new conversation topics[10]
- Handling miscommunication[11]
- Taking turns when conversing[12]
- Inferring intentions and feelings from gestures and facial expressions[13]

A huge part of socializing involves making good decisions based on available information, verbal and nonverbal. Social cognition encompasses this decision-making process, including the interplay between deciphering social cues and making social decisions. We see such decisions take many forms with students in our school, ranging from choosing the best way to introduce oneself to a game or activity in progress to thinking through how to forge a better relationship with a chemistry lab partner. Social cognition also encompasses the political acumen needed to forge positive relationships with important people, like teachers and other adults in a student's life. Table 3.7 lists some of the positive signs and trouble signs for social cognition.

> **PICTURE THIS!**
>
> Effective teachers are adept at forming and nurturing positive relationships—with their students, with colleagues, with administrators, and with parents. Social cognition is part and parcel of this aspect of teaching. Consider ways in which you, as a learning leader, are currently encouraging and fostering the development of these relationships.

Table 3.7 Social Cognition: Positive Signs and Trouble Signs

Positive Signs	Trouble Signs
Collaborates effectively	Is too pushy or too detached during group work
Navigates the "give and take" of conversation	Dominates conversations or is too passive
Detects the mood of others	Does not pick up signals about the mood of others
Shows appreciation for others' viewpoints and interests	Shows little appreciation for others' viewpoints and interests

Spatial Ordering

Contemplate the visual representations of the constructs used in this chapter. How helpful are they to you? When sharing the content of this chapter with colleagues, would you use the images, abandon them, or alter them somehow? What other images might you construct to convey this content?

Spatial ordering is the processing and production of material that is visual or exists in a spatial array. It is sometimes referred to as "visual processing," but that term does not capture the idea that a great deal of spatial information is not taken in visually (imagine navigating your way through a dark closet). Also, visual processing does not capture the production side of the equation, such as designing or creating artwork.

Spatial ordering is thinking in a spatial way, as illustrated in Figure 3.8. Material that may not seem to have an obvious spatial element to one person may be processed spatially by another. Driving directions, for example, could be processed in a spatial way, such as visualizing a map, or they could be thought about in terms of a series of steps (such as, "Take the first left, take a right at the fifth stoplight, look for the blue building on the right.").

Figure 3.8 Spatial Ordering

Table 3.8 Spatial Ordering: Positive Signs and Trouble Signs

Positive Signs	Trouble Signs
Readily makes sense of maps, graphs, diagrams, and symbols	Misinterprets visual information or needs support to understand it
Draws or copies well Good at building and fixing things	Struggles with drawing, copying with appropriate accuracy, building, or fixing things

In the academic realm, one student might visualize the science concepts involved, another may rely on a sequential memory of a laboratory experiment, and a third student might even do both. The use of schematic imagery has been shown to be related to success in solving math word problems; schematic imagery represents the relative quantities and relationships between a problem's elements and is very useful for setting up a solution and reality-testing the result. Weak spatial ordering can also lead to disorganized written calculations, such as not lining up numbers neatly in columns, leading to errors. Even language arts includes spatial information; for instance, correct placement of commas and quotation marks constitutes a kind of visual pattern. Table 3.8 lists a few of the positive signs and trouble signs related to spatial ordering.

Temporal-Sequential Ordering

Temporal-sequential ordering (sometimes shortened to "sequencing") is the processing and production of material that is linear or exists in a meaningful serial order. Put differently, it is thinking in a sequential way, and in many respects is the mirror image of spatial ordering. As with spatial ordering, material that may not seem sequential to one person could be processed sequentially by another (consider the driving directions example from the previous section). (See Figure 3.9.)

Contemplate the constructs you have learned about in this chapter (which were presented alphabetically). When sharing the content of this chapter with colleagues, in what order would you cover them? Temporal-sequential ordering helps to make such decisions as how to order information. Students make similar decisions, such as

Figure 3.9 Temporal-Sequential Ordering

Table 3.9 Temporal-Sequential Ordering: Positive Signs and Trouble Signs

Positive Signs	Trouble Signs
Accurately follows sequential procedures and instructions	Confuses steps of procedures and instructions
Learns sequential information like timelines	Has trouble learning sequences like the process of photosynthesis
Presents ideas in a clear, serial order	Presents ideas out of logical serial order

constructing narratives for short stories, building historical timelines, and explaining processes like respiration.

Sequential information abounds in school starting in the early grades when students need to master material such as the alphabet and number lines. Sequences become more conceptual in the later school years, such as the unfolding of historical events and the steps in a science lab experiment. Students who have trouble processing and generating sequences are at a distinct disadvantage with schoolwork. Table 3.9 includes some positive signs and trouble signs for temporal-sequential ordering.

Metacognition

You were asked to reflect upon your own neurodevelopmental constructs several times in this chapter, all of which were opportunities for metacognition. Though metacognition is not considered to be a construct in this framework, it is nonetheless a well-established neu-rodevelopmental function that is integral to the All Kinds of Minds approach. Metacognition is, simply, thinking about thinking. It includes one's knowledge about learning as well as insight into one's own learn-ing strengths and weaknesses.[14] Students benefit from good metacog-nition both in terms of keener self-insight for strategies and academic tasks and, more generally, in stronger resilience.[15]

> Metacognition is similar to Gardner's intrapersonal intelligence, which builds an accurate self-perception and uses it to make good decisions.[16]

Comparing the All Kinds of Minds Framework to Other Frameworks

Arguably, the theory of intelligence that has been most discussed by educators is Howard Gardner's theory of multiple intelligences. Gardner has described several nonhierarchical categories of intel-ligence.[17] Parallels to Gardner's intelligences, such as linguistic intelligence and language, can be found in the All Kinds of Minds framework. Also, the All Kinds of Minds framework can be used to more deeply and specifically understand why individuals exhibit vary-ing degrees of Gardner's intelligences. For instance, what Gardner describes as musical intelligence could stem from a combination of strengths in temporal-sequential ordering, higher-order cognition, fine motor function, and attention; for some individuals and cir-cumstances, social cognition may even be important for developing musical ability. Viewing Gardner's intelligences through a neurode-velopmental lens—and acknowledging that individuals may exhibit a particular intelligence but for different sets of reasons—paves the way for selecting or inventing approaches that develop the various intelligences.

> "What Gardner describes as musical intelligence could stem from a combination of strengths in temporal-sequential ordering, higher-order cognition, fine motor function, and attention; for some individuals and circumstances, social cognition may even be important for developing musical ability."

The Cattell-Horn-Carroll (CHC) theory of intelligence combines Cattell-Horn Gf-Gc theory and Carroll's three-tier model. Carroll[18] developed a framework with a general intelligence factor that is divided into more specific abilities, each consisting of even narrower factors. Cattell-Horn's model was similar to Carroll's in many ways, such as in its hierarchical structure. In the 1990s, Carroll's and Cattell-Horn's models were combined by Flanagan, McGrew, and Ortiz to create CHC.[19] The middle layer of CHC abilities include fluid reasoning (forming and recognizing logical relationships among patterns, inferencing, and transforming novel stimuli) and comprehension-knowledge (using language and acquired knowledge). Several of these CHC abilities are similar to constructs in the All Kinds of Minds framework, but CHC includes a general intelligence factor.

Luria organized brain functions into familiar categories, such as memory and attention.[20] The PASS model (for Planning, Attention, Successive, and Simultaneous) includes both a global index of ability and specific cognitive processes.[21] For example, *simultaneous* refers to perceiving, interpreting, and/or remembering material as a whole (such as a picture or diagram) and *successive* refers to perceiving, interpreting, and/or remembering information that is in a serial order (such as language). Table 3.10 displays the constructs in the All Kinds of Minds framework with similar elements from Gardner's multiple intelligences, CHC, Luria's framework, and the PASS model.

Table 3.10 All Kinds of Minds Framework Compared with Other Frameworks

All Kinds of Minds Framework	Howard Gardner's Multiple Intelligences	CHC Broad Cognitive Abilities	Luria's Framework	PASS Model
Attention		Processing speed	Attention	Planning Attention
Higher-order cognition	Logical-mathematical	Fluid reasoning	Thinking	
Language	Linguistic	Comprehension-knowledge Auditory processing	Speech	
Memory		Short-term memory Long-term retrieval	Memory	
Neuromotor function	Bodily-kinesthetic		Movement and action	
Social cognition	Interpersonal			
Spatial ordering	Spatial	Visual processing	Perception	Simultaneous
Temporal-sequential ordering				Successive

The CAST model includes a recognition network, strategic network, and affective network,[22] each of which represents somewhat similar functioning to certain aspects of the All Kinds of Minds framework. For example, the strategic network (planning, executing, and self-monitoring) is analogous to the attention production controls. Table 3.11 lists other constructs and functions along with related brain networks from the CAST model.

The All Kinds of Minds framework is not at odds with other frameworks, especially those that do not include a global intelligence factor. The value of a framework is that it can facilitate organizing evidence about learners' profiles. Each of the frameworks described in this section, including others not listed here, can serve this purpose.

Table 3.11 All Kinds of Minds Framework Compared with the CAST Model

All Kinds of Minds Constructs/Functions	Brain Networks from the CAST Model
Attention, Mental Energy Control	Recognition, Strategic, Affective
Attention, Processing Controls	Recognition, Affective
Attention, Production Controls	Strategic
Higher-Order Cognition	Recognition, Affective
Language, Expressive	Strategic
Language, Receptive	Recognition
Memory, Active Working	Strategic
Memory, Long-Term	Recognition
Neuromotor Function	Strategic
Social Cognition	Affective
Spatial Ordering	Recognition, Strategic
Temporal-Sequential Ordering	Recognition, Strategic

Educators even may use more than one framework at a time. The All Kinds of Minds framework has many features that are attractive to learning leaders, including

- *Approachability.* Several constructs, like memory, are actually lay terms.
- *Specificity.* Most constructs are broken down into components.
- *Validity.* It draws from research in multiple domains.
- *Applicability.* Its components link to academic skill development.

Thinking with a framework can boost the efficacy of school or district initiatives. For example, a district investing in a literacy and comprehension program for all elementary schools could help educators hone their observation skills through knowledge of the neurodevelopmental functions necessary for reading development. A school that chooses critical thinking as the theme of the year could use the framework to explore tasks requiring critical thinking.

The All Kinds of Minds framework is supported by a strong foundation of research, some of which is provided in Table 3.12.

Table 3.12 Examples of Research on the Neurodevelopmental Constructs

Attention

Mental Energy Controls

Learners who struggle with attention may experience a more general deficit in energy state regulation.[23]

Mental fatigue is one of the hallmarks of students with weak attention.[24]

Processing Controls

Distracting auditory stimuli can hinder children's listening comprehension.[25]

Limited attention interferes with memory of visual material.[26]

Production Controls

Brain imaging studies indicate that previewing (or planning) and facilitation-inhibition (or impulse control) improve steadily throughout adolescence.[27]

Improvements in self-regulation (including planning and self-checking) brought about improvements in fourth-grade students' composition skills.[28]

Higher-Order Cognition

Eighth graders who performed well on a reasoning test also demonstrated successful achievement in science.[29]

Four- to eleven-year-olds' scientific misconceptions (such as confusing heat with temperature) steadily decreased with age, indicating that development of scientific concepts undergoes change throughout childhood.[30]

Elementary students and adults all distinguished reasoning from nonreasoning in scenarios, but age-related improvement occurred for identifying problems solved with nonreasoning approaches, like guessing.[31]

Language

Receptive

The processing of word sounds (phonological awareness) is one of the components of word decoding and efficient text reading.[32]

Morphological awareness (knowledge of meaningful word parts) was found to make a significant unique contribution to reading vocabulary, spelling, decoding accuracy, and decoding rate.[33]

Learners with reading difficulty often have limited vocabulary.[34]

Expressive

Expressive language emerges when infants are about one-year-old and develops to include single words, sentences, and connected discourse.[35]

The capacity to generate sentences has been shown to be integral to writing.[36]

Memory

Long-Term

Memory for visual-verbal pairs (that is, a sound linked with a symbol) is a factor for learning phonics for reading decoding.[37]

Long-term memory is important for the learning of multiplication facts.[38]

Active Working

Children show age-related improvements in visual working memory; in fact, ten-year-olds perform at adult levels on some tasks.[39]

Results from an extensive meta-analysis of eighty-six studies indicate that active working memory capacity correlates with many different abilities within the information processing system, but that working memory may be best placed with the lower cognitive abilities rather than higher order abilities like reasoning.[40]

Neuromotor Function

Graphomotor

Children with handwriting difficulty generate more letters with added strokes, produce smaller letters, and exhibit more variability in spacing and alignment.[41]

Students who struggle with handwriting use more space to construct individual letters, reverse the direction of letters more often, and tend to hold their pencil aloft longer between the writing of the letters.[42]

Fine Motor

Research into structured drawing tasks has shown that performance improves with age, including less frequent stopping of movements, shorter drawing times, higher speeds, and fewer errors.[43]

Mental representations of hand localization (used for movement perception, planning, and control) are developed to adult levels by seven to ten years of age.[44]

Gross Motor

Children without gross motor function difficulties were more accurate at mentally rotating images than the students with such difficulty, suggesting that they do not have sufficient mental models for how to control movements.[45]

Weaknesses in gross motor function may limit children's abilities to obtain good information about objects and to perceive sensory-motion feedback, thus restricting their social play behaviors.[46]

(*Continued*)

Table 3.12 (Continued)

Social Cognition

Social cognition and language affect each other.[47]

Children who overestimate the extent to which they are socially accepted by their classmates were also described by peers as aggressive, while children who underestimate their social acceptance were the most prone to aggressive behavior in response to social criticism.[48]

Spatial Ordering

Sixth graders with high spatial visualization ability tend to produce images that are primarily schematic in nature, and students with low spatial visualization ability tend to produce pictorial images that do not bolster thinking about math problems.[49]

Findings from a study involving fifth graders suggested that weak spatial processing can lead to difficulties such as not accurately lining up numbers during math calculations.[50]

Temporal-Sequential Ordering

Evidence was found of a temporal information processing factor with male adolescents.[51]

Participants used mental representations that organized visual material in a time sequence, enhancing memory.[52]

Readers greatly value the time dimension that is described in most narratives; readers engage in an active process of mentally organizing described events into a temporal sequence and then remember the events in this fashion.[53]

Metacognition

Metacognitive understanding develops gradually between four and twelve years of age.[54]

Developmental improvements in comprehension monitoring occur between fifth and sixth grades, comprehension monitoring is a significant predictor of reading comprehension, and students use metacognition to choose and apply learning strategies.[55]

Key Ideas

- Attention is a multifaceted construct that maintains mental energy for learning and work, absorbs and filters incoming information, and oversees the quality of academic output and behavior.
- Higher-order cognition includes several abilities, including understanding concepts, evaluating ideas and opinions, generating original ideas, and applying logical approaches to complex problems.
- Language has two sides: understanding incoming information (oral and written) and communicating ideas orally and in writing.
- Memory includes briefly recording new information, mentally juggling information while using it to complete a task, and storing and then recalling information at a later time.
- Neuromotor function involves the two-way connections between the brain and muscles, including those needed for handwriting.
- Social cognition has several facets, such as navigating conversations, working and playing with others in a cooperative manner, and nurturing positive relationships with influential people.
- Spatial ordering (sometimes referred to as visual processing) is the interpretation and generation of material that is visual or exists in a spatial array; it is thinking in a spatial way.
- Temporal-sequential ordering (sometimes shortened to "sequencing") is the interpretation and generation of material that is linear; it is thinking in a sequential way.
- Metacognition is thinking about thinking.
- The All Kinds of Minds framework, while distinctive, has similarities with other learning frameworks, but does not include a global intelligence factor like IQ.
- The All Kinds of Minds framework can be used in conjunction with school or district initiatives, such as literacy development programs.

Learning Leadership in Action

Working independently, with a group of colleagues, or an entire staff, use the information below to explore your learning profile. Read the indicators provided and determine areas of strengths and weaknesses for each construct. Then consider how the profile of an individual or team affects instructional decision making, learning climate, or school/district policies.

Example: A team of secondary language arts teachers individually reflect on the common indicators of strengths and discuss their insights at their next team planning period. As they review their own profile of strengths and weaknesses, they discover that everyone on the team has strengths in higher-order cognition, language, and memory. The team wonders how their strengths affect the curriculum and instructional decisions they make as a team. With new insights from the science of learning, they consider what they can do to ensure the language arts curriculum and their lesson plans meet the needs of all learners, not just those who have similar strengths.

Neurodevelopmental Constructs	Common Indicators of Strengths	Strength or Weakness?
Attention	I stick with demanding work without brain fatigue setting in. I can keep my focus and steer clear of distractions. I routinely control impulses, plan, take my time, and check my work.	

Neurodevelopmental Constructs	Common Indicators of Strengths	Strength or Weakness?
Higher-Order Cognition	I usually understand ideas and concepts quickly and easily. I apply logic and reasoning to most challenges. I readily generate innovative ideas.	Strength for team
Language	I gather and understand a lot of information through words and text. I express myself well with words, sentences, and passages.	Strength for team
Memory	I can juggle mentally lots of information and many ideas. I readily memorize information. People can count on me to recall important information and events.	Strength for team

(See blank template on next page.)

Neurodevelop-mental Constructs	Common Indicators of Strengths	Strength or Weakness?
Attention	I stick with demanding work without brain fatigue setting in. I can keep my focus and steer clear of distractions. I routinely control impulses, plan, take my time, and check my work.	
Higher-Order Cognition	I usually understand ideas and concepts quickly and easily. I apply logic and reasoning to most challenges. I readily generate innovative ideas.	
Language	I gather and understand a lot of information through words and text. I express myself well with words, sentences, and passages.	
Memory	I can juggle mentally lots of information and many ideas. I readily memorize information. People can count on me to recall important information and events.	
Neuromotor Function	I have good control of large body movements, such as for sports or dance. I have good control of hand movements, like for art or playing musical instruments. Handwriting comes naturally and easily to me.	
Social Cognition	I collaborate effectively in a range of settings. I nurture positive relationships with others. I am good at reading the mood of people and situations.	
Spatial Ordering	I am drawn toward visual and graphical material. I easily recall shapes, symbols, and images. I work well with diagrams and maps.	
Temporal-Sequential Ordering	I remember processes and work well with them. I am comfortable following steps and sequences. Numbered lists and sequences help keep me on track.	

4

Digging Deeper
Knowing Students as Learners

Jan had discussed the science of learning with Brian and the other middle school principals in their cohort meeting last week and she knew she was ready to take the next step. She was confident that reaching the school goals would depend on the whole staff getting better at understanding the learning needs of their students. As the learning leader in the school, she needed to harness the talents of her staff to know more about their students, work collaboratively across subject areas, and focus on learning across the school. "How can we better know our students as learners?" was the theme of the plan. Jan felt fortunate that Mr. Chapman had already agreed to work closely with her to demonstrate the strength of this approach to the entire staff.

For Eastville Middle School's next professional development meeting, Jan wanted to provide her staff with an example that would show the power of this approach, so she asked Mr. Chapman to discuss Paul's neurodevelopmental profile and how he had come to know Paul as a learner. He started by describing Paul's overall strengths and affinities. Then he shared a story with the group about Paul's struggles, particularly the difference between his class participation and how he performs on tests. He described how Paul makes rich and valuable contributions during class discussions, shines during team projects, and develops creative and effective work products. In addition, Paul often takes on a leadership role when working in groups and encourages his team members with his positive attitude. Conversely, he struggles with tests, often achieving disappointing results. Mr. Chapman also made a point of weaving multiple examples of how he had observed Paul's peer interactions, talked with his parents, looked closely at his work samples, reviewed his cumulative folder, and talked with Paul's other teachers.

One specific example he shared with the Eastville staff was Paul's class notes. Mr. Chapman made a copy for each teacher to look at as he discussed some interesting clues that work sample revealed. While Paul had a few key words related to the various science topics they had discussed in class, the pages of his notes consistently included pictures drawn in the margins. For example, on the day they discussed force and friction, Paul had drawn a detailed image of a machine that used force to propel an object through the air. While his written notes were scarce, his picture demonstrated many of the elements of the concepts they had learned that day. This was Mr. Chapman's first concrete clue that one of Paul's strengths was in spatial ordering.

By this point in the meeting it was readily apparent to the entire Eastville staff that Mr. Chapman knew Paul well. Ms. Cox, who was Paul's social studies teacher, skeptically commented, "I have Paul for the same amount of time you do each week, and I didn't know that he belonged to the local soccer league and was good at spatial things. That's somewhat interesting, but it sounds pretty time consuming to figure out."

Jan had been watching her staff's body language as they listened to Mr. Chapman's description of Paul's learning profile, and she wasn't surprised that Ms. Cox had asked that question. She knew that there would be varying degrees of acceptance among her staff, which was one of the reasons she was so pleased that Mr. Chapman was already finding success with this approach in his classroom. He would be a key asset to gaining staff buy-in this year. His response to Ms. Cox's question seemed to alleviate some of her anxiety, especially when he explained that Paul was currently his most puzzling student and acknowledged that it did require more time and effort to get to know him deeply. Mr. Chapman concluded his portion of the meeting by reinforcing the need to know students better, especially the struggling ones, and how helpful a depth of knowledge about the science of learning was to the process.

As the staff broke into small groups and began their discussions, a common theme emerged. Jan's staff recommended that they all learn more about the science of learning and the neurodevelopmental framework. It seemed to be an essential element to getting to know students more deeply, and it was evident that Mr. Chapman had a great command of that body of knowledge. There were a few people who wondered about their ability to learn the scientific concepts to the degree that Mr. Chapman had, but Jan was pleased that there was no real division among her staff. They had collectively made a recommendation to her, which was a large improvement over the pedagogical wars of past initiatives. She felt confident that she could act upon their recommendation, but she would definitely be enlisting the help of the principals' cohort to think through a realistic plan.

This chapter will explore
- Developing a student's neurodevelopmental profile
- Mining sources of data to inform a student's profile
- The art of "kid watching": being careful observers of students
- Establishing a "trust fund" among members of a student's learning community

---

A Portrait of a Student

Every student has a unique combination of strengths, affinities, and weaknesses; each is an individual masterpiece. Our future leaders think differently, work differently, and share their strengths in individual ways, diversity that will enable us to meet the needs of a global economy and workforce in years to come.

Educators have the privilege and responsibility of celebrating and nurturing the unique minds that come into classrooms and schools. One might think of schools and classrooms as galleries for the many masterpieces entrusted to our care—care that involves not only protection and nurturing but opportunity for growth. In the same way we appreciate art for its unique qualities, we can also come to appreciate learners for their individual learning profiles—the strengths, affinities, and weaknesses that influence how students engage with the demands of school. There is the student whose receptive language supports a voracious appetite for reading, particularly mysteries. Another student exhibits strengths in expressive language, effortlessly using words to eloquently share an idea or experience. Another student struggles to generate words and sentences but can use images and diagrams to communicate ideas and feelings as effectively as his language-oriented peers. Each of these students adds value to the classroom, especially when her or his strengths and affinities are acknowledged and nurtured.

Teachers like Mr. Chapman are continually seeking to understand the unique learning profiles of their students—to paint a portrait of what enables each student to be successful. An appreciation for and desire to better understand diverse learners are essential to creating learning environments that are learner centered. Across the grades, students encounter rigorous academic expectations. A deep understanding of students' learning needs enables a teacher to develop the strategies necessary to support them in successfully achieving these expectations. At the same time, rigorous content must be relevant to those who are learning it. Leveraging students' affinities amplifies the connections between content and interest, making the learning more relevant and increasing the

> ## PICTURE THIS!
>
> In the same way teachers acknowledge and nurture variation among their students, your school staff represent diverse strengths and weaknesses. Consider the teacher whose strengths in social cognition combined with years of experience make her ideal for mentoring new teachers. There is also the media specialist who uses her creativity to develop top-notch technology activities for teachers to use with their students. Both teachers add value to the culture of the school.

> *Affinities*: Topics that a person pursues with a passionate interest (for example, whales) or skills and activities that a person loves to do, even if they are not particularly good at them (for example, cooking). Read more about leveraging affinities in Chapter Five.

motivation of students to engage in scholarly pursuits, both now and throughout life. Rigorous and relevant learning experiences require healthy student-teacher relationships—relationships that are built on teachers knowing students well.

Educators are equipped with a variety of tools for understanding students, including data from assessment, grades, and observation. For many years, IQ scores have served as a widely accepted component of measuring ability and achievement. While this type of information can certainly help inform the picture, it is far from the full description of any student. As Douglas Reeves states in his book *The Learning Leader,* "Not everything that counts can be counted, not everything that can be observed can be expressed in quantitative terms."[1] Applying this concept to understanding students, we have to consider what can be learned from multiple sources of information.

Keys to Knowing Learners

Mining Data from Multiple Sources

Lorna Earl presents a model of thinking about assessment along three dimensions: assessment *of* learning (using a summative measure to document and report a student's progress at the end of a chapter, unit, or class), assessment *for* learning (gathering a wide range of data to inform and adapt instruction and learning activities), and assessment *as* learning (monitoring one's own learning and using that information to adjust one's understanding).[2] Each of these approaches to assessment provides insight into which students are learning and what is being learned (or not learned). The important information we as learning leaders must uncover is *why* students struggle and *how* they learn best. In learner-centered classrooms and schools, educators use data from many sources and use that information to uncover the learning needs of students.

A piece of the puzzle for acquiring a deep understanding of students as learners is the quantitative data we can gather from various

> The more specific the data, the better we understand how the student learns and the more targeted the intervention plan can be.

sources. Using data to make decisions about teaching and learning is not a new idea among learning leaders. Current trends in education encourage schools to make use of formative assessments as a means to take quick, frequent snapshots of student progress and use those data immediately to inform curricular and instructional decisions— what Earl refers to as "assessment *for* learning." Many schools conduct interim assessments throughout the academic year as a way to track students' ongoing progress in mastering the concepts and skills defined by state or local standards. Results of end-of-grade or end-of course tests also serve to measure student progress (that is, assessment of learning).

There is clear value in taking a periodic snapshot of student progress; important information can be gathered about what a student is learning and how well she is remembering it. Results can also serve as red flags to indicate weak skill areas and provide clues for where to begin working with a student. For example, a low score on a reading assessment may indicate this academic area as a "hot spot." Ideally, more detailed data are also available, such as performance on items related to decoding, vocabulary development, or comprehension of informational text. The more specific the data, the better we understand how the student learns and the more targeted the intervention plan can be. The use of a neurodevelopmental framework supports this level of specificity.

Making the best use of data to describe a student as a learner requires digging deep to learn more. Consider this example:

A sixth-grade student scores at a Level 2 on an interim assessment of math.

Possible hypothesis: *The student has not yet mastered particular subskills of math.*

With further investigation into the data, we find that the student has missed several items that required interpreting data from a chart or graph. His responses to word problems involving probability were also incorrect.

Possible hypothesis: *The student did not read the word problems carefully and missed critical information.*

Applying a neurodevelopmental lens opens the door to determining potential breakdown points for the student—points that can be improved with specific, targeted strategies.

Possible breakdown points:

- The student struggles with the spatial demands of reading a chart or graph (how the information in the chart or graph is related to the headings, the vertical and horizontal axes, to other information provided, and so on).
- The student finds it difficult to manage his attention processing controls in order to focus in on the relevant data in the chart needed to respond to the question.
- The student struggles to comprehend the technical vocabulary of math (for example, median, range, mode).
- The student's active working memory is overloaded when solving these types of problems (that is, there is too much information taking up too much space on his desktop), resulting in information being lost.

The more we know about a student's learning profile, the more effective we can be at determining the breakdown point that is most likely interrupting the student's performance. See Exhibit 4.1 for an example of a neurodevelopmental profile.

Exhibit 4.1 Sample Neurodevelopmental Profile

Construct/Function	Weakness ↔ Strength	Notes
Attention: Mental energy	✗ (middle)	Issues with mental energy causing her to fidget? Trying to stay alert?
Attention: Processing	✗ (weakness)	Better if interested in topic; particular problems deciding what's most important
Attention: Production	✗ (weakness)	Need to work on self-monitoring strategies
Memory: Short-term	✗ (toward strength)	Harder if oral directions
Memory: Active working	✗ (weakness)	Big impact on her writing—getting overwhelmed; causing problems with complex math problems
Memory: Long-term	✗ (middle)	Spelling, math facts
Language: Receptive	✗ (middle)	OK reader, but learning new technical vocabulary is a problem
Language: Expressive	✗ (when writing) [weakness] ✗ (when speaking) [strength]	Expressive language when talking is super—leverage this strength to work on writing
Temporal-sequential ordering	✗ (middle)	Writing is a concern
Spatial ordering	✗ (middle)	Great in class or soccer, but loses things
Neuromotor functions: Gross motor	✗ (strength)	Great strength
Neuromotor functions: Fine motor	✗ (strength)	
Neuromotor functions: Graphomotor	✗ (toward strength)	
Higher-order cognition	✗ (strength)	
Social cognition: Verbal pragmatics	✗ (strength)	Caring, compassionate
Social cognition: Social behaviors	✗ (strength)	Cooperative with teammates

At New York City's Pedro Albizu Campos (P.S. 161) in Manhattan, educators found digging deep to have a significant effect on the success of their students. Driven by the goal of helping students whose performance on standardized tests was below proficient (that is, Levels 1 and 2), principal Barbara Freeman and the staff of P.S. 161 began to look closely at their school practices. It became clear to meet the learning needs of these targeted students, there had to be a strategic approach to how classroom teachers and related service teachers worked with the students and with each other. The teachers were providing excellent instruction, but gaps existed between how students were supported in class and the services they received from the related services staff. Many of these students received help from multiple sources (for example, special education, interventionists, ELL, and so on), so coordination of efforts was essential. The teachers providing support services needed a common language so that there was a shared understanding of students' strengths and weaknesses and of the strategies that were included in each student's learning plan. In addition, these teachers needed a framework for talking about students in a specific way, moving from assumptions and generalized statements such as "She just doesn't do anything" to rich descriptions of students as learners.

Barbara introduced her staff to the All Kinds of Minds framework in 2007, encouraging her out-of-classroom personnel (including special education teachers, academic intervention team members, and ESL teachers) to join her in attending an All Kinds of Minds course. The group found the framework to be a missing link in their strategic approach to student learning. They began to rethink their approach to strategies, analyzing when best to accommodate students and at what points was it essential to intervene. "We found ourselves really thinking carefully about what we were trying to do with each individual learner," Barbara explained.

With a decision to start with the fifteen to twenty students performing at Levels 1 and 2, the staff began digging deep with new approaches for gathering data about a student. "We had to figure out why these students weren't performing at proficiency. Where was the breakdown for each of these students?" commented Barbara. The support services team, working collaboratively with the general education classroom teachers, began using tools and processes acquired through their training to identify students' learning profiles, link those profiles to weak academic skills, and develop learning plans matched to how the students learned best. Over time, they began to see progress in the classroom—progress that continued and was represented by gains for specific subgroups on end-of-year assessments. Many of the students who had previously scored at Level 1 or 2 had increased their score to a Level 3 or 4, a trend that has continued for the past two years.

P.S 161 now has a team of nineteen educators on staff who have developed a depth of understanding in this approach and who are collaborating with colleagues across the school to address the needs of students. "We were drawn to this model as a way to support our most struggling learners and are clearly making gains there," says Barbara, "but this framework helps us serve all of our students, even those who perform well on the tests. Our teachers now better understand what they are seeing in the classroom daily. As a school, we also better understand our role in addressing deficit areas. This approach has made a difference for our students and our teachers—it's now just how school gets done at P.S. 161."

The value of digging deep is seen in the experience of Liz Swearingen, a teacher in Owasso, Oklahoma. Liz, along with many of her colleagues from her school and district, attended a professional development course from All Kinds of Minds. Though her experience with the All Kinds of Minds approach was still pretty new,

---

PICTURE THIS!

Describing teachers' strengths and weaknesses and developing plans for ongoing professional development is part of the job of a learning leader. Imagine the rich data portrait you can create when you look to multiple sources for information to inform these plans. Consider sources of data such as a conversation with the teacher, classroom observations, lesson plans, parent comments, participation on school and district committees, student surveys, and peer feedback.

she was beginning to observe her students more carefully and thinking differently about what she saw.

An opportunity to try this new approach to teaching came when several students in her fifth-grade class achieved poor results on a test of thermal energy. Students who demonstrated their understanding of this science concept in class one day were unable to communicate that same understanding on a multiple-choice test the next. "Where is the breakdown for these students?" she wondered. Based on her observations of them during class activities, Liz had seen evidence that her students understood the concept, but the test scores were not indicating the same results. What was it about that test that prevented these students from showing what they know?

Liz spent a few weeks observing and reflecting on the strengths and weaknesses of her students, then applied her understanding of the framework to the information she gathered. She realized there was a mismatch between how her students learned best and how she was asking them to demonstrate knowledge. Armed with a hypothesis of her students' learning profiles, an eagerness to try something new, and the need for choices that allowed students to play to their strengths, Liz started with a simple change: allowing students to illustrate the three ways thermal energy is transferred and label where the transfer occurs and what it is called. This option for demonstrating knowledge of this concept, using a spatial approach rather than relying on language and memory, resulted in twelve students passing the test who otherwise might not have.

By creating opportunities for students to engage with curriculum based on how they learn best and to express their thinking in a way that leveraged their learning profiles, more students achieved success in this fifth-grade classroom. "Next time I'll give them options from the start and teach them more about how to choose an option that works for them," Liz said. Well-informed, inquisitive teachers like Liz recognize the value in digging deeper to discover more, of searching for information to explain *why* students are achieving (or not achieving), and using that information to create student-centered learning opportunities.

Qualitative Data

Beyond assessment data, what other sources of data are available as we describe the strengths and weaknesses of a student? Some obvious contributors include age, health, prior school experience, and exposure to concepts. So many important aspects of a student's learning profile don't show up on a test but are instead gathered through other sources such as observation, student work, and conversations with members of the student's learning community. Qualitative data gathered from a variety of sources allows us to look at a broad range of strengths, weaknesses, and affinities and identify patterns that help create a rich description of the student as a learner.

> Qualitative data gathered from a variety of sources allows us to look at a broad range of strengths, weaknesses, and affinities and identify patterns that help create a rich description of the student as a learner.

As described in Chapter Three, the All Kinds of Minds approach provides another way to deeply understand a student as a learner: utilizing a framework based on research from cognitive science and research on learning. This framework provides educators with the knowledge and tools to describe unique strengths and weaknesses of students and to consider how those strengths and weaknesses interface with the demands of school at any given time. The framework supports teachers in making evidence-based decisions without being bound by any single measure of ability. With this lens for observing students, teachers can better understand the strengths, affinities, and weaknesses affecting school performance and motivators for success.

Using this framework to appreciate learner strengths and weaknesses involves carefully observing and describing students, relying on patterns of evidence to drive instructional decisions and the use of strategies. One might compare this approach to the work of a detective who searches carefully for clues from a variety of sources—witnesses, those directly involved in the case, physical evidence—then analyzes those clues for patterns or themes. From these patterns come a hypothesis and conclusion. The search to deeply understand the learning profile of a student follows a similar path of gathering clues, looking for recurring themes, and making evidence-based decisions about strategies. The goal of this process is a rich description of the student as a learner, not a particular label or diagnosis. From this description, those involved in the learning community—educators, parents, and the student—can make informed decisions about "small wins" strategies for learner success.

A thorough description includes evidence from multiple sources: teachers, parents, students, and student work samples. Effective evidence gathering occurs in multiple settings (for example, classroom activities, related arts classes, extracurricular activities) and at various times of day. By looking for patterns across a broad spectrum, we are able to better describe students as learners. The search for patterns also helps to avoid premature conclusions brought on by misleading data points.

Kathi Howard, a school psychologist, and her colleagues at Old Trail School in Ohio, saw the value of observation and the search for patterns as they worked collaboratively with a sixth-grade student in the school. At first glance, this student appeared to be very impulsive, even careless in his work, suggesting weak attention production controls. Some perceived him as "not invested" in his learning.

Upon closer observation, they noticed the student was a few seconds behind his peers in doing most things. He got his book out later than his peers. He found and picked up his pencil more slowly. While directions were being given in music class to find certain songs and classify them as a type of music, he was still tearing his paper out of his notebook. In one-on-one conversations, Kathi noticed that when speaking with this student, he often paused a noticeable moment before answering simple conversational questions such as "How are you doing today?"

While on the surface this student demonstrated weak attention, observations revealed evidence of a student who is processing information at a slower pace than expected. For instance, his receptive language may need an extra moment to make meaning out of instructions, or his long-term memory access may lag a bit when retrieving information. So, how can a slow processor be impulsive? The group's hypothesis was that this student is impatient with himself; he recognizes that most tasks (arranging materials, understanding others) take him longer than others. His slow processing makes it difficult for him to keep up. It is likely that he completes tasks quickly in order to save face and because he is impatient with the pace of his own output.

To address this student's learning needs and help protect him from humiliation, his teachers reduced the complexity of many of the "set-up" demands of the day, supporting him while minimizing his feeling of "missing the train" on so many preparatory activities (for example, getting materials out and ready for work). They also worked to create a classroom environment that expected and rewarded "think time" before calling on students to respond; this gave the student's language and higher-order cognition more time to kick into gear. They supported his long-term memory access and expressive language by providing him with rehearsal opportunities (a twenty-four-hour heads-up on what to prepare for in-class discussions) so that his voice can be heard in class. A critical element of his learning plan also included coaching him on the importance of his taking enough time to process the information completely before he responds—challenging the notion that "fast = excellent" and teaching him about slow, deliberate, careful responders who have contributed greatly to their fields. By collaborating and sharing a common perspective for observing and understanding learners, this group of educators was able to move past the surface to the specific learning issues for this student and develop a plan that would lead him to greater success in sixth grade.

All Kinds of Minds emphasizes the importance of multiple pieces of evidence gathered over time that work together to describe a student as a learner. Evidence can include classroom observations, information gathered through conversation with parents and students, assessment data, and examples of student work. A broad range of data provides the opportunity to paint a more complete picture of a student and his or her learning profile. Grounded in the All Kinds of Minds approach and filtering multiple pieces of evidence through this lens, teachers can more fully know their students as learners.

Knowing More Through Kid Watching

The drive to appreciate students as learners starts with "kid watching." When we step back and simply observe a student engaged in an academic or social activity, what do we see? Where is he successful? Where do the breakdowns occur? Being an effective kid watcher requires suspending judgment and interpretation of the events and instead focusing on describing the phenomena that you see. Kid watching happens over time and in multiple contexts, so that we can gather as much information as possible to inform our decision making. As patterns begin to emerge from the observations and other data points, then it's time to interpret and form hypotheses about students' learning needs and make decisions about instruction. The basic four-step problem-solving model in Table 4.1 provides a way to organize one's "kid watching."

> " Being an effective kid watcher requires suspending judgment and interpretation of the events and instead focusing on describing the phenomena that you see. "

School Leaders as Observers

A district or school needs a robust, comprehensive common language of instruction shared by everyone to ensure that high-yield strategies supporting student achievement are used effectively.[3] School leaders

Table 4.1 A Four-Step Problem-Solving Model

Steps	What to Look For/Consider
1. What do we see?	Evidence of strengths, affinities, and weaknesses Avoid assumptions and early interpretations Observations at school (in various classes, different times of day, from multiple teachers) Insights shared by parents and caregivers Insights from the student Assessment data
2. What do we think?	Identify emerging patterns and themes Link patterns to related neurodevelopmental functions (see Chapter Three for help with these linkages) Form a hypothesis about student's learning profile
3. What will we do?	Strategies to try at school and/or at home Conversations about learning with students and parents or caregivers
4. What happens over time?	Identifying anticipated outcomes: What do we want to occur? Tracking actual outcomes: What changed as a result of the strategies we tried?

can use the neurodevelopmental framework to describe observations they make about students as part of the practice of walkthroughs.

PICTURE THIS!

Think about your work with the teacher you are currently coaching to improve an area of her teaching practice. Review the four steps listed in Table 4.1 and note ways this model can structure your work with this teacher.

School leaders use walkthroughs to observe various segments of teaching: lessons, routines, or things that occur in class that must be addressed on the spot. When using walkthroughs more as "instructional rounds," school leaders can provide snapshots of student observations to help inform the instructional decision making and pedagogical skill of teachers.[4] They may observe the effectiveness of a routine that helps all students with time management, or they may observe a student exhibiting an unusual response to a lesson presentation.

Teachers as Observers

Teachers are in a unique position to observe and authentically describe students. These are the professionals who see students in learning contexts for up to six hours a day, five days a week, throughout an entire academic year. Not only are teachers with the students for long stretches of time, they see them in a variety of settings—academic contexts such as class discussions, independent practice, and collaboration with peers, as well as social contexts such as in the hallways and at lunch. In some cases, several teachers share the responsibility of working with a particular student, offering yet another opportunity for observation from multiple perspectives. Within and across the various settings and times of day, at what points is this student successful and engaged? At what points is the student struggling? Are there times when he or she is completely disengaged? When the educational professionals who are part of a student's learning community share a common approach and a neurodevelopmental framework for understanding learners, these questions are more easily answered and the student better understood. This makes the teacher's work more effective, and the learner is the true benefactor.

Parents and Caregivers as Observers

The complete picture of a student as a learner includes, but is not limited to, what happens within the school day. Clues to a student's learning needs are also abundant at home, at work, or through extracurricular activities such as Boy or Girl Scouts or participation on sports teams. Observations made in these settings can reveal strengths and weaknesses that aren't evident at school but certainly affect the overall picture.

Regina, a principal from South Carolina tells about her son, Jason, who struggled with spelling throughout his elementary years. As a fifth grader, Jason continued to be challenged by spelling, and it was beginning to be a significant factor in his ability to communicate his ideas in writing. As an educator, Regina had received lots of training in literacy and instruction, but she was still struggling to help her child find success in this particular academic area. She and her staff chose to explore All Kinds of Minds as another resource for supporting student learning.

Regina's experience during the training was twofold: as a school leader and as a mother. She quickly identified many opportunities for this approach to improve their work with students across the school. At the same time, she was also coming to a greater understanding of her own child. Equipped with the framework for learning, she began to observe Jason more closely at home while helping him with his homework and noticed a trend of problems with tasks that involved temporal-sequential ordering. She also noticed some memory weaknesses, but not always. While he struggled to consolidate things like spelling words into his long-term memory, Jason really excelled with understanding, recalling, and using rules (also a function of memory). This revelation led her to take a new approach to spelling with Jason, creating a notebook of common spelling rules and using those rules to guide his spelling. This notebook became a resource that Jason used for spelling homework assignments. The more he practiced the spelling rules, the more he internalized them, and they become automatic for him. Finally, after several years, Jason is finding it much easier to communicate his ideas, thanks to a persistent and well-informed mom.

Students as Self-Observers

Chapter Two referenced research about improved self-insight—learners better understanding their strengths, affinities, and weaknesses. Self-insight occurs as a result of external feedback and self-reflection. Students can often speak very candidly and accurately about what aspects of school are easy and difficult and what strategies work best for them. This is true from young learners to secondary-level students, though the sophistication and specificity with which they describe themselves varies across ages and grades.

Students also provide us with insight into their affinities—those topics, skills, or experiences that they truly love and enjoy doing, even if they aren't very good at them. Affinities are another essential element of the data portrait; they can be leveraged to make learning interesting and fun for struggling students. When students are aware of their affinities and those affinities are leveraged and nurtured, students are more engaged in the learning process.

Learning from Student Work

The work a student produces provides great insight into patterns of strengths and weaknesses, revealing clues to how that student's mind engages with the learning demands of the task. From daily class assignments to long-term projects, the finished product is a source of data that is critical. A common task for students in all grades is written production, such as narrative writing, research papers, science lab reports, and responses to open-ended test items (see Chapter Seven for more on writing). Upon observing the student's work, a teacher may find it to be off topic or inaccurate, or it may be conceptually correct but not have the necessary explanation to clearly demonstrate the student's understanding.

Each of these outcomes tells us something about the learner. Perhaps the student whose writing is off topic is struggling to comprehend the concept, or perhaps he understands, but struggles to find the right words to demonstrate that understanding. Perhaps the student who produced a cursory explanation has a reduced supply of mental energy for writing tasks. This student may be working so hard to produce written language that he loses much of what he wants to say. These are the questions that observing student work can lead us to ask, thereby deepening our understanding of the student. Many protocols are available to educators to support the careful observation and analysis of student work, including those from the School Reform Initiative and the Coalition for Essential Schools. Combined with the All Kinds of Minds framework as a lens for analyzing and interpreting observations of student work, educators can learn a great deal from this source of data (see Table 4.2).

Tools of the Trade: Describing Phenomena Versus Using Labels

If data-driven decision making is about more than scores, and members of a student's learning community—teachers, parents, students themselves—are all critical observers, then what should we pay attention to? What information can most effectively help us support student success? Decisions we make about student learning must be

Table 4.2   The Art of Kid Watching: Getting Started

Select a student	Select a student who puzzles you (for example, has been referred for discipline issues several times, is showing signs of academic struggle in a particular content area, struggles to get along with others) Focus your data collection with a framing question that begins "I wonder . . . " (for example, I wonder why he struggles to understand what he reads even though he decodes individual words so well?)
Teachers as observers	What have I observed about this student in my classes? What information do I need from my colleagues who also teach this student? Are there others in the school who also interact with this student regularly? What quick question can I ask them, to capture their observations (not their assumptions)? Is there a short survey I can provide to guide their observations?
Parents or caregivers as observers	What information might I gain from the parents' perspective? What do I need to know about this student outside of school?

Students as observers	How aware is this student of the issue that I am wondering about?
	
	I will start a conversation with this student by asking the following question:
	
	_____?
	
	Some sample conversation starters:
	
	   I noticed you seem to get frustrated during algebra class. Tell me more about what's bothering you.
	
	   What is the best part of your school year so far? What is the worst part? What strategies have you tried, to make the difficult parts of school easier?
	
	   I really enjoyed your presentation on Mt. Everest. You shared lots of interesting information with the class through your PowerPoint slides. In fact, there was more information in your presentation than in your written report. Is writing particularly difficult for you?

Looking at student work	Are there student work samples that would provide insight into this issue?

evidence based—evidence that is gathered through observation and the search for recurring themes.

Take a moment for this brief exercise (you'll need a piece of paper and a pen or pencil): Look at Figure 4.1 and jot down what you see.

Now think about what you noted. To what extent did you capture just what you saw (such as two sets of tracks, one set larger than the

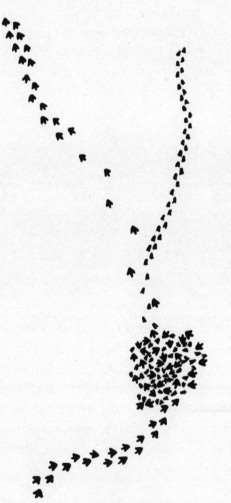

Figure 4.1 Making Tracks

Adapted from: Working Group on Teaching Evolution, National Academy of Sciences. *Teaching About Evolution and the Nature of Science*. Washington, DC: National Academies Press, 1998, p. 89. Reprinted with permission by the National Academy of Sciences, courtesy of the National Academies Press.

other, the sets converging or emanating from a circular area containing jumbled tracks, and so on)? To what extent did you go beyond strictly observing and begin to interpret the data, such as "It looks like the animals engaged physically (for example, a fight, a dance) and one emerged without the other (perhaps carrying him)?"

This exercise demonstrates the difference between observing the phenomena and making meaning of it. At times, in our efforts to find solutions as quickly as possible, we make assumptions that either lead us down the wrong path or shortchange the degree to which we understand the real issues at hand. For these reasons, it is important to observe, describe, and look for recurring themes.

> In our efforts to find solutions as quickly as possible, we make assumptions that either lead us down the wrong path or shortchange the degree to which we understand the real issues at hand. For these reasons, it is important to observe, describe, and look for recurring themes.

As mentioned before, teachers are in the best position to describe students as learners. Leveraging the opportunity to see students across settings, teachers and other school personnel have access to many perspectives and critical observations. However, educators have to be careful to stay focused on the observation and describe what they see without prematurely jumping to interpretations or assumptions.

For example, a middle school physical education teacher may notice that, during practice drills, her student demonstrates good ball-handling skills and can successfully shoot the ball from the free-throw line. She also notices that the student is coordinated in her movement up and down the basketball court. However, when the student is in a game situation, many of these skills become less refined and the student becomes frustrated, often yelling at her peers. This pattern of behavior has occurred consistently throughout the semester.

The teacher in this example has maintained a focus on the phenomena—what she has observed regarding this student. All too often, descriptions of students are colored by interpretation of what we see, not the evidence itself. Another teacher may have instead talked about this student as very talented, but a bad team player, or even a bully on the court. Labels and generalized statements such as "talented," "a bad team player," and "bully" do not give us the detailed information we need to truly understand the student. "Talented," while positive in tone, still fails to tell us about the skills and abilities that are working well for the student. She is talented in what way? It is essential that learning leaders maintain a focus on describing phenomena and avoid labels whenever possible.

Using the All Kinds of Minds framework, the teacher can deconstruct this task of basketball and begin to make some hypotheses about why this student is struggling despite her strengths with discrete skills. In a game setting, players have to process lots of information quickly and use that information to make decisions. This places a heavy demand on the player's processing and production controls of attention and on her active working memory. This basketball player may have a hard time juggling multiple aspects of the game simultaneously. She may struggle when information must be processed quickly. In practice drills, she only had to pay attention to one thing at a time and could do so at a slower pace. This perspective enables her coach to understand where the breakdown is happening and how to help her player during a game situation. This could involve gradually ramping up the complexity and speed of drills during practice so that she is better prepared for games. Table 4.3 offers some of the common combinations of neurodevelopmental functions that come into play for various academic tasks. Note that this table is organized at the construct level. Looking more deeply at the function level would reveal greater variability regarding the demands of assignments, such as the difference between the receptive and expressive language demands or the active working and long-term memory demands.

Learner appreciation is like good art appreciation. Art appreciation is not simply the ability to walk through a museum and label masterpieces by categories—that's an Impressionist piece, that's an

Table 4.3 *Neurodevelopmental Demands for Common Assignment Types*

Assignment	Language	Memory	Higher-Order Cognition	Attention	Temporal-Sequential Ordering	Spatial Ordering	Neuromotor Functions	Social Cognition
Essays	✓	✓	✓	✓	✓		✓	
Group discussions	✓	✓	✓	✓				✓
Models/dioramas		✓	✓			✓	✓	
Oral presentations	✓	✓	✓	✓	✓			✓
Lab reports	✓	✓	✓	✓	✓		✓	

example of surrealism, that's cubism—and feel you "know" art. Rather, it is the ability to continually revisit the masterpieces to view the phenomena that form the work and continually see something that you might have missed before, or didn't show up in the particular light in which you first encountered the art. It's describing the phenomena of a masterpiece that enables us to talk about art in its richness and complexity, and it is the same approach that permits us to describe and understand the complexity of our students as learners.

Establishing a Trust Fund

When members of a school faculty have a shared framework for thinking about learning, and all practice describing phenomena instead of labeling, the culture of the school becomes one that appreciates and celebrates the unique characteristics of learners. By relying on descriptions and hypotheses, teachers begin to notice common themes during conversations about the learning needs of students.

It is possible that this approach can address the issues raised by researcher Kirsten Olsen in her book *Wounded by School.* Her research with accomplished adults revealed an unexpected, disturbing, common theme about schooling: many carried stories of being harmed and humiliated.

What she repeatedly heard was a feeling of being lost and anonymous. "In most schools you're just passing through," stated a student newly enrolled in a charter school. "They don't even know who you are unless you are a real problem." Olsen argues that knowing students as individual learners and permitting passion by embracing affinities is a key element to increasing engagement, persistence, and performance of all learners.[5]

This culture also begins to spread beyond the walls of the school to relationships with parents and caregivers. Through these kinds of conversations with parents, schools are able to establish a rich "trust fund" with parents and students, with members of the learning community contributing to the fund by focusing on strengths, describing *specific* weaknesses, avoiding labels, collaboratively identifying strategies, and embracing learner diversity. This fund becomes a rich foundation for a sound relationship among all members of the student's learning community and for an optimistic future.

> Schools are able to establish a rich "trust fund" with parents and students, with members of the learning community contributing to the fund by focusing on strengths, describing *specific* weaknesses, avoiding labels, collaboratively identifying strategies, and embracing learner diversity.

Imagine being part of such a community for a student you know who is struggling with the demands of school. It may be your son or daughter, a relative, or a student you have worked with during your career. You are part of a team of people who appreciates how this student is wired to learn and who are solely focused on helping this student be successful—both now and in the future. When the student falters, the team is there to remind him of his strengths, use his affinities to make learning relevant, and identify strategies for shoring up areas of weakness. When learning gets hard, the trust built through this alliance fuels the motivation to continue trying.

GETTING STARTED WITH SMALL WINS

Small wins = *concrete, significant tasks that produce a visible result while moving one step closer to a new vision or one step away from an unacceptable condition*

How might Jan Stewart, the principal at Eastville, lead her staff to better know their students as learners? How might you create a learning environment that appreciates diverse learners and seeks to know them well? Some first steps include

- Begin conversations about learners by talking about strengths and affinities before talking about weaknesses (for example, in child study teams, with parents during a parent-teacher conference)
- Intentionally look for the unique qualities a student brings to the school and classroom (for example, when assigning students to cooperative groups)
- Use a neurodevelopmental framework to describe students as learners (Chapter Three provides helpful resources for connecting common observations to neurodevelopmental constructs and functions)
- Leverage students' strengths and affinities to accomplish goals
- Start with careful observation before jumping to assumptions (for example, when examining student work in collaborative learning groups)
- Gather information about a struggling student from a variety of sources, including teachers, parents and caregivers, students, assessments, and student work
- Invite members of a student's learning community to establish a trust fund, working together toward achieving success

Learning Leadership in Action

Consider commonly used statements that represent interpretations, inferences, or labels of students, or think of some specific students that are currently puzzling you. Determine additional sources of information that would allow you to dig deeper to really get to know a student and be able to paint a data portrait of him or her. Use this tool independently, with teams, or the entire staff as a catalyst for creating a student-centered learning environment.

Example: The school psychologist meets with a team from the elementary school to discuss their concerns about a particular student. They suspect he may have a learning disability and want to start the referral process. The psychologist wants to facilitate a conversation to gather more evidence and try more strategies prior to considering a referral.

Common assumptions, interpretations, or labels	What data, observations, and evidence exist?	How can we paint a richer, more thorough data portrait?
Student attention span is so short that he isn't able to listen to or understand instructions, can't focus on reading to gain understanding, and often can't sit still long enough to complete a task.	Classroom work is often incomplete, resulting in failing reading, social studies, and science. Is often out of seat, or moves out of group and walks around class prior to completing assignment. Hasn't made "proficient score" on state assessments in reading and science. Is very fidgety in class, rocks back in chair.	Ask, "When is attention NOT a problem?" Gather data from multiple sources: Talk with the parents. Consider insights from multiple teachers (for example, art, physical education, teaching assistants). Talk to the student and ask for his interpretations about his challenges and affinities. Look deeper at work samples from all subjects, including the incomplete assignments. Look at what is going well for the student, his strengths and affinities.

(See blank template on next page.)

Common assumptions, interpretations, or labels	What data, observations, and evidence exist?	How can we paint a richer, more thorough data portrait?

5

Building on Student Assets

"Impressive," Jan thought as she passed by the middle school's closed-circuit television studio, struck by the range of talents she saw at work. The students were in charge of the school news every morning. John and Sarah anchored the news desk, Kevin ran the equipment, and Paul created the digital images in PowerPoint to illustrate each story. "These students are all doing jobs that play to their strengths and that they really enjoy. What an opportunity to show off their assets."

Jan paused to reflect on the last professional development meeting where the staff shared ways they were effectively and intentionally recognizing the strengths and affinities of their students. Ms. Cox, the social studies teacher, was responsible for the school's television studio and had presented this example during the meeting. Mr. Chapman had elaborated on his story about Paul by first reminding the staff of Paul's neurodevelopmental profile. Then he explained how he put all his pieces of evidence together in ways that allowed him to take advantage of Paul's strengths in conceptualization, spatial ordering, and social cognition in order to increase his consolidation of information into long-term memory. Mr. Chapman knew that other students in the class could also benefit from seeing Paul's visual representations of scientific concepts, so he began having Paul share his diagrams with classmates. Leveraging Paul's strength in spatial ordering increased Paul's overall confidence with scientific concepts, which *translated into improved performance on all his science-related work. The meeting concluded with a few other staff members sharing some rich examples of classroom activities and group projects.*

Next, Jan had challenged her staff by asking, "How can we do more? How do we take advantage of those assets to help these students learn? Do our school policies encourage or discourage students to showcase their assets?" An energetic professional dialogue ensued. One outcome of their vibrant discussions was the staff's recommendation to further examine the policies and schoolwide practices. Jan was pleased that her staff continued to be engaged enough to make thoughtful recommendations and even more pleased that the initiative was gaining momentum as the year progressed.

It was more than halfway through the year and all the teachers had learned about the neurodevelopmental framework, were taking time to get to know the students who were struggling in their classes, and were appreciating the unique profiles of their students. Jan knew that a big part of this initiative's success could be attributed to the ongoing support she received from the principals' cohort. Each principal was approaching his or her charge of increasing student achievement slightly differently, but the cohort continued to provide opportunities for collaboration that resulted in practical solutions for Eastville Middle School.

In fact, when Jan had shared the recent recommendation that her staff made for their next discussion topic, her cohort suggested a multitude of ideas for schoolwide policies and practices that would celebrate students' strengths and affinities. She was going to combine those with the ideas she collected from her staff; they would discuss these ideas and determine which ones felt right for Eastville Middle School. Jan smiled. She was very pleased with the types of conversations that she was hearing these days in the classrooms and halls of Eastville and was looking forward to the upcoming discussion focused on student assets.

This chapter will explore
- The importance of focusing on strengths and affinities
- Ideas for nurturing and leveraging students' assets
- An All Kinds of Minds approach to learning plans

Assets as Part of the Data Portrait

What are your strengths? When you read about the eight constructs in Chapter Three, which ones do you consider your assets?

What are your affinities—those topics, activities, or skills that you pursue with great passion?

Now think about your career path, hobbies, personal interests, or tasks on which you do well and that create a sense of personal satisfaction. Chances are your choices allow you to excel in areas that play to your strengths and, ideally, permit you to pursue interests, causes, or activities for which you hold a passion.

Everyone has neurodevelopmental strengths—those brain functions that enable us to effectively perform certain tasks and skills with relative ease. Paul's strengths in spatial ordering and conceptualization enable him to make sense of what he is learning and can be leveraged to support his memory weaknesses. When Mr. Chapman focuses on Paul's assets, uses those assets to help manage his weaknesses, and allows him to share those assets with his classmates, Paul's self-esteem and motivation to learn increases. Equally important, Paul's classmates see another way to learn scientific concepts through the visualization strategies Paul can offer.

Professional athletes typically showcase exceptional strengths in neuromotor functions and spatial ordering. Individuals in the public relations field usually demonstrate excellent expressive

PICTURE THIS!

Knowing Mrs. Walker has an affinity for learning about NASA and space exploration, you ask her to lead a school-wide project culminating in two astronauts visiting the school. Knowing Mr. Wilson has great spatial ordering combined with strong neuromotor functions and social cognition, you ask him to lead a group of students in the design and construction of a greenhouse for the science department. Using your understanding of Mrs. Gallagher's amazing time management and attention production controls, you recommend her for the PTA planning committee. Thinking of your faculty's strengths and affinities is an essential element of building on assets throughout the school.

language and social cognition. A computer programmer relies on well-developed temporal-sequential ordering and higher-order cognition. Our individual strengths are the traits that help drive our career decisions. When coupled with an affinity (like a love for football, building relationships, or video games), the likelihood for career success and satisfaction greatly increases.

An Assets-Based Approach to Teaching and Learning

Educators have a responsibility to continually search for what is going right for students (strengths) and to help students discover their natural passions or interests (affinities). Sometimes strengths and affinities are the same for students, but not always. A student may be good at writing poetry but not have a strong interest in it (and vice versa). However, a student's strengths may match the social demands of running for student government, an activity that also allows him to leverage a true passion for public service and leadership. We often ask our successful friends, "How did you know you wanted to be a cabinet maker [or chef, florist, biologist, teacher]?" The typical response is, "I don't know, from the time I was a kid I just loved building things [cooking, flowers, animals, sharing ideas]." Parents are often the first to point out the strong interests of their children, such as noting how they drag every wounded insect into the house, keep basketball statistics and play in a fantasy league, or love looking at and collecting old family pictures, scrapbooks, and documents.

> " Educators have a responsibility to continually search for what is going right for students (strengths) and to help students discover their natural passions or interests (affinities). "

Affinities can play an important role in boosting student success, often providing the foundation upon which educators can make school learning relevant and inspire rigor in study. In academia and adult life, when affinities have been nurtured, they are referenced as scholarship and expertise.

When students begin to falter and miss the benchmarks established for success, educators often rush to fix the problem. In the quest for problem identification and remediation, the more important questions and observations such as "What's going right in this student's life?" are too often overlooked. It is the answer to these kinds of questions that will generate strategies for a learning plan that will have a longer-term effect on success in school and life. Educators are good at diagnosing the challenges. The next step is to more effectively and consistently slow down and see where the strengths and affinities lie and develop a picture of possibility for a student in learning plans.

> In the quest for problem identification and remediation, the more important questions and observations such as "What's going right in this student's life?" are too often overlooked.

John was a student in Karen Jordan-Jarrett's fifth-grade class in North Carolina. He was talkative and frequently enjoyed sharing his humorous stories and ideas with his classmates, though not always at the appropriate time. John also struggled with getting and staying organized. In fact, he rarely had what he needed when he needed it, resulting in many missing assignments. His lack of production had become a real problem. He and his family had heard for years about John's challenges, but Karen believed John had a contribution to make. Karen was concerned that John's lack of production would be perceived mistakenly as a lack of ability. As a teacher with many years of experience using a neurodevelopmental approach as a basis for her teaching practice, Karen began observing John and taking notes on what she saw. After the first few weeks of the school year, Karen asked John and his mom to come in after school so they could talk about what John was doing really well. This was a different kind of conversation than his mom was used to, so it took a while to get everyone talking, but soon the threesome spent 45 minutes talking only about John's strengths! By only discussing his strengths, Karen sent a powerful message to John and his mom about the culture of her classroom—that strengths were as important as weaknesses. This approach strengthened the relationship among Karen, John, and his family, creating an alliance among the members of this student's learning community.

With a shared understanding and appreciation for his learning profile, Karen and John could now start to address his struggles with production, particularly in the area of managing his materials for school and staying organized that had been caused by a weakness in spatial ordering. Karen had learned through her observations that John had strengths in other areas of spatial ordering that enabled him to easily interpret and use information from graphs, charts, and other visuals. Using this area of strength, she provided John with a picture of an organized desk as a visual reference for keeping his learning space organized. Among several other strategies they identified for John's learning plan, they began using an expandable folder with subject-specific files to hold all his papers in one place. Even if the papers were in the wrong slots, at least they were all there. While these strategies didn't solve every problem, they moved John in the right direction. Because she took an assets-based approach to teaching, Karen was able to provide John with greater access to school success by valuing his strengths and helping manage his weaknesses.

Valuing Students' Assets

Nurturing and Leveraging Affinities

Imagine the possibilities if every teacher spent a few minutes each day asking, "But what does he do well?" or "When have I seen her succeed?" How would the hallway conversations be different if, in the midst of solving what's wrong, everyone stopped to describe what's going right?

Affinities provide educators with a vehicle for personalizing a student's educational experience and increasing motivation to engage in learning. Educators throughout the school have the privilege of not only helping students to identify areas of passion but also helping nurture those passions. Affinities can be leveraged as part of instruction, as was the case with Jake, a student at Ferguson Middle School who really struggled with learning, including reading and math. Jake was an avid skateboarder. Janet Boucher, one of Ferguson's intervention specialists, decided to leverage his interest in skateboarding for all it was worth. She asked him to give a class presentation about skateboarding and write a research paper about it. They explored the science and math behind skateboarding, such as the relationship among velocity, distance, and ramp angles involved with jumps. She gradually encouraged Jake to connect skateboarding to broader topics. For example, he researched the history of transportation, including skateboarding. He also went from building his own skateboards to building a bike. Now in high school, he is building a car.

"Affinities provide educators with a vehicle for personalizing a student's educational experience and increasing motivation to engage in learning. Educators throughout the school have the privilege of not only helping students to identify areas of passion but also helping nurture those passions."

Janet leveraged skateboarding as a metaphor as well; Jake has an easier time learning when he breaks down large amounts of information into smaller chunks, and Janet likens this to his working on the numerous small parts that are in skateboards. Never an enthusiastic reader, Jake now understands that reading is a great way for him to learn about skateboarding, bikes, cars, and mechanics. Jake routinely comes back to visit Ferguson. "I think he likes to show his appreciation for the help we gave him," says Janet, "and he's also proud of the path he's on."

Jake's success demonstrates the power of attending to students' affinities as part of their educational experience. Sometimes a student's affinities are obvious—the student talks about the topic all the time or it is the theme of most every drawing and story! At other times, the process of helping a student discover his affinities may need to be more deliberate, coming as the result of careful observation and conversations about preferences, interests, and dreams. As teachers build relationships with students around learning, more information about these intense interests naturally emerge.

Take the 60-second challenge! Give every student one minute of your attention each week just to explore their strengths and affinities. These questions can get you started:
- If you were to design the perfect day, what would you be doing?
- What parts of school are easiest for you? Why?
- What are your affinities—those things you love to do or learn about?

Nurturing and Leveraging Strengths

Think about a student you know who struggles in school. What does this student do well? Perhaps this student's strengths aren't academic but instead are athletic, social, or artistic. Gather insights outside the school as well. The student may work and take on responsibility in his home, reflecting great time management, or participate in community activities. Which constructs seem most directly related to this student's strengths? How are these aspects of the student's learning profile being nurtured and strengthened?

In our urgency to achieve goals and help students succeed, it's easy to overlook those aspects of students' learning that are already working well. This oversight is unfortunate, because the result is missed opportunities to continue to strengthen those strengths—to find ways for the student to refine and celebrate what's going right. Also missed are opportunities to leverage those strengths—to use them as a tool for working on areas of weakness. For example, a student may be struggling with the active working memory demands of reading—of holding on to the characters, plot, and themes while deciphering challenging vocabulary. At the same time, this student easily processes information spatially and works well with charts and graphic organizers. We can leverage this spatial strength to help with the active working memory demands of the task by encouraging the student to create a story map as he reads, stopping periodically to sketch out or briefly describe the big ideas of the story.

> **PICTURE THIS!**
>
> Imagine walking into the teacher's workroom and instead of overhearing conversations about how poorly students are doing, you hear anecdotes about what students are doing well. When teachers gather to brainstorm interventions, you hear them searching for ways to leverage their student's strengths and affinities. You visit a classroom down the hall where students are practicing research skills as part of a project to explore a personal affinity. These are just a few signs of a school culture that embraces strengths and affinities.

Nicole, a special education teacher in South Carolina, provides opportunities for her students to leverage and strengthen strengths while they are working on weaknesses. One sixth-grade student, Anthony, while making progress academically, works to make good choices and behave in a way that is appropriate and effective for school. Meeting behavioral expectations is not always easy for Anthony, particularly when he is asked to tap into his social cognition and collaborate with other students. Nicole has worked with Anthony for two years, and while she is still learning about his learning profile, she has seen enough evidence to know that he has great strengths in long-term memory. "Once the information is in, it's there to stay," says Nicole as she describes Anthony's memory. Keeping this in mind, Nicole creates learning experiences that allow Anthony to leverage his long-term memory, such as a Jeopardy game in science to test his knowledge of the atmosphere. At the same time, this activity requires Anthony to work with a team of classmates. Nicole uses this opportunity, a time when Anthony's memory is serving him well, to focus on strategies to improve collaboration. Prior to engaging with his classmates in the game, Nicole spends time talking about collaboration and discussing with the students the kinds of behaviors that support collaboration. She and Anthony also role played various scenarios so he can try on these new behaviors. "We're making progress," says Nicole. "He feels good about his performance during the game, and we are able to work on his social cognition. It's a win-win."

Nicole could have easily overlooked Anthony's terrific memory and focused solely on the social cognition issues. Instead, Anthony is the beneficiary of a teacher who took the time to know him well, including his strengths.

Three ways to think about strengths:

1. *Advanced ability:* Exceptionally well-developed and exceeds expectations for a given developmental stage
2. *Solid functions and skills:* Operate as expected for a developmental stage and enable one to perform most expected tasks with relative ease
3. *Relative strengths:* Work effectively for a particular student in relation to weaknesses but may not be at the same level as other students the same age

As with affinities, sometimes neurodevelopmental strengths are obvious—they drive how students approach tasks or what is seen in day-to-day activities (for example, the student whose social cognition strengths allow her to work collaboratively with most students in the class and who is the first to befriend a new classmate). For other students, teachers find themselves having to dig past the student's struggles to mine the valuable resource of strengths. It is important in these instances to remember that everyone has learning strengths and it is worth the time and effort it takes to discover them. This discovery process is often a collaborative one, including conversations with the student, the parent or caregiver, and other teachers who are members of the student's learning community. The student may be achieving great success in other classes or in extracurricular activities. She may be involved in activities at home that tap into strengths, such as caring for siblings or planning family vacations.

It is also important to remember that strengths are relative—a student does not have to be the lead player on the soccer team to have strengths in neuromotor functions or be the head of the debate team to have strengths in higher-order cognition. When identifying strengths, think about what is working well for a student in the context of his experience and find ways to strengthen and leverage those characteristics.

> Think about what is working well for a student in the context of his experience and find ways to strengthen and leverage those characteristics.

Opportunities to nurture and leverage strengths and affinities are limited only by the creativity of the members of a student's learning community. There are innumerable ways to build on students' assets to make learning more accessible and more enjoyable. Katharine Brown is a third-grade teacher in North Carolina and Jim is one of her students. As a third grader, Jim's academic skills were below grade-level expectations, and his behaviors often interfered with his—and others'—learning. As his resource teacher, Katharine focused on

Jim's strengths and affinities, particularly his language strengths, by positioning him as the editor of the new school newsletter. This leadership role and the responsibilities of editing the newsletter provided Jim with a more concrete purpose for learning the skills of reading and writing. At the same time, his responsibilities of interviewing teachers and students became authentic opportunities to work on his weak areas in social cognition. In Katharine's words, Jim has gone from "not doing anything to a willingness to try, but he is no longer defiant and resistant to class lessons. He is feeling proud!" By appreciating Jim's learning profile of strengths and weaknesses and investing in knowing him well, Katharine has built a foundation for success for Jim.

Educators employ many techniques for recognizing and celebrating students' greatest assets, such as exploring how one's assets will create opportunities for success in a future career. Techniques can be simple day-to-day activities like identifying the spelling whiz or geography guru in the class and encouraging students to tap into these peers as resources. Assets can be leveraged around special occasions, like having the student with great social cognition serve as host for visitors to the school. Many times community organizations become outlets for celebrating strengths, such as encouraging students to participate in a local theatre group. At the Purnell School in New Jersey, students participate in the Affinities Program, a curriculum built on the foundational belief that the best way to help students grow is to help them discover and use their strengths. Strengthening strengths while supporting students' weaknesses must frame how we educate our students.

The development of the Affinities Program was led by Jenifer Fox, who has since started the Strengths Movement (www .strengthsmovement.com), which seeks to change how we see ourselves and our students, moving from a focus on weaknesses to a focus on strengths.

When Student Assets and School Demands Differ

Sometimes a student's strengths and interests are not aligned with the demands of school. For example, a second-grade student may demonstrate exceptional vocabulary, using sophisticated language to talk about interesting ideas that his classmates don't understand. This strength will serve this student well in years to come but may make it hard to make friends in second grade. The teacher's role is to help this student think about his audience and what kinds of words work best in different situations (like the school cafeteria versus the classroom) without discouraging his interest in learning new words. Equally important is helping this student see the long-term benefits of this area of strength.

Many students in today's classrooms are well wired for the demands of working in a global economy but not matched to the current demands of school. Students with strengths in higher-order cognition, who are creative problem solvers, exceptional evaluative thinkers, and whose language and social cognition abilities are well developed, are prepared to take leadership positions in a twenty-first-century workforce, where these competencies will be in high demand.[1] Students who rely on strengths in long-term memory may achieve positive results on tests and be able to easily recall facts, but those strengths will not play a prominent role in the kind of thinking required for the future. Students who are struggling today can have hope for what the future holds when they are able to focus their energy in areas that more closely align with their strengths. The cultivation of optimism—inspiring these students to see the hopes and possibilities of their future—is critical to their self-esteem and motivation.

A New Approach to Learning Plans for Struggling Students

In a learner-centric school, the goal of a learning plan must be to equip the student for success—to provide him with the insight and tools to manage his learning profile and advocate for his personal learning needs. In many of today's schools, intervention plans are written to define targeted weak skills and strategies to support the struggling student in improving those skills.

> *Learning plan:* A defined action plan including accommodations, interventions, and resources for meeting the learning needs of a student

Learning plans written from an All Kinds of Minds perspective focus on opportunities to build on students' assets while including strategies for targeted areas of school performance. Table 5.1 describes characteristics of an All Kinds of Minds learning plan compared to those of a more traditional learning plan, like an individual educational plan (IEP).

Table 5.1 Keys to Effective Learning Plans: Building on Assets

Traditional Learning Plan (for example, IEP)	• Defines prescription for services (for example, occupational therapy, speech therapy, special education services) • Includes description of current performance (often includes social/emotional and academic performance) • Description often focused on skill deficits • Provides documentation of evaluation results for reading, writing, and math • Includes annual goals with short-term objectives to address weak skill areas

All Kinds of Minds Learning Plan	• Defines recommendations for strategies to support learning profiles (for example, memory, higher-order cognition, neuromotor functions)
	• Defines targeted school performance areas (academic or social)
	• Includes areas of strength and strategies to strengthen strengths
	• Links elements of student's learning profile to targeted areas of weakness
	• Identifies strategies that connect to student's learning profile:
	  • May include accommodations and interventions for school and home
	  • Accommodations and interventions leverage strengths and affinities

When students succeed in a particular area, it is important to encourage that success. This means identifying opportunities for the student to practice and continue to improve her areas of strength. For example, a student with strengths in oral expressive language may find pleasure in being part of the school's drama club or being the anchor of the school's daily newscast. By engaging in these activities, this student's expressive language strengths continue to improve. Strengths can also be leveraged when selecting strategies. Exhibit 5.1 contains an example of a learning plan that leverages strengths.

Keys to Effective Learning Plans

Strategies to Minimize Learning Challenges

Part of equipping students for success is teaching them strategies to manage their learning profiles. Good learning plans nearly always include a balance of accommodations and interventions.

Some educators are reluctant to make accommodations for students, feeling this lets the student "off the hook." Another way of looking at accommodations is to think of them as supports while students work to improve skills. The decision to use an accommodation or intervention often stems from the goal of the lesson or task. If the objective of a lesson is to demonstrate how to determine the area of a rectangle, then the accommodation of using a calculator to support a student's memory of multiplication facts doesn't interfere with that

Accommodations: Strategies designed to bypass an area of weakness so that the student can continue to perform (for example, providing a student who struggles with reading decoding to listen to a book on tape so that he can learn the necessary information)

Interventions: Strategies designed to improve an area of weakness (for example, teaching word attack skills to a student struggling with reading decoding)

Exhibit 5.1 Sample Learning Plan

Strengths	**Strategies to Strengthen Strengths**		
Social cognition Math problem solving/Higher-order cognition Creativity/Rich oral vocabulary/ Social cognition	Serve as a peer mediator or student counselor (strengthen social cognition) Serve as math tutor for younger students (strengthen math problem solving and leverage compassion for others) Encourage participation in drama productions (strengthen creativity, oral vocabulary, and ability to get along well with peers)		
Affinities			
Animals Soccer Video and board games Reading biographies and fiction novels Technology			
School Performance Weaknesses and Underlying Neurodevelopmental Functions and/or Constructs	**Accommodations:** **(Strategies for Bypassing Weak Functions)**	**Interventions:** **(Strategies for Strengthening Weak Functions)**	
School Performance Weakness: *Writing (elaboration, cohesion, spelling)* Neurodevelopmental Functions and/or Constructs: *Expressive language* *Active working memory*	Separate revisions (elaboration, cohesion) from editing (spelling) *[reduce active working memory demands of writing]* Digitally record oral telling of stories to friend or partner, then review to write *[leverage social cognition]* Use word processing software with word recognition *[leverage affinity for technology and support active working memory]*	Use graphic organizers with guiding questions to plan writing *[intentional steps to improve elaboration, support active working memory]* Read favorite novels and identify story elements that elaborate on plot and make events interesting; also identify transitions that tie elements together *[leverage affinity to improve elaboration and cohesion]*	
School Performance Weakness: *Easily distracted/trouble following directions* Neurodevelopmental Functions and/or Constructs: *Attention processing controls*	Use a listening buddy when receiving directions: She must first tell what she heard Buddy fills in the gaps	Give prior notice when appointing her as class paraphraser *[leverage oral expressive language while working on processing controls]* Engage her in problem-solving brainstorming about how to filter distractions Talk about strategies she uses in soccer to stay...	

objective. If the goal is to recall multiplication facts, then an intervention focused on consolidation and retrieval of these facts from long-term memory is more in order.

Another consideration to make when selecting strategies is to find those techniques that will provide the necessary support for students while protecting them from humiliation. Students put a significant amount of energy into avoiding humiliation, and educators have a responsibility to all students, and to struggling students in particular, to support them in these efforts. For example, placing a checklist on the desk can be helpful for a student who struggles with the sequential and active working memory demands of multistep directions or processes. However, that checklist will also be visible to other students in the class, which, depending on the age of the student and the culture of the classroom, may be a source of humiliation for the student who needs it. An alternative would be to place the checklist in a less conspicuous location such as the inside of a notebook or on a clipboard. This still provides support but is not as obvious as a checklist on the student's desk.

Teachers should also consider the effectiveness of teaching selected strategies to their entire class. Often a strategy that works well for one student will also work for others. For example, another alternative to the checklist strategy just noted is to offer it as a resource to everyone in the class, using this as an opportunity to talk about sequences and the memory demands of keeping steps in order. Typically, the students who find the strategy helpful will continue to use it, while other students won't. Either way, the idea of using a strategy to support learning has been destigmatized and the classroom culture is more accepting of learning differences. By sharing the strategies with the whole class, the targeted student maintains his self-esteem and the whole class benefits.

Collaboration

Chapter Four introduced the notion of establishing a "trust fund" among the school, the parent or caregiver, and the student. An essential component of maintaining a healthy, secure trust fund is collaboration among those involved with it. In order for a learning plan to be meaningful, everyone involved in implementing it must have a shared understanding of the goals and strategies. This shared understanding is the result of clear and frequent communication and mutual respect for the insights of the teachers, the parents, and the student.

Collaboration begins with conversations among members of the student's learning community—the student, his parent or caregiver, and other teachers who work with this student in a learning environment. Through open dialogue, the resulting learning plan can represent a comprehensive view of the student's strengths, affinities, and weaknesses and strategies to address recurring themes. This collaboration continues throughout the implementation of the plan, with ongoing communication about progress and any necessary adjustments to strategies.

School Policies That Support Student Success

School policies are a set of rules established for a collective body. Often, an educator's sense of fairness assumes that rules should be enacted uniformly. When we use a more comprehensive set of data about a struggling learner to map out a plan for success, it can often reveal situations in which the policy doesn't work to support an individual student. Suppose a student is in eighth grade, but due to weak language and memory, is reading at a third-grade level. This is affecting all aspects of his academic performance, as evidenced in failing grades in all classes except physical education and art. He's had a growth spurt and is one of the starting players on the junior varsity basketball team.

Unfortunately, the school policy states that a student must maintain an average of C+ or better to play on a school team. The policy is well intended, put in place to motivate students to get good grades. However, this opportunity to play basketball is the one thing going right for this young man, who is desperately trying to learn to read and who is embarrassed and feels stupid during this vulnerable time in adolescence. Do you enforce the policy in the name of fairness and take away the one thing going well for him in school? Or do you make an exception and use this as an opportunity to try to revise policies to better accommodate and support struggling learners? This is a dilemma school leaders must manage as they create learning plans that will boost student success. It has no easy answer. But a comprehensive assessment of the learner, with a rich array of evidence viewed through a science of learning framework, helps with a more accurate diagnosis and understanding of the struggling student. A subsequent learning plan that is dedicated to working on learning challenges while building the student's assets provides a starting point. Learning leaders are charged with helping colleagues make the most informed decisions they can about how best to use school policy to support student learning.

GETTING STARTED WITH SMALL WINS

Small wins = *concrete, significant tasks that produce a visible result while moving one step closer to a new vision or one step away from an unacceptable condition*

What's a learning leader to do? How can you build on student assets in your school? How can you, like Jan Stewart, more effectively and intentionally recognize the strengths and affinities of your students? How do we take advantage of those assets to help these students learn? Some first steps might include

- Look around your school for opportunities for students to showcase their strengths and affinities. Determine ways to shine a brighter light on these opportunities and to create new ones.
- Examine the learning plans of your struggling students. If students' strengths and affinities are missing, add them as part of these plans. List ways you plan to nurture and leverage each student's strengths and affinities.
- Reflect on your school policies and the ways in which they encourage or discourage students to celebrate their strengths and affinities.

Reflection Exercise

Learning Leadership in Action

Contemplate the format, requirements, process for creation, and decisions about the content of individual learning plans in your educational setting. Then select one, several, or all of the statements about the All Kinds of Minds approach to reflect on individually or discuss with colleagues.

Example: The superintendent and middle school principals have formed a study group around this book. They individually read the chapters and reflect on the Learning Leadership in Action activities and then meet during early release days to share their thoughts and discuss ideas.

All Kinds of Minds Approach: Building assets through individual learning plans	How do your learning plans reflect this statement?	What could you do to enhance your learning plans?
Inspire optimism in the face of learning challenges	Success stories are shared and celebrated.	Engage students in conversations about the possibilities and opportunities for success beyond middle and high school.
Leverage strengths and affinities	Our learning plans don't explicitly include strengths, but sometimes we talk about them.	Include space to document strengths before listing weaknesses. Choose interventions that leverage strengths and affinities in the strategies.
Promote collaboration and a shared understanding	We meet annually with students and parents to discuss learning plans and progress. We must get parent's signature.	Engage in ongoing communication (at least once per quarter) with students and parents about strengths, progress, and effective strategies.

(See blank template on next page.)

All Kinds of Minds Approach: Building assets through individual learning plans	How do your learning plans reflect this statement?	What could you do to enhance your learning plans?
Inspire optimism in the face of learning challenges		
Discover and treasure unique learning profiles		
Eliminate humiliation, blaming, and labeling of students		
Leverage strengths and affinities		
Empower students to find success		
Align with an individual's learning profile		
Promote collaboration and a shared understanding		
School policies that support student success		

6

Looking Deeper
A Fresh Perspective on Behavior

"It's going to be one of those days!" thought Jan, frustrated with the seventh-grade discipline reports she had received that morning. One was about Billy, who was late for class for the third time, activating the "Three strikes and you go to in-school suspension" policy. She sighed; discipline was definitely not her favorite part of her job as principal of Eastville Middle School. Jan knew she shouldn't jump to conclusions about Billy or enact the discipline policy before trying to understand the underlying reasons for his pattern of behavior. Jan was pondering her next steps, when she saw Jeremy take a seat outside her door.

Jan glanced up at the clock and confirmed that Jeremy was supposed to be in algebra class right now. His teacher had informed Jan that for the past few weeks Jeremy consistently failed to turn in his work and spent class time off task, trying to engage other students in conversations about the basketball team (of which he is a member) or the latest horror movie. Jan walked to her door to invite Jeremy in for a discussion. She asked him why his Foundations for Algebra teacher had sent him to the principal's office, and he looked sheepishly at his lap for a few moments. Then he mumbled, "I guess I was rude when I said that percents were stupid. I just don't see why we need to know about those things." Jan prompted Jeremy a bit more and then he began to open up. He talked about his frustration with mathematics, how hard it was for him to understand what the teacher was talking about, and the pressure of needing a good grade in that class. "I just don't get why I need to know this stuff," he kept saying. Jan thought about the recent professional development meetings that were focused on strengths and affinities and got out a piece of notebook paper. She shared with Jeremy the relevance of understanding percentages to basketball statistics and sketched out a few sample problems. As she was explaining, Jeremy began to ask good questions and successfully worked a few of the example problems that Jan had written on her notepad. Then he asked, "Can we figure out my basketball stats before I go back to algebra today?" Of course, Jan said yes.

Once Jeremy had left her office, Jan turned her attention back to Billy. She knew that she needed more background information on his situation before addressing his discipline report. He had both Mr. Chapman and Ms. Cox for teachers, and they both had a lunch break coming up in a few minutes. She sent them a quick e-mail asking if they could meet briefly at the beginning of their lunch period. She also looked through her in-box and located a recent e-mail from the principals' cohort. It was requesting agenda items for their next meeting. Jan hadn't had any noteworthy ideas when she received it, so she hadn't responded yet. However, now it occurred to her that an interesting discussion topic would be how behavior policies relate to student learning and achievement. Feeling satisfied with her suggestion to the cohort, she hit Send and got up to go talk to Billy's teachers.

This chapter will explore
- Neurodevelopmental suspects, or factors that commonly affect behavior
- Key ideas about social cognition, an often misunderstood construct
- Tactics for preventing behavior problems, in the classroom and at the building level

---

THINGS AREN'T ALWAYS WHAT THEY SEEM ON OUR FIRST OBSERVATION. Behavior problems (such as not following instructions, disrupting class, distracting peers, acting aggressively, and so on) may not be character flaws, acts of moral turpitude, evidence of negative peer pressure or problematic parenting. Rather, they may be observable phenomena related to weak neurodevelopmental functions. Just as reading, math, or writing can be undermined by a profile, so too can behavior. In order to identify such weaknesses, it is necessary *first* to gather information and *then* to hypothesize, because initial impressions may miss the mark. Also, educators need to look for opportunities when students are not exhibiting behavior problems; those moments also provide important clues.

Diane Heffernan is a kindergarten teacher at Cape Fear Academy in Wilmington, North Carolina. One of her students, Will, came to her class with a reputation from his pre-K class as a behavior problem. He was unable to sit still without touching the children near him. He would not participate in activities. He frequently did the opposite of what was asked of him. As Diane watched Will and got to know him, she found out that he didn't understand directions like his classmates and had significant trouble reading; his receptive language was the likely culprit behind his comprehension difficulties, both when listening and reading. She took a very positive approach with Will, celebrating his small achievements. After experiencing so much failure the previous year, he responded fantastically to Diane's frequent praise (she gives him high-fives all the time). She discovered that he learns much better through hands-on experience and emulating models, neither of which overwhelm his receptive language. He loves all of the projects he gets to do in her class, which allow him to showcase assets in higher-order cognition and spatial ordering. He now participates appropriately in group discussions and activities. But more important, his peers no longer see him as a disruptive force, but rather as a friend and fellow classmate.

Neurodevelopmental Suspects

What are some of the functions that, if weak, could lead to behavior problems? The science of learning has identified several. To be sure, not all behavior problems are rooted in neurodevelopmental weaknesses. Educators should consider the potential culprits described in the following sections of the chapter (examples of supporting research are provided in Table 6.1), certainly before making judgments about a student's character, personality, or upbringing.

Table 6.1 Neurodevelopmental Causes of Behavior Problems

Neurodevelopmental Construct or Function	Research Examples
Attention Production Controls	
Overseeing the quality of academic output and behavior; previewing likely outcomes; inhibiting impulses and working at appropriate rates; self-monitoring output and work	Students with attention deficits are perceived by their teachers as being more limited in prosocial behaviors than comparable students without attention deficits[1]
	Impulse control has been found to be a major factor in antisocial and delinquent behavior in juveniles[2]
	Eight-year-olds previously identified with behavior problems were coached to self-monitor their own behavior by observing themselves on tape actively participating and using proper behaviors; each showed dramatic and sustained improvements[3]
Language	
Understanding incoming oral and written information; communicating ideas orally and in writing	Language problems and social skills deficits are related[4]
	The co-occurrence of social-emotional/behavioral problems and language weaknesses ranges between 50 and 70 percent; children with primary language weaknesses have been tracked over time and found to have elevated rates of social, emotional, and behavioral problems; children with primary diagnoses in the emotional-behavioral realm have been found to have moderate to severe language difficulties[5]

Graphomotor Function

Coordinating muscles needed for handwriting; recalling handwriting movement patterns and letter shapes; getting adequate feedback about hand/pencil location during writing motions

Students who lack adequate handwriting abilities to complete school assignments satisfactorily are at risk for behavioral problems due to frustration[6]

Social Cognition

Knowing what to talk about, when, with whom, and for how long; working and playing with others in a cooperative manner; nurturing positive relationships with influential people

One reason aggressive children act aggressively is that they more frequently attribute hostile intentions to others, particularly in scenarios in which the intent of others is ambiguous[7]

A meta-analysis found a robust and significant association between hostile attribution of intent and aggressive behavior[8]

Individuals who associate themselves more with the victim role in conflict (a view that may be implicit or outside of conscious awareness) very quickly conclude that they are under threat and have more frequent experiences of victimization[9]

Children who overestimate the extent to which they are socially accepted were identified by their peers as more likely to be aggressive; on the flip side of that coin, children who underestimate their social acceptance were the most prone to aggressive behavior in response to social criticism[10]

Matthew, a student at Ferguson Middle School in Beavercreek, Ohio, was showing behavior problems as well as academic struggles, particularly with reading. He frequently got so angry at school that he hit lockers with his fists. Janet Boucher, one of Ferguson's intervention specialists, invested time to better understand Matthew. Knowing the importance of affinities, she sat with him at a computer and asked him to show her things that interested him. He shared his passion for all things mechanical. She then provided him with kid magazines about robots; he read them voraciously. He enthusiastically talked about the stories he'd read, giving him practice with summarizing. He progressed to writing his own stories about robots, including keeping a journal with story ideas. Within a few months, his reading progressed multiple levels.

Janet determined that Matthew needed extra time to process information, a learning phenomenon that cut across several of the neurodevelopmental constructs, including his language, higher-order cognition, spatial ordering, temporal-sequential ordering, and even social cognition. His slower rate of processing led to his difficulty adjusting to new settings, so Janet made sure that he had time at the beginning of long classes to keep to himself and settle in, especially when he had had a rough day. He got angry much less frequently and stopped punching lockers. Some of Matthew's peers asked why he got this special time to himself, but Janet explained that he needed it because of the way his brain was wired. Instead of being resentful, the other students reflected on their own profiles of strengths and weaknesses. By developing a deeper understanding of Matthew's learning profile and by tapping his affinities, Janet helped him to significantly improve his behavior and experience more success in school.

Attention Production Controls

Weaknesses in the production controls can lead to impulsivity, limited foresight about decisions, and inadequate self-monitoring of one's actions. Weak production controls can be like a dashboard that has gone haywire, resulting in an out-of-control automobile. When this occurs, educators need to hold off on assuming the student is out of control as a matter of choice. It can be very difficult for a student, for example, to resist certain impulses due to weak attention. This doesn't mean educators should just forget about the behavior problems that result. But students will likely better respond to strategies that explicitly target a neurodevelopmental weakness. The research has shown that because attention can be improved through various strategies, so too can the behavior problems that result from weak attention. Table 6.2 contains some questions that can guide this information-gathering process.

Weaknesses with other aspects of attention can also lead to behavior problems. Robert was a special educator at Silverthorne Public School in Mississauga, Ontario, Canada. Marshall, one of his second graders, read and wrote enthusiastically and displayed excellent spatial ordering when building a variety of structures. However, he sometimes displayed defiant and aggressive behavior when asked to complete tasks, particularly in the morning and after lunch, when he often appeared exhausted. Robert interpreted Marshall's lack of stamina and apparent inconsistencies in effort as signs of a weakness in attention mental energy control.

Robert put strategies into place to improve Marshall's behavior by addressing his mental energy controls. For example, his teachers encouraged Marshall to produce work in smaller, more manageable chunks. They also gave him play dough to help him remain alert during individual and group activities (a little bit of physical activity, even as small as manipulating play dough, can help boost mental energy). They explained to the other students that these accommodations helped Marshall get

> **PICTURE THIS!**
>
> Think about how you might use the questions in Table 6.2 to think differently about behavior problems in your school. Opportunities to explore these potential neurodevelopmental culprits can come in formal student staffings as well as more informal conversations about behavior problems. Work with your colleagues to reframe these questions for use with students.

Table 6.2 Questions to Ask About Behavior Problems

Questions to Ask About a Student with Behavior Problems	Neurodevelopmental Weaknesses to Consider	Potential Strategies to Address Behavior Problems
How impulsive is the student across settings and tasks? How well does the student think ahead or plan, including on academic tasks like writing and math? To what extent does the student self-monitor, such as catching mistakes in school work?	Attention Production Controls	Play "what-if" games requiring the student to think ahead about social situations Provide positive reinforcement when impulses are resisted Debrief after challenging situations to improve self-monitoring of behavior
Does the student have difficulties with reading comprehension? Listening comprehension? Does the student have trouble with expressing thoughts in writing? When speaking? How extensive is the student's vocabulary? How well can the student comprehend or generate complex sentence structures? To what degree does the student understand abstract or figurative language?	Language	Provide the student with scripts, including phrases and sentences for expressing needs and feelings Give the student opportunities to find success in activities such as music and art that do not place heavy demands on language
How legible is the student's handwriting? How much effort does the student need to exert to generate handwritten material? Is the student's oral expression noticeably more elaborate or sophisticated than written expression?	Graphomotor Function	Make accommodations available for weak handwriting, such as abbreviated writing assignments, providing copies of notes (or outlines for notes), and voice-recognition software

Questions to Ask About a Student with Behavior Problems	Neurodevelopmental Weaknesses to Consider	Potential Strategies to Address Behavior Problems
How easily does the student make or keep friends? How well does the student do with entering a game, conversation, or activity? What is the student's capacity to collaborate and resolve conflicts? How sophisticated are the student's conversational skills, such as selecting and shifting topics, turn taking, and giving feedback (like eye contact and nodding)? How well does the student read situations and other people? Does the student show appropriate affect for the mood of the situation or group?	Social Cognition	Role-play situations that routinely bring about misbehavior, giving the student practice with accurately interpreting social language, reading social cues, and making good decisions View scenes from television shows or movies and talk about how characters relate to each other (positively and negatively) and behave (or misbehave)

through his daily tasks and that he was not merely "playing" with the play dough.

Months later, Marshall continued to show improved behavior. He independently asked for breaks while working, making statements and asking questions such as, "I can't do it right now," and "May I take five minutes off?" Robert noted that Marshall had deepened his understanding of himself as a learner. Marshall responded more positively in social situations, including those that had previously brought out the worst in his behavior.

Language

Considerable research has demonstrated a link between language problems and negative behavior. Why? Language is the main way that a person's needs can be expressed and met. So students with weak language might get caught in a negative spiral in which communication difficulty leads to inappropriate ways to meet needs (like aggression), in turn leading to negative experiences (such as peer rejection) and then to feelings of inadequacy. Language also can serve as brakes on behavior, because internal dialogue helps one to think through behavioral choices and ponder options; as a consequence, limited language can contribute to impulsivity and poorly reasoned decisions. As is the case with attention, improving language holds the promise of also improving behavior. But the first step is to reveal the nature of the student's difficulty. When students show behavior problems, the possibility of weak language (receptive or expressive) should be considered (Table 6.2 contains questions to help identify neurodevelopmental constructs and functions that might be affecting behavior).

Graphomotor Function

What would it be like to go through your entire school career with your writing hand in a wrist cast? Weak graphomotor function can be as frustrating as writing in a wrist cast—pencil control is difficult, legibility is poor, hand fatigue sets in quickly, and written output can be excruciatingly inefficient. So it stands to reason that weak graphomotor function can lead to behavior problems when handwriting is expected of students. School is a student's career. When adults struggle in their careers, especially when they are forced to do things that are very difficult and unpleasant, negative side effects result, some of them quite serious. When students display behavior problems in school, consider whether a mismatch between task demands (like handwriting) and a neurodevelopmental function (like graphomotor function) may be a cause.

Social Cognition

Put simply, social cognition is thinking about relating to other people. We use it to process social information and navigate social situations.

It has an input side that has to do with reading people and situations. For example, we regularly interpret verbal and nonverbal signals to discern dispositions, intentions, and moods of others. Social cognition also has an output side in terms of decision making about relationships and interchanges. As with input, we use tools that are both verbal (such as greetings, questions, and compliments) and nonverbal (such as eye contact, gesticulations, and posture) when relating to others. For some students, these abilities to read others or accurately express thoughts and feelings are underdeveloped, unreliable, or frequently break down under pressure (time or situational pressure).

Social cognition, a neurodevelopmental construct, is distinct from socialization, which can be viewed as an applied skill (like reading) that involves several neurodevelopmental functions, several of which were discussed in previous sections of the chapter. Someone can struggle with socialization despite having good social cognition; that person's relationships may get derailed by impulsivity due to problematic attention production controls, for example. However, weak social cognition could be the culprit when language, attention, and other constructs are functioning solidly. Because social cognition is multifaceted, a person may struggle with one aspect of this construct while exhibiting strengths in other aspects of it. Table 6.3 lists some specific aspects of social cognition, all of which have been identified and explored through research.

Research has demonstrated that limited social thinking, directed toward situations and others as well as to oneself, leads to behavior problems. For example, individuals may misread situations and think

Table 6.3 Components of Social Cognition

Comprehending how complex emotions operate[11]
Recognizing emotions in ourselves and in others[12]
Understanding another's perspective[13]
General interpersonal understanding[14]
Managing the initiation, rate, intensity, and duration of social interactions[15]
Perceiving one's effect on others[16]

others are being aggressive toward them when that might not be the case. Information about social cognition and other functions affecting behavior can be gathered by educators.

Preventing Behavior Problems

This section explores how to prevent behavior problems by incorporating beliefs about teaching All Kinds of Minds into a school climate:

- Inspire optimism in the face of learning challenges.
- Discover and treasure learning profiles.
- Leverage strengths and affinities.
- Eliminate humiliation, blaming, and labeling of students.
- Empower students to find success.

Inspire Optimism

Preventing many behaviors entails seeing the flip side of the coin, or appreciating how a neurodevelopmental function that is a liability in school may be an asset in the future. For example, a language weakness could lead to unique ways of communicating and heretofore hidden assets, such as spatial ordering. Attention weakness could be the seed of entrepreneurial spirit, risk taking, or decisive decision making.

In fact, a survey of U.S. entrepreneurs found that about a third of them identified themselves as having reading difficulties. These individuals reported being more likely to delegate authority and to excel in oral communication and problem solving. They also were more likely to own multiple businesses, to grow businesses more quickly, and to employ more staff.[17] Growing up with significant learning problems may promote the development of compensatory abilities that translate to useful career and life skills. Such abilities include the capacity to trust others (for delegation), read other people, process or generate visual material (in lieu of text), oral expression (to bypass written expression), creativity, and political savvy. In addition, experiencing learning problems can build resilience, leading to heightened determination even in the face of substantial obstacles to success.

> "Growing up with significant learning problems may promote the development of compensatory abilities that translate to useful career and life skills. Such abilities include the capacity to trust others (for delegation), read other people, process or generate visual material (in lieu of text), oral expression (to bypass written expression), creativity, and political savvy."

Paul Orfalea, founder of Kinko's (now FedEx Kinko's) views his learning challenges as instrumental to his tremendous business success: "My learning disability gave me certain advantages, because I was able to live in the moment and capitalize on the opportunities I spotted." Entrepreneurs are often noted to have an insatiable nature—for experience, success, action—that is typical of many students with attention deficits. Orfalea attributes his intense curiosity to his "weak" attention controls: "I get bored easily, and that is a great motivator."

So one challenge for educators is to address behavior problems without crushing the underlying causes that might end up being assets. This requires a paradigm shift of sorts, to view students' learning profile functions as characteristics (such as insatiability or impulsivity) that may be mismatched for current demands rather than as outright weaknesses. A student's language may not be weak, for example, but rather not well suited to ninth grade (but that student's language ability may not be an impediment in the future, or it could indirectly lead to the development of other abilities).

Discover and Treasure Unique Learning Profiles

Understanding the nature of learning profiles can go a long way toward the prevention of behavior problems. Specifically, educators should adopt the mind-set of looking carefully at the available evidence (as in the "Making Tracks" exercise in Chapter Four) before jumping to conclusions. As the previous sections describe, behavior problems may stem from the same neurodevelopmental functions that underlie academic skill development. A first-year teacher in a New York City public school went to a workshop to learn how to use a neurodevelopmental perspective to better manage the behavior of her fifth-grade students. After taking a closer look at what might be at the root of some of the behaviors that were interfering in the classroom, she commented that "it never crossed my mind that he didn't want to misbehave. I had thought his motivation was to drive me crazy. Now I know it is a weakness with his attention production controls and more important, I know how the two of us are going to make it better." A student doesn't choose to struggle with writing or math, so he may not choose to misbehave either.

Keenan was a seventh grader at Old Trail School in Bath, Ohio, who repeatedly got himself into hot water by telling his peers and teachers alarming stories about his home life. Kathi Howard, Old Trail's school psychologist, confirmed that all was indeed well with his family, but she realized that Keenan's mind was overly active when learning information. This was revealed, for example, on a list learning task in which she read about a dozen words to Keenan, who then had to recite them; he tended to give a lot of words that were not on the list but were tangentially related (such as saying "sock" rather than "shoe"), although he was convinced that his errors really were on the original list. This pattern was seen across tasks and activities, such as memorizing a story, during which he consistently inserted his own details and later mistook them for details that had been in the story.

Kathi connected this overactive processing to Kevin's creating false memories. Bringing his awareness to this pattern was an important first step. Then he was asked to practice differentiating information he encounters from his own invented ideas; this could have been accomplished by having him relate a recent experience and to sort details into three categories: things that he is certain really happened, those that did not really occur but could have, and things about which he's not certain and needs to discuss with someone else who was there to clarify. Being aware of his active processing and practicing better

Overactive processing of information relates to the attention processing controls. In a sense, the student is extremely distracted by his or her own thoughts, which can lead to daydreaming and mind trips. For example, a class may be discussing Arctic marine animals and the student starts thinking about animals that live in the Pacific Ocean, then New Zealand, then Australia, then a movie about Australia, that one of the actors also played a superhero in a different movie, and then getting a new comic book after school. The student has mentally traveled from the Arctic Ocean to the local book store in a matter of moments. Active processing can boost creativity, but overactive processing can lead to distractions from the task or topic at hand.

control of it led to more accurate performance on memory tasks and, just as important, the alarming stories became a thing of the past.

The process of discovering students' profiles should include the search for strengths. Many students who have struggled with behavior or learning problems have been told only the bad news about themselves. Merely hearing that they have strengths can be beneficial. But strengths and affinities can also be utilized to improve behavior.

Leverage Strengths and Affinities

One way to leverage strengths and affinities—the assets mentioned in the previous chapter—is to use them to prevent behavior problems. Many educators have used the tactic of offering "affinity time" (such as playing computer games) as positive reinforcement for appropriate behavior. But students need and deserve ample opportunities to develop strengths and pursue interests. Recall the success of Katharine Brown with her third-grade student, Jim. At the beginning of the year he was resistant, angry, and defiant. But she illuminated his excellent verbal abilities and made him editor of the fledgling student newsletter. After a few months, he was like a different child—no longer resistant and defiant, and very proud of his success.

A school experience devoid of any exposure to weaknesses is not realistic or even desirable. Learners have to meet certain benchmarks and improve their skills, even in the face of challenges. But the trick is to build in enough opportunity to use strengths and affinities to sustain learners as they take on those challenges.

Eliminate Humiliation, Blaming, and Labeling

A school climate that is free of humiliation, blaming, and labeling will promote positive behavior while minimizing negative behavior. Again, not all behavior problems are rooted in neurodevelopmental weaknesses. Regardless, students should also be held accountable for their actions. But consequences for misbehavior can be meted out in tandem with efforts to understand *why* a student misbehaves. That understanding can help make decisions to improve behavior or to prevent future problems, as was the case with Keenan, the seventh grader at Old Trail School in Ohio.

Eliminating humiliation, blaming, and labeling requires a mindset that can influence the continuous decision making of an educator. Understanding that a child has difficulty with word retrieval helps the teacher refrain from spontaneously calling on her for an answer in class. Knowing that a student has both neuromotor and spatial difficulties sets a different set of expectations for physical education and mandatory competitive sports. Most important, it shapes the kind of communication educators have with students and parents.

Table 6.4 includes two kinds of statements about a student's learning challenges. Those in the first column are grounded in a neurodevelopmental framework and can inform decisions about strategies. Statements in the second column lack specificity and, possibly, rushed conclusions.

Table 6.4 *Statements About Learning Challenges*

Specific Statements About Learning Challenges	Nonspecific Statements About Learning Challenges
"His attention production controls don't work well for eighth grade."	"He's ADHD."
"Her language problems affect how she makes decisions and interacts."	"She's got oppositional defiant disorder."
"Let's bypass his weak graphomotor function as much as possible so that writing isn't so frustrating."	"He's going to get a demerit every time a homework assignment isn't handed in."
"We need to help her improve her social cognition so that she can more accurately read her peers and situations."	"She's clueless as to what her peers think about her."
"Different parts of his learning profile really interfere with his behavior."	"He's one of those kids who are up to no good."
"Her weaknesses make learning schoolwork extremely hard for her."	"She just rushes through homework with the smallest amount of effort."

Empower Students

One of the best ways to empower students for behavioral success is to deepen and expand both their self-insight and their knowledge about learning. Students who understand their learning strengths and weaknesses are better equipped to advocate for themselves. Self-advocacy is a positive course of action that replaces problematic tactics like aggression, withdrawal, or avoidance. Students will be more likely to employ strategies because they will know the rationale behind why those strategies were selected.

> " One of the best ways to empower students for behavioral success is to deepen and expand both their self-insight and their knowledge about learning. "

Getting the student's viewpoint on learning or behavioral troubles not only provides additional perspective on the situation but also helps the student learn about learning. Katharine Brown got important information about her third-grade student Jim's learning from Jim himself, and in the process he made discoveries about himself, including his excellent language and shaky social cognition. By enlisting the seventh grader Keenan in his assessment process, his teacher helped him acquire a better understanding of how his attention interfered with his memory. This understanding then increased Keenan's motivation to try the strategy of journaling to differentiate real facts from his ideas.

Brent was a seventh- and eighth-grade teacher at Sequoyah Middle School in Broken Arrow, Oklahoma. He worked extensively with one of his students, Chris, who frequently missed or misunderstood instructions, did not complete his work, and responded to the stress and tedium of difficult tasks through misbehavior. Chris often asked of whoever would listen, "What is wrong with this school?" But Brent wondered if the question Chris really was asking was, "What is wrong with me?"

Brent looked at information from a range of sources, including Chris and his parents, and was able to get a better handle on his strengths and weaknesses. Brent was anxious about sharing what he'd learned with Chris, specifically about his attention weaknesses. Would Chris's reaction be a sarcastic, "No kidding? We had to go through all of this to figure that out?" When describing his weaknesses, would his problems gain some new validity or power to him, so that the words would become another label that he didn't want and couldn't escape?

Brent began with, "I have really good news," and they talked about the incredible strengths Chris exhibited in language, higher-order cognition, and social cognition. He went on, "Now, I have some other good news," and they talked about the weaknesses Chris had struggled with *and* the many things that could be done about them—the list of strategies that they could use to strengthen those areas and minimize their interference with his life at school. They chose together those that would be most practical and effective for Chris.

During the discussion Chris didn't offer much that could be interpreted as approval. But the next day he finished his work and seemed very clear on all the instructions. No disruptions. No attempts to escape his work. Brent watched closely, looking for an opportunity to intervene with one of the strategies they had planned, but there was really no need. In the ensuing weeks and months Brent hardly had the chance to implement strategies for Chris, as the behavior problems had largely dissipated. Brent likened the positive effect on Chris to what often happens when we go to the doctor. We go in feeling sick but come out feeling better even before a single dose of a prescription. We feel better just knowing that a headache is due to an easily treatable infection and not a rare tropical disease or ruptured blood vessel. Instead of confirming Chris's worst fears, Brent affirmed his highest hopes.

Preventing Problems at the Classroom Level

The beliefs described in the previous sections can be utilized in various ways at the classroom level to prevent behavior problems. Teachers have ample opportunities to empower students with better self-insight and knowledge about learning. Preview assignments and activities in terms of neurodevelopmental functions that will be involved. Be open about how strategies address weaknesses, which not only can increase buy-in but also promotes learning about learning.

There are more ways to leverage and develop strengths and affinities than can be listed in a series of books, let alone just one. The only limitations are an educator's creativity and willingness to innovate. Students should have multiple paths to success in terms of how they access information, engage with it, and demonstrate their knowledge. Topics and activities that may at first seem beyond the academic realm can be brought into the classroom experience to create opportunities for success.

All classrooms should be filled with a "can do" spirit that is cultivated by authentic, specific, and concrete praise (both from the teacher and students). Optimism can be nurtured by a future orientation, such as by connecting assets (including those that may temporarily be liabilities) with potential life paths. Educators, especially those in high schools, should think about such paths and the neurodevelopmental demands involved in them. For example, journalism requires good language and social cognition, while engineering places more demands on spatial ordering and aspects of higher-order cognition.

> "All classrooms should be filled with a "can do" spirit that is cultivated by authentic, specific, and concrete praise (both from the teacher and students)."

Watch out for labels of all kinds: systematic (such as "pullout student"), clinical (such as "LD kid"), and vernacular (such as "lazy"). Labels are seductively easy, so don't settle for them. Push yourself and others to dig deeper for answers, question thinking, and challenge assumptions. Be open to seeing something *different*, and be open to seeing something *differently*.

Preventing Problems at the Building Level

The bifocal lens described earlier in this book is a metaphor for thinking globally and acting locally. Most educators can act locally in their classrooms, but they should also think globally at the school or district level. School policies can be adopted that ramp up and protect opportunities for students to experience success. Educators need to fight against the tide of cutbacks in the arts, music, and physical education. Younger students, in particular, need more recess rather than less. Schools should forge connections to their communities, which offer many ways to develop strengths (such as internships and apprenticeships). Community connections can showcase adults who represent success stories and different ways to develop and work with learning profiles.

Positive Behavior Support (PBS), or Positive Behavioral Interventions and Supports (PBIS), is an example of a system that can be adopted on a school or district level and that can be compatible with the beliefs about teaching all kinds of minds. In general, such systems should focus on increasing positive behaviors by understanding behavior through a problem-solving process.

When schools adopt wholesale systems for behavioral support, emphasizing the positive reinforcement of good behaviors (building strengths) is preferable to punishing negative behaviors. For instance, schoolwide token economies could provide rewards for behaviors such as resolving conflicts without aggression, fair play, supporting peers, and following rules without prompting. Such systems should be instituted in such a way as to respect student privacy (eliminating humiliation), like keeping behavior scores confidential. Also, multiage activities and groupings can provide younger students with role models and older students with the positive experience of mentoring others (inspiring optimism).

GETTING STARTED WITH SMALL WINS

Small wins = *Concrete, significant tasks that produce a visible result while moving one step closer to a new vision or one step away from an unacceptable condition*

What's a school leader to do? Jan Stewart had an *aha!* moment when she began to differentiate between real behavior problems and learning problems that look like behavior problems. What about your school? Is it common practice to rush to an assumption, or do you take the time to dig deeper? Here are some small

(Continued)

wins that can lead away from behavior myths and move toward a learner-centered approach to managing behavior:

- Learn about neurodevelopmental weaknesses that can lead to behavior problems, including
  - Attention production controls
  - Language
  - Graphomotor function
  - Social cognition

When students struggle with behavior problems, explore these possible culprits and help students to understand their own learning profiles.

- Explore the possibility that a learning profile that leads to behavior problems in school may lead to success later in life. Preview potential life paths in terms of neurodevelopmental functions that will be needed for success.
- Look for opportunities to leverage strengths and affinities in order to give students chances to experience success rather than frustration and failure.
- Analyze instruction and task demands to determine when students with certain neurodevelopmental weaknesses will be particularly at risk (such as during extended lectures for students with weak attention processing control or receptive language).
- Avoid labels, whether they are rooted in education systems (such as "resource student"), clinical practice (such as "ADHD" kid), or lay terminology (such as "unmotivated").
- Challenge and modify school or district policies that are not conducive to an All Kinds of Minds perspective on behavior.

Learning Leadership in Action

Working individually or with colleagues, list some common but undesirable behaviors students exhibit in the classroom or school environment. Then think about how those behaviors are addressed and how that might look different with an understanding of the neurodevelopmental framework and All Kinds of Minds beliefs.

Example: A small, rural elementary school has one class of each grade level and a discipline process that is consistent across K–8. The teachers in the early grades are concerned that the school policies don't take enough into consideration about learning profiles. They also wonder how to have fair and consistent policies that allow for professional judgment. They decide to pair up to look at the school policies and their own classroom management practices. They plan to use the All Kinds of Minds approach to make recommendations to their principal.

Common undesirable behaviors	Current ways of addressing these challenges (specific strategies, approaches, policies, and so on)	What would it look like if the All Kinds of Minds approach were used in addressing these behavior challenges?
Disrupting peers during class	Demerits given for misbehavior; detention if enough demerits are given	Task-analyze, on a student-by-student basis, where and when disruption occurs. During high language demand activities? When attention is stretched?

(See blank template on next page.)

Common undesirable behaviors	Current ways of addressing these challenges (specific strategies, approaches, policies, and so on)	What would it look like if the All Kinds of Minds approach were used in addressing these behavior challenges?

Boosting Writing Achievement
Through the Science of Learning

Springtime in a public school always features thinking about and making final preparations for testing, including the annual writing assessment in targeted grades. This was the case for Eastville Middle School. "We have worked hard all year to integrate writing into every class and subject," thought Jan, "and the school has seen some terrific results of that effort."

At one of the early professional development meetings last fall, Jan's staff had unanimously recommended that they wanted a literacy coach to collaborate with and help them with writing across the curriculum. Jan had initially been worried about funding for a new position but was able to put together a plan to share this resource with another principal in her cohort group. Fortunately, the superintendent saw the value in their plan, and the part-time literacy coach was making a positive impact on Eastville teachers and students.

Jan and the literacy coach met monthly to discuss progress, concerns, and insights that she gained from her work with the teachers and students at Eastville. The coach shared with Jan the impressive work of Mr. Chapman's science students as she worked with them on their group projects. She was helping the students understand writing as a means to express their thoughts about a topic, which required them to organize their thinking as they write. Many groups were incorporating digital presentations into their projects to show what they learned about various scientific concepts, like global warming. She was helping them plan, draft, refine, and record the scripts for these presentations. But what really impressed her, the literacy coach told Jan, was the way that Mr. Chapman worked with her to break down the different learning demands of the various assignments. Working closely with him helped her to deepen her understanding of the neurodevelopmental framework, although she wasn't confident she would ever have it mastered as well as Mr. Chapman did. He could tell the students what tasks would stress their active working memory, or their sequential or spatial ordering, for example. He helped some of his students understand how to monitor assignments to match up with their attention abilities. Even more impressive was the way he suggested strategies to use if students' minds weren't especially wired with those strengths.

The literacy coach also worked very closely with the English/language arts teachers throughout the year and assured Jan that they were providing a broad range of writing opportunities for their students. Students practiced expository and persuasive writing, working through the process of defining an issue, explaining their perspective, presenting facts to back it up, and choosing words appropriate for a particular audience. In the eighth-grade classes, the students wrote letters to their legislators regarding a proposal to extend the school year by six weeks, with many students choosing to mail their letters and even visit their representatives to talk more about the topic. This engaging assignment really helped the students see the use of writing for real-life purposes.

Jan always enjoyed her conversations with the literacy coach. "We're making progress," thought Jan. "We're making the learning relevant, leveraging student's strengths and affinities, and working with each one to demystify the writing process. Now if we can only get them to do well on the annual writing test." She knew the literacy coach was meeting with the language arts department this week. They were going to discuss their final efforts toward helping Eastville's students apply the skills they have learned to the state assessments that were coming up this spring.

This chapter will explore
- The neurodevelopmental functions most closely associated with writing
- Common observations related to weaknesses in written production
- Ways to improve writing in your school
- A tool for assessing writing breakdowns

Role of Writing

What's the last written communication you composed? Was it an e-mail? An article for a newsletter? A note to a parent? A proposal for funding? A report for your supervisor? A comment on a social networking site? A blog?

What about the students in your school—how is writing part of their daily experience? Is it journal writing? Book reports? An answer to a test question? A text message to a friend? Content for their MySpace or Facebook pages? Twitter?

Why do students write in your school?
- For pleasure?
- To show what they know?
- For social networking?
- To express an idea or opinion?
- As a form of assessment?

Whether it's a report for your employer, an e-mail to a parent or colleague, a student's response to an essay question, or for literary pleasure, the skill of writing is part of most everyone's daily experience. For adults, writing is a frequently used means of communication, both personally and professionally. A report from the National Commission on Writing indicates that writing is viewed by many employers as a threshold skill for candidates seeking professional-level positions.[1] For students, writing is increasingly becoming the foundation of their digital social world as well as being tied to academic standards, twenty-first-century skill requirements, annual assessments, SAT and college essays, and job applications. Dr. Kathleen Yancey, past president of the National Council of Teachers of English, stated that writing has moved from submission to participation.[2] Bottom line, written literacy in its many forms is a foundation for success in the academic and social aspects of our lives.

This chapter focuses on writing in order to illustrate the connections among academic tasks, learning framework underpinnings, and the All Kinds of Minds approach for all of the reasons stated and because every school leader, teacher, and student is involved in the task of writing. They do their own writing and critique and support the written output of others, whether in peer conferences, student work analysis groups, or collaboratively preparing presentations, reports, or grants. Every district and school is also faced with state tests that either directly assess writing or use constructed written responses as a means of assessing content knowledge.

Why Talk About Writing

Mel Levine has stated that "writing is the largest orchestra a kid's mind has to conduct."[3] When students write, they are engaged in thinking, reasoning, and analyzing. The act of writing helps build and maintain the brain pathways that connect diverse functions, such as language, memory, temporal-sequential ordering, and neuromotor control. This building process is similar to the effects of exercise. Engaging in cardiovascular activities (for example, running) and strength training (for example, weightlifting) not only improves overall health and well-being, it simultaneously strengthens muscles of the body. Each of the neurodevelopmental constructs described in this book is called upon to some degree when we write. Therefore, when students write, they not only improve their use of the academic subskills related to writing (for example, mechanics, ideation) but also strengthen the brain functions specifically called on for writing (for example, language, temporal-sequential ordering).

> " Mel Levine has stated that "writing is the largest orchestra that a kid's mind has to conduct." "

There is an additional reason why learning leaders should target writing as a key strategy to produce greater achievements for all students. Schools demonstrating the greatest gains in achievement and equity include consistent nonfiction writing instruction and practice.[4]

And while the benefits of nonfiction writing (description, analysis, persuasion with evidence) for student achievement gains is hardly a new research finding, it is a time-consuming instructional endeavor, and many schools still resist the writing across the curriculum effort. Best-selling author Stephen King has said that "writing is thinking through the end of a pen."[5] Schools making achievement gains use writing across the curriculum not to divert time from math, science, music, or the arts, but with the conviction that "if these subjects are worthy of thinking, they are worthy of writing."[6]

For educators, a student's written production can provide great insight into his learning profile, presenting clues to the weak functions that might be derailing the desired outcomes. As we analyze this critical academic skill in this chapter, we look at writing expectations and the underlying neurodevelopmental functions that affect writing ability. We also explore the phenomena common to struggling writers and strategies for boosting student achievement in this academic area.

A Neurodevelopmental Approach to Writing

If writing comes easily to you, you may not have stopped to consider how complex this skill really is. For you, it may seem as simple as sitting at your computer and the words and ideas just flow. What you may not realize is that, in order for that flow to occur, myriad brain functions work simultaneously and efficiently to generate your written output. Your brain is wired for this kind of work, making it relatively easy and perhaps even enjoyable.

When writing doesn't come so easily, this same myriad of functions are at work, but somewhere among the interactions between functions, a breakdown occurs. When teachers understand the neurodevelopmental demands of writing, they can more easily isolate the breakdown point and find strategies to help. Research on writing and its development has shown that the demands of writing vary depending on age (writing in elementary school is vastly different than senior year in high school). However, the research has also revealed that a core set of functions is important for writers of all ages.

> " When teachers understand the neurodevelopmental demands of writing, they can more easily isolate the breakdown point and find strategies to help. "

Writing and communication are essential elements for developing students' critical thinking and their ability to conceptualize and organize their own knowledge and thinking. Whether individual forms of writing (for example, journaling or narrative writing) or writing that introduces a social element (for example, e-mail and chats), all forms of writing require the organization of thought and the application of basic skills such as developing ideas, word choice, and appropriate voice. Through the writing process, students develop and refine their critical thinking as they select the most effective words to convey a message, use conventions that will resonate with their targeted audience, and evaluate how well the content of their writing answers the question or addresses the prompt. These processes and strategies come into play at varying degrees of breadth and sophistication, whether a writer is posting to a social networking page, contributing to an online discussion thread, writing a research paper, or responding to a prompt for a writing assessment. It is one of the most difficult tasks we ask of students and written production taps into a complex combination of functions to support these basic skills.

Take out a piece of paper and respond to the following prompt.

Write a three-sentence paragraph describing where you would like to spend your next vacation. Be descriptive and vivid, so someone reading it will understand why you want to go there.

But, here's a catch. You cannot use the letter *w*!

Finished? Now switch hands, and respond to the prompt again.

Neurodevelopmental Suspects

If you tried the exercise suggested in the box, you have two of your own writing samples to consider as we explore the common neurodevelopmental weaknesses (or "usual suspects") that can undermine students' writing. Chapter Three described these areas; a sampling of the research on writing and the science of learning is included in Table 7.1.

Attention

Writing is work that requires sufficient mental energy. Anyone who has taken an essay exam, written a term paper, or had to produce "copy" under a deadline can appreciate how draining writing can be. Learners who have small "fuel tanks" to begin with will have more trouble sticking with writing tasks. Such learners may have trouble activating the vigilance they will need and can benefit from "kick-starter" activities (like collaborating on an outline or being provided with the opening phrase of a sentence or opening sentence of a paragraph) to initiate momentum.

Learners with limited mental energy also have endurance issues and have trouble writing for extended stretches of time. Sometimes these learners exhibit behaviors—such as tapping, rocking in a chair, fidgeting with fingers—to compensate for and replenish their mental energy drain. Paying attention to the patterns of peak performance of such students, offering frequent breaks (perhaps involving physical activity) or changes in routine (such as shifting to math or reading) can boost student's mental energy.

> Paying attention to the patterns of peak performance of such students, offering frequent breaks (perhaps involving physical activity) or changes in routine (such as shifting to math or reading) can boost students' mental energy.

Table 7.1 *Writing and the Science of Learning*

Neurodevelopmental Construct or Function	Research Support
Attention: Mental Energy Controls	
Maintaining mental energy for learning and work; allocating a reliable flow of energy	Handwriting accuracy deteriorates following sleep deprivation[7]
Attention: Production Controls	
Overseeing the quality of academic output and behavior; previewing likely outcomes; inhibiting impulses and working at appropriate rates; self-monitoring output and work	The capacity to inhibit impulses and to plan contributes to writing success[8]
	Students can improve their writing through strategies that promote planning during prewriting[9]
Expressive Language	
Communicating ideas orally and in writing; utilizing words and word components; building sentences and extended pieces of language; using language to develop and extend thoughts	Writing involves understanding meaningful word parts (or morphemes) and word retrieval[10]
	The complexity of the sentences that adolescents composed was found to be a significant factor in the overall text quality in their writing, especially for certain genres[11]
Active Working Memory	
Mentally juggling information while using it to complete a task; handling simultaneous task components	Text composition places large demands on both visual and verbal active working memory[12]
	Writing involves several independent tasks (like spelling or vocabulary use); the more efficient those tasks, the less they burden working memory and the more cognitive resources are available for other processes necessary for quality writing[13]
Graphomotor Function	
Coordinating muscles needed for handwriting; recalling handwriting movement patterns and letter shapes; getting adequate feedback about hand or pencil location during writing motions	Motor abilities for handwriting (controlling a pen or pencil with efficiency and legibility) have connections to generating text[14]
	Characteristics of legibility include spacing between words, spacing between letters in words, alignment, letter size, and slant[15]
	The more complex sequential motor movements needed to form the loops and connecting strokes of cursive writing place more demands on graphomotor function than does manuscript writing[16]

Higher-Order Cognition
Comprehending concepts; generating original ideas; using logical approaches to address complex problems

Certain words promote the use of imagery in writing, which in turn leads to higher quality of writing[17]

Story mapping improved writing performance by bolstering students' conceptual understanding of text structures[18]

Writing has been found to promote the formulation of scientific concepts and to get students to challenge their ingrained misconceptions, such as that the sun orbits the Earth[19]

Social Cognition
Knowing what to talk about, when, with whom, and for how long; working and playing with others in a cooperative manner; nurturing positive relationships with influential people

Instruction including the establishment of audience awareness goals led to greater consideration of opposing perspectives for persuasive writing[20]

Spatial Ordering
Understanding information that is presented visually; generating products that are visual; organizing materials and spaces

Spatial demands of writing stem from how writers mentally represent the layout of the text as well as the use of visual strategies such as concept maps[21]

Temporal-Sequential Ordering
Understanding the order of steps, events, or other sequences; generating products arranged in a meaningful order

Measuring the accuracy of word sequences was the most reliable and valid way to predict student writing proficiency, as measured by teacher ratings and a district writing test[22]

Instruction that included coaching on sequencing ideas led to improved schematic structure of stories and longer papers for students with writing difficulty; these improvements generalized to persuasive essay writing as well[23]

The complexity of writing also places high demands on the attention production controls, which include impulse and rate control, previewing and planning, and self-monitoring. Most writers agree that the prewriting stage is crucial. Learners with weak production controls often impulsively jump right into their writing without first developing outlines, however basic. Once writing has begun, working at the right pace (without rushing) can be problematic if the production controls aren't operating reliably. Ernest Hemingway once commented that "writing is re-writing." Early drafts are almost inevitably filled with mistakes and opportunities for improvement. If the self-monitoring aspect of the production controls is not doing its job, then the writer may miss a large number of those mistakes and opportunities. Overall, the writing of learners with weak production controls tends to be disorganized, unplanned, and filled with mistakes.

Attention processing controls can affect writing in two functions: saliency determination and satisfaction level. Students demonstrating weaknesses with these aspects of attention are often distractible, and their writing can often miss the most important aspects and points. Students have to manage their satisfaction level and focus on the writing task even if it is not interesting—as many nonfiction writing pieces can be. Students with attention weaknesses are particularly challenged by nonfiction writing, which research shows to be a critical component of increasing academic achievement.[24]

Another challenge is focusing on the most relevant and important message to convey and making it clear to the audience, a task that taps into saliency determination, one of the processing controls of attention. One strategy to help students strengthen this function of attention in writing is the "six-word" challenge. The origin goes back to a challenge to Ernest Hemingway, who was asked to tell a story in only six words. He nailed it with "For sale: baby shoes, never worn."

Expressive Language

Expressive language is the output side of language and includes communicating and producing ideas in writing as well as orally. In a sense, expressive language is the translator that converts the mind's ideas into

Decades later, an online writing community offered a variation to the six-word challenge: "Tell your life story in six words." The resulting favorites were published in *Not Quite What I Was Planning: Six Word Memoirs by Writers Famous and Obscure*, edited by Rachel Fershleiser and Larry Smith. Visit www.sixwordmemoirs .com for ideas and prompts (for example, favorite holiday tradition, milestone birthdays) for writing six-word stories.

words, sentences, and discourse. Ironically, some struggling writers have good expressive language, which would be revealed in the clarity of their *oral* expression. For such writers the difficulty lies with some other aspect of their profile, such as the production controls of attention. In these instances a contrast is usually noticeable between oral expression and much less effective written expression. But many writers struggle because of weak expressive language, in which case oral expression would not be appreciably better in quality than written expression.

Language weaknesses can present themselves in writing through content that is overly simplistic or when there are significant gaps in word usage. Writing samples may reveal that the right word wasn't selected for a particular situation. At times, syntax problems are evident: the use of clauses isn't quite right, meaning gets lost because of vague pronoun references, or the sentences are poorly constructed.

The neurodevelopmental functions described in this chapter affect writing directly. But other functions, namely those related to how learners take in information, might affect writing more indirectly. For example, problems with the processing controls of attention may lead to distractibility, which can derail a writer when extended work sessions are needed. Also, weak receptive language might affect the quality of information input (such as reading comprehension), which in turn will affect the quality of output (such as written expression).

Memory

The complexity of writing, for all age groups, means that a considerable amount of information has to be juggled mentally, which is the role of active working memory. The two main categories of information juggled by working memory are verbal information (words, sentences, and so on) and visual material (such as a diagram or illustration). Verbal working memory is needed for writing tasks such as sentence generation (like recalling key facts while also following punctuation rules and thinking about word usage). Additionally, visual working memory is needed for planning (such as constructing a graphic organizer or cluster diagram) and image-based conceptual content (such as a Vincent van Gogh painting, which could be the subject of an essay).

Working memory is needed for coordination of simultaneous writing processes. As a writer, you need to remember what you are currently working on without losing track of the overall core ideas you want to express. The written work of learners with weak active working memory is often messy, unplanned (similar to that of those with weak attention production controls), and of lower quality than the learner's oral expression (assuming no problems with expressive language). Students who can copy neatly from a board but have poor legibility in a composition or can edit punctuation in a peer paper but have glaring mistakes in their own work are flashing "memory weakness": they are challenged to hold all the multiple writing task components together when they are writing.

Long-term memory plays an important role, as writing requires the rapid retrieval of words, information, and rules. There is an argument to be made for the benefits of automatizing as many of the mechanics of writing as possible in the elementary years: spelling, capitalization, punctuation, grammar, letter formation, and so on. Episodic memory, or memory for life experiences, is often one of the stronger aspects of long-term memory, as research on adults is revealing. While there is scant research linking this finding to other developmental stages students can begin to strengthen their memory functions by alternating narrative writing from life experiences (that is, from episodic memory) with persuasive writing that requires more factual recall and analysis. There is research that shows that elementary students have less difficulty with narrative writing than persuasive writing.[25]

Teachers who observe students who verbally express eloquent and perceptive thoughts in discussion but not on paper may be encountering a long-term memory weakness. Careful observation can reveal clues to memory weaknesses. (Refer back to Table 3.5 of common observations of memory.)

> "Careful observation can reveal clues to memory weaknesses."

Graphomotor Function

Graphomotor function is the manual dexterity needed for writing—the motor abilities used to control a pen or pencil and form letters. During writing, the brain must send messages to small muscles to direct finger movements. For some students, the communication between the brain and handwriting muscles is slow or unreliable. These specific muscles are not the same ones used in many fine motor activities such as drawing or playing a clarinet, explaining why some students may excel as artists or musicians and yet have difficulty with handwriting. As you learned when you used your nondominant hand in the earlier writing exercise, graphomotor weaknesses can undermine other important aspects of writing. Written production for students who struggle in this area is often brief, uses simplistic language, and reflects poor application of many rules of spelling, punctuation, and grammar.

Expressive language and graphomotor function work together like a computer and a printer—a shaky connection can lead to problems getting words, sentences, and passages down on the page, despite what has been generated by the computer. Learners with weak graphomotor function often are very frustrated by writing because it is such an inefficient and ineffective way of communicating; they would much rather communicate through talking or illustrating, or avoid writing altogether. While printing is less taxing than using cursive for those with weak graphomotor function, often the main strategy to support such learners, especially adolescents, is to circumvent handwriting and promote keyboarding or voice recognition software.

Keyboarding, or typing, is an important writing skill that can significantly improve efficiency of output, especially for students with weak graphomotor function. In addition, putting writing in digital formats (such as word processing) opens the door to numerous tools and platforms for collaboration and sharing of knowledge.

Higher-Order Cognition

Depending on the specific requirements of a writing assignment, complex and sophisticated thinking play a huge role in written expression. One aspect of higher-order cognition is creativity, which certainly affects the generation of stories and poetry; expository writing, such as coming up with an innovative way of describing a scientific idea or literary theme, also involves creativity. The understanding of concepts is important for writing, such as in science (writing up the results of a chemistry lab experiment) and history (when drawing connections between socialism and communism). In elementary and middle school grades, learners are asked to write about concepts such as water cycles, free speech, and the solar system.

Higher-order cognition, particularly the functions of conceptualization and evaluative thinking, is called into play whenever learners are asked to tackle complex issues and take a stand to defend their point of view. Selecting the best topic to write about, knowing how to research and find appropriate factual material to support a position or topic, brainstorming (necessary for producing original thoughts and elaboration), and analytical thinking are all components of writing that rely on functions of higher-order cognition. Students who struggle with these demands of writing often produce pieces with overly concrete language and a lack of persuasive content and supportive detail.

While weaknesses in aspects of higher-order cognition can take many different forms, the general theme is that the writing is lacking in sophistication; it may be cleanly written from a punctuation standpoint, be well organized, and even contain clear language, but weak higher-order cognition renders it devoid of much substance. It will be characterized as being very concrete, and void of symbolism and abstract concepts.

Spatial Ordering

Although writing is a task that inherently involves a great deal of verbal information, research has also established the importance of spatial ordering (processing and production of material that is visual or exists in a spatial array). It affects writing in two critical ways: how a student organizes materials for the task and how the words and images get placed on paper.

Writers often benefit from visualizing the different components of a piece of writing, like the introduction, body, and conclusion. Educators often promote highly visual strategies for planning, such as graphic organizers, yet this approach is difficult for learners with weak spatial ordering to use. The written work of students with weak spatial ordering may have a disordered appearance—for example, misaligned margins—that often makes it challenging to read. In the later stages of writing development, problems with spatial ordering may show up when the writer cannot differentiate the unique visual conventions of poetry, reports, or text presentation within media such as PowerPoint or other multimedia applications.

Temporal-Sequential Ordering

Sequences abound in writing—letter patterns in words, series of words to form sentences, sequential arguments in expositions, plot narratives, and so on. Temporal-sequential ordering involves organization—organizing time to complete the writing task and organizing ideas in a logical, stepwise manner.

Learners could have trouble with writing sequences on several different levels. At the on-the-page level, errors include confusing letter sequences within words, word order within sentences, and the proper placement of punctuation. At the thought level, problems include not structuring narratives clearly in short stories and making poor choices about the order in which to present a series of points in support of a hypothesis. Teachers often find that students with memory burdens, attention challenges, and language weaknesses struggle with some of these sequencing demands as well.

Social Cognition

Social cognition is increasingly playing a more important role in the act of producing text, particularly with the explosion of digital media and social networking. The use of instant messaging, microblogs (for example, Twitter), e-mail, Web sites, and multimedia productions as forms of communication require writers to consider the social implications of the words and images they choose to share with their audiences.

Perspective taking, an element of social cognition, is critical for both digital media and more traditional forms of written production. Understanding who the reader is and what that reader needs or expects from the writer is essential to developing an effective product. Teachers often forget to prepare students for the "audience" of their state writing exam responses, a key insight that can help improve the presentation of the response for evaluation.[26] The full effect of social cognition on written production is an area that will need further investigation and research in the near future.

Common Observations of Poor Written Output

Students struggle with writing for a variety of reasons—most often due to a misalignment between the demands of the task and the student's

As the world of writing continues to expand with new technology, research will need to explore the brain functions related to these new formats. For example, the opportunity for collaborative writing in a virtual classroom has implications for social cognition, the limited text capacity of texting and instant messaging places a burden on the processing controls of attention, and the ability to consolidate one's thinking to the most salient points, melding writing and multimedia, will forge new connections with spatial ordering, and so on. New ways of writing require new scientific inquiries and research.

learning profile. This misalignment can occur with all types of writing, from standardized writing assessments to composing an e-mail. To understand the demands of writing, we can apply the learning framework to subskills of writing and identify common breakdown points. Table 7.2 describes subskills that can be problematic for writers and related neurodevelopmental breakdowns. In addition to the connections listed in the chart, some functions are inherent in all elements of writing and should be considered when working with struggling writers. For example, all writing tasks tap into expressive language

Table 7.2 *Common Writing Subskills and Related Neurodevelopmental Functions*

Weak Writing Subskills	Possible Neurodevelopmental Breakdowns
Ideas are disorganized or lack elaboration	Expressive language, higher-order cognition (conceptualization)
Word choice is inappropriate for target audience	Attention production controls, social cognition
Story events lack logical sequence	Temporal-sequential ordering, higher-order cognition
Overuse of one sentence structure	Expressive language
Capitalization and punctuation errors	Memory, attention production controls
Poor letter formation	Graphomotor function

and require mental energy. A note of caution: the linkages noted in Table 7.2 are *possible* breakdown points. Just because a function is listed does not necessarily mean it is a weaknesses for an individual student. Understanding why an individual student struggles with writing requires careful observation and data gathering and looking for patterns of strengths and weaknesses.

A body of research focused on the stages of writing development serves as another source of developmental expertise for learning leaders seeking to better understand how to assess a student's strengths and weaknesses in writing. This synthesis of research on writing development has resulted in a comprehensive description of writing stages and what is expected within various grade ranges (see Table 7.3).[27] The implications of this research suggest that certain abilities and skills must be acquired and consolidated before a student can successfully progress to the more advanced writing demands—a stepwise process that involves accumulating layers of writing subskills. The challenge is that neurodevelopmental functions develop in children independently from the writing stages and contribute to the mismatch that we often see with writing developmental stages.

With the pressure to demonstrate strong written production, combined with the complexity of the task, it's not surprising to see why some students struggle significantly with written output. There are innumerable points at which a breakdown could affect the process of writing. For some students, their expressive language functions are fine-tuned, but memory breakdowns get in the way. For others, they know lots of interesting words and use them well, but the flow of the story events is off. There aren't many points in a school day where students get a break from writing demands. On the one hand, this is helpful because to gain proficiency at writing, students need to write.[28] On the other hand, if a student's mind isn't wired for successful writing, this part of school can become overwhelming.

For a student in Julie Brothers's fourth-grade classroom in Owasso, Oklahoma, narrative writing was definitely an overwhelming task. When faced with a writing assignment, Carl would stare at the blank page for quite a while before finally writing three or four sentences. When asked to read this "finished" story aloud, Carl would do

Table 7.3 Stages of Writing Development

Stage	Grade Range	Descriptors
Imitation	Preschool to first grade	Prewriting focus, inventive spelling, letter and number formation
Graphic presentation	First and second grade	Visual processing and production focus, introduction of conventions like capitalization and punctuation
Progressive incorporation	Late second to fourth grade	Integration of conventions (rules) with language, cursive writing introduced
Automatization	Fourth to seventh grade	Focus on planning and revisions, writing in different genres (poetry, report, expository); conventions should be made more automatic to create greater mental capacity to think, remember spatially, and write
Elaboration	Seventh to ninth grade	Organization of information from multiple sources, extensive use of transition and cohesive ties, writing for problem solving and idea development
Personalization and diversification	Ninth grade and beyond	Development of different writing styles and conventions (lab reports, poetry, newspaper article, essay, research paper), uses irony, symbolism, and figurative language

so and then respond, "But that's not all of my story." Carl and Julie both knew that he had more ideas and meaningful things to say, but the process of getting those ideas on paper was not working.

Julie began the process of careful kid watching, observing Carl during writing tasks as well as during other subjects over several weeks. "It was like peeling the layers of an onion," said Julie regarding the process of observing and getting down to the core of how Carl learned best. She tracked her observations, noting patterns such as trouble with completing the steps of math problems in the correct order and recalling concepts taught previously in order to apply them to new problems. "There were pieces he knew, but it was as if everything was jumbled up in his head and he just couldn't get it out in an effective way to accomplish a task, especially with writing," reported Brothers. Applying her knowledge of the framework to the evidence she had gathered, she began to realize that active working memory was a weak area for Carl, particularly for sequential tasks like writing. He understood the steps but couldn't keep track of what information went where. Carl was an avid reader of mysteries, so Julie used that as an analogy to help explain writing to Carl—how he could build suspense for his readers through the different events in his story. They began breaking up the parts of his story (introduction, events, and conclusion) across individual pages. On the side of each page, Carl had prompts for questions he could ask himself along the way, a strategy that supported his active working memory and sequential ordering while encouraging his creativity. Simple questions such as *who, what, when, where*, and *why* began to spark additional questions for Carl, and his writing improved. He was able to manage the flow of information from his mind to his paper and was able to truly tell his story. By January, Carl was producing elaborative stories and was very proud of his writing. Carl is a student who could easily have fallen through the cracks, not because of a disability, but because of an ability that he was struggling to share and that Julie was able to help him release.

Learning More from Student Work

Julie used careful kid watching and questioning to learn more about Carl's thought processes while he was writing. She then used these data to identify specific strategies that would accommodate Carl's weaknesses and make writing easier. Using a neurodevelopmental framework, teachers can also acquire similar information from a student's written output. Used in conjunction with observable phenomena, student work can provide great insight into a student's learning profile and can support teachers in selecting targeted, effective strategies. The examples in Figures 7.1 and 7.2 demonstrate the use of a neurodevelopmental lens to analyze student writing and select intervention strategies.

North Carolina Lighthouses — Diamonds Along the Shore.

Stretched along the beautiful coastline of North Carolina are seven majestic beacons of light, each with a history of guiding sailors to safety. With many still in use today, these lighthouses have helped ships navigate the treacherous inlets, rivers, sounds and ocean waters since the 1800's. The shifting sandbars and shoals beneath the surface of the water and intersecting currents create hazardous waterways for commercial shipping boats. The lighthouses provide a warning to captains that danger lurks near.

Figure 7.1 *Student Writing Sample: Lighthouse Report*

Strengths	Weaknesses	Strategies
Deep understanding of concept (higher-order cognition)	Handwriting very difficult to read (graphomotor function)	Allow student to compose using a computer
Effective organization of ideas (temporal-sequential ordering)		Offer alternative modes of demonstrating knowledge of concept (for example, oral presentation, digital presentation)
Use of descriptive vocabulary to convey thoughts (expressive language)		Allow use of a scribe upon completion

One Incredible Dream

The light was so bright, yet I couldn't see anything. Slowly, slowly it inched closer to my bed. My little brother was excited about Halloween and reading scary stories before bedtime. I told my Mom about my dream. She said not to read scary stories right before bedtime, that it would make me have crazy dreams. I realized that the light must have been my brother trying to scare me with the flashlight. I jumped out of bed and said, "You can't scare me!"

Figure 7.2 Student Writing Sample: Incredible Dream Story

Strengths	Weaknesses	Strategies
Creative ideas (higher-order cognition) Accurate mechanics (expressive language) Introduction sentence engages the reader (expressive language, social cognition)	Sequence of story events out of order (temporal-sequential ordering)	Encourage use of concept map prior to writing Ask student to write story events on sentence strips and manipulate as telling story to determine best order

When assessing writing, it's important to observe the student during the writing process, as Julie did, and analyze samples of the student's writing, as demonstrated in the previous examples. This dual approach enables teachers to gather data about the student's thought processes and assess the results of the student's implementation of that thinking. If a student's higher-order cognition or active working memory functions are weak, the breakdown may be at the point of consolidation and organization of an idea. If a student's writing demonstrates good ideas that are poorly executed, that may be an indication of weak temporal-sequential ordering, expressive language, or attention production controls. The more information a teacher can gather, the more specific the analysis and selection of strategies.

> ### PICTURE THIS!
>
> You join a Professional Learning Community meeting in which a group of teachers are working together to help a new faculty member uncover the breakdown points that are causing her students to struggle with writing assignments. Everyone in the group is looking at examples of student work, making observations, linking evidence to neurodevelopmental functions, and asking questions to help this new teacher think differently about her instruction and strategies she is using with various students. This kind of professional conversation is reflective of the collaborative culture of your school.

Improving Writing in Your School

Being familiar with the demands of writing, searching to find the breakdown point, analyzing student work and instructional practices—these are all key elements of taking a neurodevelopmental approach to writing, an approach that allows learning leaders and educators to be specific and targeted when working with struggling writers. Consider three perspectives on writing: assessment, instruction, and school practices.

What opportunities are currently available in your school for teachers to reflect on their approach to writing instruction and students' progress in this area?

- Professional Learning Communities?
- Grade-level and cross-grade-level planning sessions?
- Critical Friends groups?
- Department meetings?

Assessing Student Writing

A Small-Wins Approach: Moving from a 2 to a 3

U.S. Secretary of Education Arne Duncan holds high expectations for all students. In 2006, as superintendent of Chicago public schools (CPS), Mr. Duncan presented a powerful idea to CPS teachers: "the Power of 2 + 2."[29] Mr. Duncan wanted to raise the CPS test scores on the ISAT (the Illinois state proficiency exam). As a district, students were achieving below the state average on extended response test items that required a level of proficiency in writing to adequately demonstrate what knowledge students had gained from a text. Mr. Duncan had a hunch that for many Chicago students, producing the written response was an inhibitor to accurate assessment of reading, and he set out to remove that barrier.

Year after year, Chicago teachers had heard that their students scored lower than other districts in the state, and Mr. Duncan didn't want to limit his encouragement to cheerleading that all CPS educators had to do better. He wanted a specific challenge that wouldn't overwhelm teachers. He figured out that if each teacher could move two students to "meets standards" (the 3 score point) and if they could move another two students to "exceeds standards" (the 4 score point), the yield would be a 5–7 percent increase in the number of students who were meeting or exceeding expectations in this area, an indicator of increased student understanding and improved written communication. A brilliant use of the small-win strategy!

Knowing that support was needed to meet the challenge, he went further, offering summer writing institutes for CPS teachers and providing "Writing Every Day" handbooks. During the school year, monthly "Looking at Student Writing" talks took place, and the ISAT writing showcase was made available to teachers to assist them in understanding the anchor papers and rubrics used to score the response. Literacy coaches assisted teachers in analyzing the prompts and rubrics from retired ISAT prompts and guided them through analysis of responses that scored a 2 ("does not meet expectations") and what the feedback revealed.

Test scores did improve in Chicago public schools the following year, although not the dramatic 7 percent gains Mr. Duncan hoped to achieve. However, this practical approach to improving writing is a sound one. The strategies teachers learn while targeting a few students for specific intervention can be incorporated into whole class lesson and instruction. Learning leaders who desire a plan that both addresses an immediate concern of any administrator—proficiency by all students on a high-stakes test—along with targeting writing for the role it plays in overall academic achievement have a good chance for success when the approach includes building deeper expertise among teachers in their ability to both analyze writing and to expand their repertoire of writing strategies.

Analyzing Writing Expectations

A key step to increasing student achievement is developing a clear understanding of the expectations. For assessments of written production, this means knowing the criteria by which students' work is measured and the skills they will be asked to demonstrate. This level of understanding—on the part of teachers and students—gives the final score greater meaning and makes it easier to talk about academic strengths and weaknesses.

> " A key step to increasing student achievement is developing a clear understanding of the expectations. "

Layering this understanding with a neurodevelopmental lens allows for more specific feedback to a struggling writer about the barriers and breakdowns as well as some discovered strengths. Educators want their students to meet the standard for proficiency—commonly referred to as the 3 score on state tests. Educators also want students to increase their self-insight regarding their learning profiles and their academic strengths and weaknesses. A more specific approach leads to this insight and strategies to manage difficult academic tasks.

A tactic for building greater capacity for analyzing written work and helping students prepare for high-stakes tests is to work with the rubrics and anchor papers available from your state department of education. Another option, particularly for those working with secondary students, is the use of retired prompts and anchor papers from the Scholastic Aptitude Tests as a source for investigating expectations, considering the learning demands, and thinking about strategies.

Understanding the Neurodevelopmental Demands of Proficient Writing

Writing assessments provide clear rubrics of what constitutes an acceptable—and exceptional—presentation of a student's ideas. The Texas Education Agency has six criteria for scoring a 3, which are described in the Texas Assessment of Knowledge and Skills (TAKS) scoring guide.[30] Each composition earning a score point 3 is a generally effective presentation of the writer's ideas. Elements assessed are focus and coherence, organization, development of ideas, voice, and conventions.

Before a student even begins to approach the task, the rubric reveals subskills of writing that will require the constructs of temporal-sequential ordering, expressive language, higher-order cognition, social cognition, and memory to work well to respond to this task. For example, the effective organization of this composition taps into the writer's temporal-sequential ordering (elements of communication in a logical progression), expressive language (strong discourse production and elaboration to communicate about the topic), and higher-order cognition (ability to link ideas into a cohesive concept in a developmentally appropriate way). Using an effective voice comes from strong expressive language and social cognition (choosing words that are appropriate for the reader). The task also assumes that the graphomotor functions required for producing written text are not a barrier, or if they are, they have been addressed with other accommodations (for example, use of a scribe, permission to use a word processor).

This level of understanding is most useful when compared to the learning strengths and weaknesses of the writer. Educators want to discover if the struggling writers they are targeting have some weaknesses in those areas. While this will likely be revealed in the analysis of writing, simple writing interviews with students using the tool provided in this chapter can help narrow the possible breakdown points. See Exhibit 7.1 for a sample interview template.

Uncovering the Neurodevelopmental Suspects in Student Writing

Figure 7.3 shows a student's response to a TAKS narrative prompt: *Write a composition about your favorite memory.* (The analysis of the learning demands of the prompt will be discussed when we consider the instructional components of writing.)

This sample paper was judged to receive a score of 2, for the following reasons cited in the scoring guide:

> **Score point 2:** *In this focused response, the student describes a family trip to Miami. Although there is an attempt to develop depth using sensory*

(Continued on p. 169)

Exhibit 7.1 The Writing Interview
Part One

> **Key to Part One**
> 0 = Always True for Me; 1 = Mostly True for Me;
> 2 = Sometimes True for Me; 3 = Not True for Me

Statements				
Graphomotor Function	0	1	2	3
1. Kids sometimes complain that their hand gets very tired when they have to write a lot.				
2. Some students have an unusual way of holding a pencil or pen.				
3. There are kids who think they write too slowly on tests and homework.				
4. Some people can print much better than they can use cursive.				
5. Lots of students say forming letters is not as easy for them as it is for other kids.				
Expressive Language	0	1	2	3
6. There are students who find it hard to get their ideas into words when they speak in school.				
7. Some kids make too many grammar mistakes when they write.				
8. While they write, some students have to think too long about how to say their ideas on paper.				
9. When some people write, they have trouble using good vocabulary; they use a lot of easy words.				
10. Some kids have trouble describing things well in a class discussion.				
Ideation	0	1	2	3
11. Some students find it very hard to think up topics or decide what they want to write.				
12. There are kids who would hate to have to write a story.				

	0	1	2	3
13. It can be very difficult to know what to write or include in a report.				
14. A lot of kids say it's not easy for them to come up with their own original ideas about things in school.				
15. Some people say it's really hard to write about their opinions or what they think about things.				
Memory	0	1	2	3
16. It is confusing to remember so many things at once (like spelling, punctuation, vocabulary, and so on) while writing.				
17. Some kids have much neater handwriting when they copy from the board than when they write a paragraph.				
18. When writing a report or story it's not always easy for some kids to remember what they wanted to write.				
19. Some kids have said that they have much better ideas when they speak than when they write.				
20. Problems with spelling make writing especially hard for some people.				
Organization	0	1	2	3
21. It can be really hard to get started with a writing assignment.				
22. When they write, some students have trouble getting their thoughts down in the right order.				
23. Some students don't think much in advance about what they are going to write; they just start writing.				
24. There are students who have trouble getting together the books, paper, and other tools they need to write things.				
25. It is hard to know how long it will take to write a report or a story.				

Comments:

Part Two

1. Is there any kind of writing that you enjoy in school?

2. What's the hardest part about writing for you? What's the easiest?

3. Is there anything you've learned to do that makes writing easier for you?

4. Do you ever feel embarrassed when other kids look at things that you've written?

5. If you were having trouble writing a report, what could you do?

6. Have you used a computer for writing? Has this made writing easier for you? Are there problems for you in using a computer?

7. You need muscle coordination for writing, for playing sports, and for doing art or fixing things. Which of these things do your muscles work well for and which are problems for your muscles?

8. What does a kid have to be good at to write well?

Source: Levine, M. *Educational Care: A System for Understanding and Helping Children with Learning Differences at Home and in School.* Cambridge, MA: Educators Publishing Service, 2002, pp. 321–323.

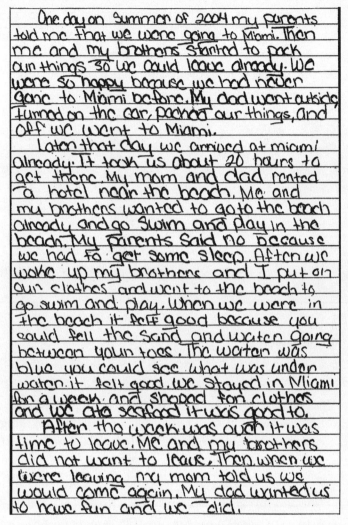

One day on summer of 2004 my parents told me that we were going to Miami. Then me and my brothers started to pack our things so we could leave already. We were so happy because we had never gone to Miami before. My dad went outside, turned on the car, packed our things, and off we went to Miami.

Later that day we arrived at miami already. It took us about 20 hours to get there. My mom and dad rented a hotel near the beach. Me and my brothers wanted to go to the beach already and go swim and play in the beach. My parents said no because we had to get some sleep. After we woke up my brothers and I put on our clothes and went to the beach to go swim and play. When we were in the beach it felt good because you could feel the sand and water going between your toes. The water was blue you could see what was under water. it felt good. we stayed in Miami for a week and shoped for clothes and we ate seafood it was good to.

After the week was over it was time to leave. Me and my brothers did not want to leave. Then when we were leaving my mom told us we would come again. My dad wanted us to have fun and we did.

Figure 7.3 Sample Narrative Writing Response

Source: Texas Education Agency, 2006. Copyright © and trademark ™ 2000. All Rights Reserved.

imagery (*you could feel the sand and water between your toes*), much of the development remains superficial. (*We stayed in Miami for a week and shopped for clothes and we ate seafood*). The overall fluency is weakened by the run-on sentences and frequent awkward wording (*Then me and my brothers started to pack our things so we could leave already . . .*).

The response tells why the paper was scored a 2, but it doesn't help the teacher or the student determine what steps will help improve the writing. Adding a neurodevelopmental lens to the analysis of the writing sample can provide the following depth of detail and suggestions for learning and teaching:

Strengths:
- Good sequential ordering (related the events of the trip in a logical order, story has a beginning, middle, and end)
- Strong memory for experiences (events describe key experiences—beach, shopping, eating seafood)
- Graphomotor function (letter formation legible)
- Hints of creativity (one example of using imagery to describe the beach)

Weaknesses:
- Expressive language: Semantic use (the frequent and awkward use of *already*, use of nonspecific vocabulary such as "play in the *beach*" and "put on our *clothes* and went to the beach")
- Expressive language: Discourse production and higher-order cognition (superficial quality of composition and lack of elaboration)
- Expressive language: Sentence formulation (several times used "me and my")
- Attention: Mental energy (mechanics were more accurate at the beginning, then increased number of punctuation and capitalization errors throughout the composition)

Using the feedback from the scorer coupled with a neurodevelopmental lens, the teacher sees a possible course of action for the writer. See Table 7.4 for a summary of this feedback.

Educators often employ a "see, think, and do" approach when they analyze student work, much like the four-step problem-solving model

Table 7.4 Feedback to Student

Strengths	Weaknesses	Strategies
Memory for life experiences makes story more interesting (strong memory)	Story needs more interesting details to enable the reader to share your experience (weak expressive language, higher-order cognition)	When planning story, select two or three of the most memorable events from your trip, and using a concept map, identify characteristics that made them memorable (for example, what you saw, who you shared the experience with, how it felt to be there, how it reminded you of other experiences) Imagine you are making a movie of your memorable experience. What would you be sure to include in the movie? What background or props? What scenes would you be sure to include? What would the characters say to one another? Create a storyboard of the movie scenes, then use your images as a reminder of what components to include in your narrative.
Example of using imagery to build a picture for the reader (*you could feel the sand and water between your toes*) (use of creativity)	Story needs words and phrases that create pictures for the reader (weak expressive language—especially at the word and sentence level)	Before you start writing your composition, think of all the words and phrases you can related to your memory. Think of feeling words, action words, words that describe how things looked, and so on. If possible, use a thesaurus to expand your list. Use these words and phrases to talk about your memory. After writing your story, go back and add adjectives (describing words) to create a more interesting picture for the reader. For example, describe the color of the ocean, the feel of the sunshine, or the fish you saw under the water.

presented in Chapter Four (refer back to Table 4.1). When asking the question "What do we see?", observers should be careful to avoid judgments and interpretations; instead, describe the evidence of strengths and weaknesses in the work sample. With the evidence in hand, they consider the second step—"What do we think?" They look at the evidence and ask, "What additional questions did this raise?" These guiding questions permit a thoughtful and well-informed process of selecting the strategies that have a good chance of helping students improve their writing.

Strengthening Writing Instruction

Neurodevelopmental analysis can be applied to writing prompts and instructional strategies.

In addition to the prompt, students responding to the TAKS assessment were also provided with the information in Exhibit 7.2, a list "to help you remember what you should think about when you write your composition." This kind of list provides a starting point to demystify the demands that are required to be successful on this task and to help all students better prepare for this type of on-demand writing.

When a student's learning strengths match the demands of a writing task, the student likely finds writing a fairly easy task. When the opposite is true—when the student's strengths do not match the demands—the task is much more difficult. By looking at both the demands and the student's profile through the same neurodevelopmental lens, a teacher can begin to uncover the potential "trip wires" for the student and adjust accordingly. For example, we have determined that, to be proficient with the TAKS writing assessment, temporal-sequential ordering is required. If a teacher knows that one of her struggling students has temporal-sequential ordering challenges, she can predict the potential breakdown points with this task. Explicit strategies for addressing sequencing issues that contribute to written production problems become part of writing instruction and test preparation.

Exhibit 7.2 Checklist for TAKS Writing Assessment

Remember—You should:

- ✓ Write about your favorite memory *[requires long-term memory access, particularly episodic memory]*
- ✓ Make your writing interesting to the reader *[requires higher-order cognition—creativity and social cognition—verbal pragmatics and code switching, realizing that the audience is an adult educator]*
- ✓ Make sure that each sentence you write helps the reader understand your composition *[requires sequential ordering and expressive language-sentence formulation and discourse production]*
- ✓ Make sure that your ideas are clear and easy for the reader to follow *[requires sequential ordering and attention production controls]*
- ✓ Write about your ideas in detail so that the reader really understands what you are saying *[requires attention production controls]*
- ✓ Check your work for correct spelling, capitalization, punctuation, grammar and sentences *[requires attention production controls—self-monitoring and long-term memory access—recalling rules]*

Note: Italics inserted by *Schools for All Kinds of Minds* authors.

Source: Texas Education Agency, 2006. Copyright © and trademark ™ 2000. All Rights Reserved.

For strategies to support students in writing, as well as other academic areas, visit the LearningBase at www.allkindsofminds.org.

This approach can be used with writing instruction strategies, such as the 6 + 1 Trait writing process that is common practice in many schools. The Northwest Regional Education Laboratory has done extensive work in this area, and one of the best sources describing this process can be found at www.thetraits.org. 6 + 1 Trait Writing is an analytical model for assessing and teaching writing, based on the qualities that research has shown define strong writing. As we have seen with the TAKS example, assessment rubrics and instruction are often designed around the seven elements described in the 6 + 1 Trait model. In schools where this writing model is used, educators can use a neurodevelopmental framework as an overlay to support instruction.

6 + 1 TRAIT WRITING MODEL

Ideas: The main message
Organization: The internal structure of the piece
Voice: The personal tone and flavor of the author's message
Word choice: The vocabulary a writer chooses to convey meaning
Sentence fluency: The rhythm and flow of language
Conventions: The mechanical correctness
Presentation: How the writing looks on page

A treasure trove of resources that provide insights into specific learning profiles of students and to guide decisions about individual and group instruction is available for learning leaders. Some examples include

- National Writing Project (www.nwp.org)
- The School Reform Initiative (www.schoolreforminitiative.org)
- Looking at Student Work (www.lasw.org)
- Center for Applied Special Technology (CAST) Teaching Every Student page (www.cast.org)

Strategies for Writing Assessment and Instruction

Whether it's moving a student from a score of 2 to a score of 3 on a traditional writing assessment, helping a group of science students plan, draft, refine, and record the scripts for their multimedia presentation on the effects of global warming, or supporting their persuasive argument to the school board for extended recess periods to support exercise, today's learning leaders are faced with the need to support students in using writing effectively to show what they know or express unique ideas. Meeting this need requires schools to create learning environments that empower students, strengthen and leverage strengths, and celebrate unique profiles.

When working with diverse learners, teachers must take the critical step of improving student writing by helping students see the purpose of writing: to teach the reader. Whether it's explaining a personal position through a persuasive text or sharing experiences and ideas in a blog, writing is a mechanism for teaching others. By shifting the student writer's mind-set to that of teacher, the purpose for writing

> " When working with diverse learners, teachers must take the critical step of improving student writing by helping students see the purpose of writing: to teach the reader. "

becomes clearer and students can more effectively organize their ideas. This shift of mind-set empowers students and creates a sense of optimism that they can achieve when it comes to written output.

Another essential component of improving written output is encouraging students to write frequently and in many different ways. Just as a chef becomes a better cook by cooking, so too a writer becomes a better writer by writing. By focusing on both the thinking and mechanical aspects of writing, students can begin to make connections between various writing experiences and apply writing skills in multiple venues. This strategy enables students to continue to strengthen their strengths while working on weak areas.

Writing support can come in the form of instructional techniques and through accommodations and interventions designed to bridge the gap between the demands of the task and an individual's learning profile. Examples of strategies include

- Provide scaffolds (for example, concept maps) for students to preview and plan their writing, including key message points (supporting higher-order cognition), target audience (supporting attention and social cognition), and sequence of events and communication (supporting temporal-sequential ordering)
- Teach strategies for independent brainstorming, including the identification of a central theme (for example, a trip to

Miami) and ways to track ideas and details related to that theme, such as a tree diagram (for example, each new aspect of theme is noted as a "trunk" with details branching off as limbs)

- Provide examples of many types of written output, noting similarities and differences and encouraging students to make predictions about the author's purpose (supporting attention and higher-order cognition)

- Leverage a student's strengths and affinities in other areas to help with writing. For example, allow a student with strengths in drawing and graphics to create a visual depiction first, then add words to the pictures before finally transitioning to text. Help this student see the lifelong potential of his strengths, such as becoming a graphic novelist (leveraging strengths and affinities, celebrating unique profiles)

- Teach students about the active working memory demands of writing and strategies for managing the number of tasks they are juggling at once (for example, staging the writing process) (supports active working memory)

- Provide students with writing samples that include ineffective word choice, weak sentence structure, or minimal idea development. Support students' expressive language and higher-order cognition by asking them to identify the weak aspects of the story and offer suggestions for improving it. Consider having the student revise the story, adding interesting details

- Encourage students with weak expressive language to keep a writing journal that includes grammar rules, a personal dictionary of favorite and creative words, story maps, and so on (also supports memory)

- Encourage students to take advantage of the new writing opportunities emerging with technology when possible; this especially can empower students with an affinity for technology

School Practices and Writing

Learning leaders are well aware of the heightened emphasis on literacy in today's classrooms and the role that all teachers, regardless of subject area, now assume in developing reading and writing skills. Most districts and schools have embraced writing across the curriculum as a core strategy. Research supports this, offering specific guidance on types of writing instruction that effects student academic achievement. One such finding concludes that an increased emphasis in schools on nonfiction, analytic writing has a positive impact on student achievement.

There are new studies examining the most effective instructional strategies to support struggling writers with this kind of persuasive writing as well as examining various writing instructional programs. Research indicates that the most effective approach is a balanced one that stresses both high-level skills (planning and revising) along with basic writing skills (spelling, grammar, and so on).

> ### PICTURE THIS!
>
> Teachers in your school are beginning to use instructional practices that prepare students for success in a twenty-first-century world. You are seeing greater use of technology, global learning and collaboration, and students as investigators and teachers of their peers. Through customized project-based activities, students are leveraging their strengths while simultaneously acquiring new skills, particularly the use of written communication to gather and share information. As part of their graduation requirements, students in your school produce a multimedia presentation describing their school experience and how it compares to that of a peer in another region, state, or country.

All learning leaders who guide instructional decisions need to stay abreast of the emerging body of research on digital media and learning. New questions are being raised about the student's use of technology and media and overall impact on the mind, brain, and learning. Clearly, educating students in this twenty-first-century environment requires both instruction in and through digital media, and today's educators are the pioneers in this educational frontier.

GETTING STARTED WITH SMALL WINS

Small wins = *concrete, significant tasks that produce a visible result while moving one step closer to a new vision or one step away from an unacceptable condition*

What's a school leader to do? How can you start a new, more specific conversation about writing in your school? As in Eastville Middle School, are there teachers in your school who effectively analyze the demands of writing and support students in meeting those demands? How do we help students do well on writing assessments, as well as other writing tasks? Some steps for getting started might include

- Explore students' perceptions of the purpose of writing, including the many writing formats in which they engage, both in school and outside of school. Discuss the similarities and differences of various forms of writing and how the demands change based on the format (for example, research paper, expository writing, newspaper article, Web page, MySpace).
- Explore teachers' perceptions of the purpose of writing at your school. Consider the variety of ways students are asked to produce written content. Determine points during the day at which students who struggle with writing might get a break from those demands.
- Divide into small groups (grade levels or departments) to investigate protocols for analyzing student work. As you are observing and talking about the work, try to apply a neurodevelopmental lens to what you are seeing. Some suggested resources for protocols include Looking at Student Work (www.lasw.org) and the School Reform Initiative (www.schoolreforminitiative.org).

Learning Leadership in Action

Identify current writing activities and assessments in your educational environment and reflect on how they embody the All Kinds of Minds approach. Then consider how to better support students to develop strong writing skills that prepare them for the various forms of twenty-first-century writing, academic tasks, and assessments.

Example: *A team of fifth-grade teachers in an urban Texas school constitute a Professional Learning Community focused on writing. They first consider the neurodevelopment demands of the Texas Assessment of Knowledge and Skills that are presented in this chapter. Then, they select a writing activity from their own fifth-grade curriculum and analyze it through a neurodevelopmental lens. Next, they look at the alignment of their instruction and determine how their instruction could better support writing production on the state assessment.*

Writing Activities	What are the neurodevelopmental demands of this writing activity?	What are some small wins you could use to better support writing production?
Texas Assessment of Knowledge and Skills	Temporal-sequential ordering—logical progression of ideas Expressive language—discourse production and elaboration Higher-order cognition—ideas are linked to a cohesive concept Social cognition—choosing the right words for the audience Memory—retrieval of information stored in long-term memory	Each time our PLC meets, discuss one writing activity in our curriculum, understand the neurodevelopmental demands of the activity, and consider the alignment to the state writing assessment.

Writing Activities	What are the neurodevelopmental demands of this writing activity?	What are some small wins you could use to better support writing production?
Fifth-grade writing activity: "My Summer Vacation"	Social cognition—choosing the right words, tone, and messages for the audience	Support social cognition by increasing understanding of writing for different purposes and audiences Write three different versions of "My Summer Vacation": 1. Blog three entries for your classmates 2. Compose an essay for your teacher highlighting your favorite aspect of the vacation 3. Write an article for the local newspaper's "Best Vacation Spots" column.

(See blank template on next page.)

Writing Activities	What are the neurodevelopmental demands of this writing activity?	What are some small wins you could use to get started?

8

Getting Started
Creating Schools for All Kinds of Minds

I would like to see schools change in response to what we know about the legitimate differences in learning that abound among students at every grade level in every community. . . . To build a mind requires that you understand it.[1]

—Mel Levine, *A Mind at a Time*

This chapter will explore
- Examples of schools and educators implementing the All Kinds of Minds approach
- The alignment between the All Kinds of Minds approach and a futuristic vision of education
- The implications of a learner-centric model on school culture and practices
- Actionable steps for creating a school for all kinds of minds

---

PEDIATRICIANS, NEUROSCIENTISTS, ACADEMICS, JOURNALISTS, AND FILM MAKERS are providing educators with many of the most thought-provoking arguments and practical ideas to transform schools.[2] They all share a quest to orient our educational practices and policies to support what we know about learning, the changing world we live in, and innovation.

John Medina makes the point succinctly in his book *Brain Rules*. Rule #3: "Every brain is wired differently." Medina argues that

> Being able to read a student's mind is a powerful tool in the hands of a teacher. . . . It is defined as the ability to understand the interior motivations of someone and the ability to construct a predictable "theory of how their mind works" based on that knowledge. This gives teachers critical access to their students' interior educational life. It can include knowledge of when students are confused and when they are fully engaged. It gives teachers valuable feedback about whether their teaching is being transformed into learning.[3]

Tom Friedman writes about the new global world we live in and believes that the aims of education need to change because "being adaptable in a flat world, knowing how to 'learn how to learn,' will be one of the most important assets any worker can have."[4] Many education and business leaders have responded to this charge by defining and advocating that schools organize around twenty-first-century learning skills.[5] But as Clayton Christensen and his colleagues assert,

> If we acknowledge that all children learn differently, then the way schooling is currently arranged—in a monolithic system where all students are taught the same things—won't allow us to educate children in customized ways. Few reforms have addressed the root cause of students' inability to learn. And most attempts have not been guided by an understanding of the root reasons why the (education) system functions as it does. Without this guidance, we've been destined to struggle. This also means, however, that we now have a great opportunity for progress.[6]

School leaders and teachers work within our current monolithic educational system and can't convert to a new architecture or modular structures in a few months. But when they work as learning leaders, they can explicitly orient education to a focus on learners and learning. When educators accept what studies from neuroscience show—that there are a variety of different kinds of learners—they realize that communities must work toward developing different kinds of schools. Learning leaders can begin conversations in their district and community around a new and continuous search for the best instructional and educational architecture for different kinds of students.[7] Learning leaders who begin having these conversations are leading with a "bifocal lens." They have a clear vision for a learner-centric school of the future; by considering the demands of their current situation, they continually make decisions that move them forward toward that vision. This dual focus allows them to shift instantaneously between the present and the future.

All Kind of Minds has developed an approach that many schools have used to achieve the hopeful mantra of those many mission statements: "All children can learn." The transformation to a learner-centric school takes time, and the schools undertaking this initiative are at different points in their journeys. Their stories told throughout this book help us visualize what starts to happen with this approach, and we begin to see the impact on four elements that are key to integrating this approach into today's schools:

1. *Teachers and educators:* New roles, new work, new focus
2. *Pedagogy reframed:* Learning and technology
3. *Practices and policies:* Humane decisions that support a sense of educational care
4. *Pathways to success:* A greater array of accepted and celebrated outcomes

The All Kinds of Minds approach is not a unique comprehensive school reform strategy or another school improvement option. Educators in turnaround schools, charter schools, independent schools, parochial schools, Montessori schools, and the spectrum of rural, urban, and suburban K–12 public schools have used the framework and ideas described in this book. It is an approach that can personalize student learning at a deep and constructive level, and it represents a comprehensive diagnostic approach to supporting the work teachers and students do. Perhaps the slogan of BASF, The Chemical Company, best describes what All Kinds of Minds does: "We don't make a lot of the products you buy. We make a lot of the products you buy better."

The All Kinds of Minds approach:
- Educator expertise in a science of learning
- Evidence gathered from multiple sources
- A problem-solving model to uncover the complexity and richness of how a child learns
- A set of beliefs about how our students, who all learn differently, should be treated
- A commitment to align educational practices and policies to the ways students learn and vary in their learning

Introducing Learning Strategies Is a "Small Win"

What does classroom pedagogy that incorporates a neurodevelopmental approach look like? Often, it is surprisingly simple. A middle school science teacher from Jenison, Michigan, explains:

I focus on two of the eight constructs: attention and memory. These are often misinterpreted as laziness. I wanted to help my students focus, divert attention problems, and build memory muscle. A simple way to divert attention problems is to give students a stress ball with which to play, particularly during lectures or times that taxed attention. This displaces the energy that a student might use to act out and distract others. It has cut down on classroom distractions tremendously.

I've worked on building our memory muscles. I taught how memory is like a muscle that has to be trained and used on a regular basis. We do memory muscle building activities as daily warm-ups. We may look at a diagram and have to redraw it. We may be asked questions about a very detailed picture, or recall what was on the bulletin board last week. The warm-up exercises allow my students to work their short-term and long-term memory on a daily basis.

Schools and teachers are starting to better match education to the specific learning profiles of students in other ways. Incorporating Universal Design for Learning (UDL) principles with the design and delivery of curriculum, instruction, and assessment helps customize many of the visual, spatial, and auditory presentation of text materials for students.[8] The Center for Applied Special Technology (CAST) Teaching Every Student Web site (www.cast.org/tes) provides tutorials of UDL in action, model lessons, and other resources to support teachers as they apply this complementary approach in their classrooms. Using UDL principles also helps to reveal the complexity of the learning mind.

An explosion of creative and personalized learning journeys are being driven by technology—online courses, gaming strategies, simulations and multimedia content presentation. Virtual classrooms such as the Virtual ChemLab at Brigham Young University show how educators can use digital media and learning objects to create simulations that allow students to do experiments that they may never have been able to do before. The Internet has enabled access to content and subject matter resources that have never before been available to students or teachers. When content can be found and stored on a hard drive, it doesn't necessarily need to be stored in one's brain, thus freeing the student and teacher to explore information and content at a deeper conceptual level than simple recall. Web 2.0 technologies and expanding Internet access provide learning leaders with options not only to employ alternative pedagogical methods for diverse learners but also to support learners who want to pursue a depth of scholarship in areas and topics matched to their affinities.[9]

Universal Design for Learning calls for

- *Multiple means of representation,* to give learners various ways of acquiring information and knowledge along with comprehending questions and tasks
- *Multiple means of action and expression,* to provide learners alternatives for constructing responses and demonstrating what they know
- *Multiple means of engagement,* to tap into learners' interests, challenge them appropriately, and motivate them to learn

Clearly technology is part of the answer to creating learner-centric educational opportunities and schools where educators can help students master material in ways compatible with the way they best learn. One doesn't need to wait until a school is completely wired; Fort Salonga Elementary School on New York's Long Island began their transformation with a focus on changing the pedagogy and the current curriculum in the school. Changes in their practices and policies to support multiple pathways to student success followed. Fort Salonga's learning leader, Arlene Mullin, illustrates how a school can begin to act on Tom Friedman's recommendation: teach students how to "learn how to learn while they are learning."

One Elementary School Is Determined to Teach Children How to Learn

As you walk through the front doors of Fort Salonga Elementary School, you sense that this school is somehow different from a typical K–3 school. The hallways and classrooms contain colorful posters of neurodevelopmental constructs, students talk about their own learning profiles, the faculty feels empowered and engaged, parents are actively involved in their children's education, and conversations about learning abound. Fort Salonga is truly a learner-centric school that embraces the learning differences of its students, but it wasn't always this way.

The transformation began a few years ago when principal Arlene Mullin asked her faculty what they needed to do in order to adopt a learner-centered approach. They agreed overwhelmingly that they needed to empower learners to start dialogues about learning, and they got busy defining their mission: teach children how to learn. But that was just the beginning step toward changing the culture and practices of the school. Through Arlene's leadership as a learning leader, teachers and staff began discussing how to make this shift happen. The teachers' lounge, hallways, and faculty meetings were abuzz with excitement and ideas. "Training from All Kinds of Minds was the first step for us," says Arlene. "It actually was exciting to create our own blueprint for changing our culture." The training gave the faculty the design principles for a learner-centric school, but the resulting architecture was clearly of their own invention.

With the mission established and training completed, the faculty conversations zeroed in on defining their core beliefs. They started with the beliefs from the All Kinds of Minds course and began having passionate conversations about what values reflected their community, a learner-centric approach, school and district goals, parental desires, and of course, their cherished students, who came to them with unique learning profiles and high expectations for their four years at Fort Salonga. Through lots of collaboration and a few revisions, faculty were able to create a set of core beliefs that reflected Fort Salonga's culture and values.

Teachers continued to meet regularly, using their monthly in-service time to figure out how to implement a learner-centric approach. They quickly realized that if conversations about learning were going to become part of the day-to-day life at Fort Salonga, they needed a common approach and some teaching aids. To prevent this change from overwhelming the faculty, Arlene reminded them of the "small wins" strategy and encouraged them to choose a realistic, concrete action for the first year that would move them toward their vision of a learner-centric school culture. With her facilitation and guidance, the staff of Fort Salonga agreed upon an approach to start their journey: focus on one construct as a theme for a year. This would allow teachers the opportunity to infuse it into everything they did for one school year, and they could identify best practices to use for next year's construct. It was an approach that was both manageable and invigorating!

Selecting the first construct was simple. There was a district mandate to develop critical thinking, so it seemed logical that higher-order cognition would be the first theme. Several teachers eagerly volunteered to form a subgroup that would focus on creating a set of materials to communicate the important concepts of higher-order cognition throughout the school. They integrated ideas about higher-order cognition with Bloom's Taxonomy and used a skyscraper metaphor, with the highest levels of thoughts at the upper floors of the tower, to make the ideas accessible to students. The subgroup created a set of large, colorful posters that were displayed throughout the school and in the classrooms. Making physical changes in the learning environment and identifying one construct as a recurring theme for the year "helped the kids to get it," according to Arlene, who recounts an episode in which a teacher candidate was conducting a lesson in a first-grade classroom. The candidate was asking the class very basic questions, and one student said, "You have to get off the first floor!"

Bloom's Taxonomy of educational objectives starts at the most basic level of *remembering* information and progresses to *understanding, applying, analyzing,* and *evaluating. Creating* is the sixth and highest level of thought in the model.

At the final in-service meeting of the first year, the faculty engaged in a vibrant discussion around the successes of the higher-order cognition theme and skyscraper posters. They acknowledged that they needed to do more the next year; culture cannot be transformed with just a set of posters. They would need to take other steps so that all stakeholders—staff, parents, and children—could contribute to the transformation to a learning-focused school.

For the second year, the faculty chose attention as the construct of the year, in part because of the district's focus on standardized tests and test preparation. Similar to the skyscraper metaphor from the previous year, they created "trash-treasure-gold," which was a rubric for differentiating the relative importance of information. The teachers again created posters for display around the school. In lessons and hallway conversations, it was common to hear teachers talking with students about how attention can vary across individuals, settings, and tasks. Grade-level teaching teams used books (such as *If You Give a Mouse a Cookie*) to illustrate concepts and facilitate discussions about attention, and the "trash-treasure-gold" rubric was central to school-wide preparations for standardized tests.

Fort Salonga also expanded their transformation efforts by enlisting parents in the process. In the front office, visitors can find a calendar with dates for parent workshops on the learning framework and packets of parent resources on the counter. Parents have access to reading material, Web sites, and tips for developing neurodevelopmental functions at home. One of the most popular events at the school is the "All Kinds of Minds" fair for parents, where students teach parents what they know about how their minds work.

At Fort Salonga, students are knowledgeable about their own learning profiles and the constructs because teachers infuse learning about learning into everything they do. In fact, once Arlene received a phone call from a parent who asked, "What is receptive language? Johnny came home last night talking about it, and I don't remember learning about that in school." Students slowly

> ## PICTURE THIS!
>
> Just imagine the school library full of different work stations, one with a student working on a puzzle with his parents. Upon completion of the puzzle, the student proudly exclaims, "Dad, we both have strengths in spatial ordering, but Mom really struggles with it. It's a good thing she can write!"

build knowledge about their own learning profiles and the constructs when teachers share their observations about learning with their students and weave the constructs into their lessons. For example, before third graders start solving math problems, they discuss what learning functions (like active working memory or receptive language) will be needed. Once problems have been solved, the learners talk about how they solved problems, including the functions involved with different approaches. Students demonstrate knowledge about learning and their learning profiles when they select their own teams for cooperative learning projects. The teacher directs them to build their teams based on their strengths and the task demands, which reflects how this is done in the real world.

Arlene is pleased with how the students have embraced conversations about learning, but she also boasts about how engaged her faculty have become in transforming the school culture. She proudly recalls the first time she observed that report card comments contained descriptions of students' learning strengths and weaknesses. This was not something she suggested or mandated but this trend happened naturally as teachers became confident in their roles as learning experts. "That's right," Arlene confidently claims. "These teachers are learning experts."

Learning About Neurodevelopmental Constructs Can Strengthen School Instructional Initiatives

Fort Salonga has become a learner-centric school within its existing traditional school system. They committed to embracing a new focus while integrating that into existing district initiatives, standardized test, and professional development commitments.

They changed pedagogy, created new policies and practices, and their teachers have become learning experts. In fact, the faculty exemplify the new, redefined roles adults will need to play in the future education of students, as predicted by the KnowledgeWorks

Foundation *Forecast 2020: Creating the Future of Learning*. Fort Salonga demonstrated that it is possible to meet the needs of today while still embracing the possibilities of a very different future for education.

It is quite possible that an approach like Arlene Mullin's can also serve to help schools broaden the overall aims of education. The constructs shaping students' learning profiles are part of the newer aims of education for twenty-first-century skills, and those aims can be stated as an explicit reason for learning about those specific mental functions (see Table 8.1).[10]

Table 8.1 Translating the Constructs into Relevant Aims of Education

Temporal-sequential ordering	To educate students in time management and to understand how to think and act in a step by step fashion
Spatial ordering	To educate students to make good use of mental imagery and analogy for productive nonverbal thinking
Higher-order cognition	To educate students as thinkers so they become adept conceptualizers, creators, problem solvers, and critical analysts
Social cognition	To educate students to understand and practice effective interpersonal skills, including a respect for differences
Neuromotor	To educate students regarding the ways in which they can achieve a satisfying level of motor effectiveness
Memory	To educate students to be thoughtful and systematic in managing their memory "files" and components in order to merge understanding with remembering
Language	To educate students to derive knowledge from language input and become effective verbal communicators
Attention	To educate students so they can concentrate mental resources for adequate work effort; to become active processors of information, to consider alternatives, to unite previous experience with foresight

One Learning Leader Can Be a Catalyst for School Transformation

As we saw in the Fort Salonga story, transformation requires a learning leader to guide the efforts by defining a series of actionable items that progress toward a future vision. Although the learning leader is often a school- or district-level administrator, a teacher leader may credibly and effectively assume the role of lead learning expert in a school. That's what happened at Ferguson Middle School in Beavercreek, Ohio. Janet Boucher, who serves as an intervention specialist at the school, decided to become a catalyst for change by using her knowledge of the learning framework and the elements of the All Kinds of Minds approach to ignite schoolwide transformation that focused on student self-advocacy.

As you drive up to Ferguson Middle School, you are likely to see parents who are dressed in military uniforms dropping their children off. For many of these children, transitioning to new schools in new cities has become an expected part of life. The staff of Ferguson Middle School is sensitive to the challenges that are unique to military families, but they also face a common challenge shared by many schools across the country: numerous students who need learning support do not formally qualify for special education services.

In considering where to begin, Janet took into account the transient nature of her students and decided that making the students self-advocates for their learning was important to success at Ferguson Middle School, as well as other schools they would attend in the future. Janet also realized that focusing her initial efforts on the students felt like the right way to begin a broader schoolwide transformation about student self-advocacy.

Janet pondered the stack of students' cumulative folders on the corner of her desk and her charge to help those students find a pathway to success. In order to do this effectively, Janet had to first make sure she had gathered information from multiple sources, identified the recurring themes, and understood each student's unique learning profile. When her colleagues walked by her office, they would see her hunched over her desk reading through the existing information in the cumulative folders or on the phone talking with parents. They observed her talking attentively with students in the cozy reading corner of her classroom or sitting in the hallway outside her classroom, which has come to be known as the "corner office," exploring their learning through dynamic assessments. She was often seen collaborating with teachers in the teacher's lounge during lunch periods or following them back to their rooms to collect documented observations and work samples.

Once she had gathered sufficient information and felt like she had a rich data portrait of the students whose folders were stacked on the corner of her desk, it was time to craft their individualized learning plans. Janet completed the requisite district learning plan form, but she didn't stop there. It was time to take that extra step that would move her school toward a more learner-centric environment.

Knowing that a key component to a learner-centric approach is for students to truly understand their learning profile, Janet considered the best way to make this information accessible to the students so that they could be self-advocates of their learning. She immediately headed to the computer, where she made posters displaying, in words and images, each child's strengths, weaknesses, affinities, and strategies. These posters could be seen taped to the inside of locker doors, inserted in folder pockets, or clipped to the inside of students' binder covers for quick reference. One student even tacked his poster above his bed at home!

In addition to posters as a visible reminder of the unique learning profiles that existed at Ferguson Middle School, Janet set up "office visits" with individual students and reviewed their strengths, weaknesses, and the effectiveness of the selected strategies on their individual learning plans. These efforts were well received by the group of struggling students, and positive progress was evident to both teachers and students outside this initial group. In fact, other students at the school began asking if they could work with Janet and go through the process of learning about themselves. Talk about students becoming self-advocates for their learning!

Janet was making significant strides with support for individual students, but she wanted to broaden her focus so that she could positively affect the learning of all the students at Ferguson.

She launched a new program that was designed for middle school students to understand the brain and learning. As students gained this knowledge from the program, teachers became increasingly intrigued with learning about learning. Several teachers privately expressed that they didn't want to be at a disadvantage when their students began talking about their affinities or the spatial ordering demands of the geometry lesson the teachers were teaching.

> Janet used "The Mind That's Mine," a curriculum designed for middle school students focusing on the brain and learning.[11] The program includes materials and activities for self-exploration.

Janet saw this as an opportunity to move the school forward in its transformation to a learner-centric school and stepped in to provide professional development to Ferguson teachers on topics like the learning framework and the "cognitive backpack."[12] As teachers gained confidence in their knowledge, a schoolwide trend surfaced: all students began to self-advocate, and classroom conversations routinely included dialogue between students and teachers about the students' strengths, weaknesses, and task demands. Teachers and students were using a shared language, a new self-advocate role had developed for students, and educators had a new way to make decisions about curriculum and their educational practices.

> The "cognitive backpack"[13] refers to the four "I's" young adults need to develop to have the critical skills for the twenty-first-century workplace
>   1. *Interpretation*: Becoming an in-depth comprehender
>   2. *Instrumentation*: Acquiring a project mind-set
>   3. *Interaction*: Building and sustaining productive, fulfilling relationships
>   4. *Inner direction*: Attaining self-insight that informs adult and career success

These days the Ferguson learning community has expanded beyond the struggling students, general student population, and teachers; it includes the students' families. Janet recalls that one Ferguson Middle School student, whose parents were both engineers and gifted mathematicians, showed extreme difficulty with understanding and using math algorithms, which was troubling to his parents. Janet helped the parents understand that it was okay that their son's profile and interests were different from his parents. His talent and interest lay with music; he wanted to play the trumpet and be a member of the marching band. As they began to accept and respect their son's love of music, they gave him opportunities to develop musically and gain confidence in expressing his desires and abilities. With his parents' support, he began to explore other areas of interest and set out on an earnest journey of self-discovery. The learner-centric culture of the school helped a family understand that there are multiple pathways to success in school and life.

The All Kinds of Minds approach is a "mind-set that we have now," says Janet, who works closely with a team of teachers who desire to provide the absolute best instruction possible. She also believes that middle school is a great time for getting kids to better understand themselves as learners, especially for eighth graders facing a transition to high school. "Middle schoolers love learning about themselves, about their brains and how they are 'wired.'"

Janet Boucher is an example of how today's teachers can start the transformation of their roles to some of those imagined by KnowledgeWorks Foundation and described earlier in this book. Teachers can become the community's front-line experts on mind development and learning in the age groups of the students they teach. We imagine the day when parents, who are concerned about the development of their children and learning and who are seeking a lead learning expert, would seek a teacher instead of their pediatrician. Schools can build the capacity of their faculty to be these experts by strengthening the expertise they have about mind, brain, and learning integrations and also share this knowledge with the broader community, as Fort Salonga and Ferguson schools have done.

Learning Leaders Are Adopting New Roles in Schools

Teachers steeped in new knowledge about learning and its variation—using a neurodevelopmental framework—become the lead observers of the learning mind. They are in the best position to observe phenomena that provide windows into how a child's mind is wired to learn and insights that are unavailable on the standardized achievement or diagnostic tests commonly used in schools. We know the phenomena exist because educators and parents see it every day. Capturing these observations helps educators construct the richer data portrait necessary to uncover solutions and strategies for our most complex and struggling learners.

Learning leaders must manage today's testing, accountability, and assessment demands and mandates against the potential harm that our obsession with evaluation can have on students. They need to help teachers become the trusted evaluation advisors. Such leaders can do that by explaining why multiple sources of data are needed and by involving student and parent perspectives in a constructive way that builds an alliance of support for learning as an outcome of gathering and using data. They can remind their faculty—and students—that the point of assessment is to develop a deeper understanding of the student.[14]

> "The point of assessment is to develop a deeper understanding of the student."
>
> —Craig Pohlman
> *Revealing Minds: Assessing to Understand and Support Struggling Learners*

Consider that students in our schools experience a barrage of evaluation unlike any other time of life. Look at an average middle school student. His science teacher gives him weekly quizzes. The diving coach evaluates the precision and degree of difficulty of his dives. Math homework is scrutinized in class for errors. His writing is analyzed by his language arts teacher to make sure that end-of-year state examinations will show proficiency. His parents will keep finding fault—as adolescents provide plenty of fodder—with his wardrobe, his friends, and the amount of time he spends on the computer. Scores on his various computer games are posted on his social networks. Most important, his peers are forever grading him on his "fit" to the current social norm. Life can be impossibly hard on kids who do not fare well on many, if not all, of these evaluations.

This is an important reason why we need to reexamine our most judgmental practices and help ensure that feedback to students contains useful information for improvement. Learning leaders need to help establish what is an acceptable amount of data collection, testing, and formative assessment and to ensure that the evaluative practices in use are truly essential to gathering the information needed. Feedback protocols to students can be designed to help them discover what they can do well and offer constructive and hopeful guidance for their futures as learners. Such protocols need to take particular care to avoid subjective conclusions based on limited evidence that imply students are guilty of moral turpitude—such as being lazy or not working to their potential.

As lead learning experts, school leaders and teachers can strengthen their ability to become informed advisors to students and parents regarding the learning pathways and journeys that children can take. This guidance includes helping them connect the way they learn to career pathways in which they are likely to find success, while helping them find the accommodations and strategies to navigate the demands of their current school expectations.

Ongoing Commitment to Faculty Learning Supports Ongoing Focus on Student Learning

A walk across the picturesque campus of Wasatch Academy in Utah is all you need to appreciate the school's commitment to celebrating differences and promoting diversity. Students representing twenty-five states and more than thirty countries gather in small clusters to discuss an upcoming project or yesterday's soccer match. Roommates enjoy time to catch up on a reading assignment or news from home. And it's not unusual to catch an impromptu "teachable moment" when the teachers walk by on the way to their next class. This international school is in a position to truly appreciate all kinds of minds; Joseph Loftin, its headmaster, is proud of how the staff and faculty are continuing the school tradition of building each student's educational program through opportunities to develop their unique capabilities as learners. This tradition made Wasatch Academy a natural fit for All Kinds of Minds.

At Wasatch Academy, teachers encourage students to reach their greatest potential and empower them to find success. And while the school welcomes applicants who have learning differences, Max Roach, Director of Wasatch Academy's All Kinds of Minds Initiatives, is clear about one thing. "Wasatch Academy, despite its decidedly college preparatory mission, distinguishes itself by meeting students at their individual level and helping them unlock their potential. We celebrate the uniqueness of each learner and lift them up to where they want to go."

While the ethnic diversity of the student body is obvious to anyone visiting the campus, the learner diversity is just as clear to the faculty and staff of the school. With a foundation of individualization and commitment to success for every student, Wasatch Academy continues to develop and embrace a set of core beliefs and weave an understanding of students' learning profiles throughout the fabric of the school. Knowing there was a match between the mission of the school and the core beliefs of All Kinds of Minds, they chose to embrace this approach as their system for understanding and describing the learning differences of their students. Joseph and the teachers at Wasatch Academy felt this was the overarching framework that would support them in understanding and teaching to the learning differences represented throughout the student body.

Following their initial participation in the Schools Attuned (a professional development program from All Kinds of Minds) course in 2003, Wasatch Academy teachers began to observe individual students using a neurodevelopmental lens and using this information to describe student profiles and identify customized intervention strategies. While the teachers saw benefits of getting very specific about a student's profile and gains in the effectiveness of their interventions, the early implementation of the All Kinds of Minds approach faced several barriers. Staff were using the program's signature tool Attuning a Student (a systematic data gathering and analysis process) to identify student learning profiles but were struggling to efficiently implement the detailed and time-consuming process with all their students and communicate the findings among the faculty. Some of the Attuning interventions suffered from poor quality, while others were not completely finished. However, those interventions that were successfully completed produced tantalizing results. These early "small wins" served as a springboard for more faculty and staff members to engage in the All Kinds of Minds approach at Wasatch Academy and to figure out how to streamline the implementation of this process in a way that fit with the culture and teaching demands at the school.

The idea was to integrate what the faculty had learned from All Kinds of Minds with the curriculum of their Learning Strategies student course, created by Max, who also serves as a member of the All Kinds of Minds' national faculty. This year-long course is geared toward students who can benefit from developing a better understanding of themselves as learners while receiving additional support and encouragement. The Learning Strategies course provides students with an understanding of the neurodevelopmental framework and how different aspects of learning (for example, memory, language, spatial ordering) come into play during various learning experiences. The three primary goals of the learning strategies curriculum at Wasatch are (1) to help students learn about learning, (2) to learn how they learn best, and (3) to receive the support needed to succeed academically. In short, having struggling students who were taught to understand the mind and take action using shared vocabulary and tools was critical. This alignment of teacher training to student curriculum resulted in teachers being able to discuss very specific strengths and weaknesses and collaborate in developing highly specific action plans with students ... all based on a shared All Kinds of Minds approach.

The next stage in the evolution of Wasatch Academy's intervention development proceeded with the creation of the learning profile database, or LPD. All Kinds of Minds had converted Attuning a Student to a Web-based data collection and analysis tool. This new resource was a game changer for Wasatch Academy. Partnering with All Kinds of Minds, the school served as a pilot site for a novel use of the Attuning a Student Online Tool, resulting in the LPD that allows the All Kinds of Minds–trained teachers at Wasatch to have shared access to students' profile data. Wasatch Academy teachers and dorm parents go online, view learning profiles and management plans, and benefit from the work that their colleagues have done with a particular student. The learning profile database is a dynamic and powerful tool and greatly enhances the school's ability to intervene and support students' achievement.

Today, 95 percent of faculty and staff have received training to use the All Kinds of Minds approach to support student learning in classrooms and throughout the school. Teachers at Wasatch Academy have expanded the ways they use this knowledge base in their professional practice, including using a framework to consider the learning demands of content area lessons and to adapt curriculum design, lesson delivery, and assessment strategies. Teachers know that by analyzing the demands of their curriculum and instruction they more effectively differentiate their instruction and meet the learning needs of many students through their daily instruction in addition to providing one-on-one support as needed.

From the school's leadership to its teachers, students, and dorm parents, all members of this learning community share the All Kinds of Minds framework and mind-set about helping students reach their maximum potential. It has become the basis of a formal collaboration among students, dorm parents, and academic content area teachers through a structure called the Student Learning Partnership Team. This team approach brings many perspectives to the table and allows for a thorough understanding and description of the student's strengths and weaknesses as well as a cohesive approach to both academic and behavioral interventions.

Students at Wasatch lead the decisions about their academic paths and ultimately their futures. Supported by their relationships with school staff and dorm parents, students make choices based on personal goals and abilities. Students take advantage of help from on-site learning specialists who coach students to understand the demands of particular assignments, how best to approach the task based on their unique learning profiles, and strategies that may facilitate successful completion of the assignment. This experience becomes a yearlong "demystification," providing students with a new appreciation for the brain functions that affect learning.

These efforts at Wasatch are a result of the school's commitment to implementing an annual teaching and learning action plan to keep developing the learning expertise required by all faculty to make this approach work for students. Max assumes the role of lead learning advisor at the school and points out that the core components of the school plan address building capacity through summer professional development, ongoing professional development, and in-class support. He explains that Schools Attuned alone is just a body of knowledge. The key to successful integration is supporting the in-class application of the principles, strategies, and tools. "My daily activities focus on extending teachers' understanding of and ability to integrate this knowledge in daily activities. Our overarching goal of these initiatives is to improve teacher performance, student achievement, and in turn, customer satisfaction."

Wasatch Academy connects the All Kinds of Minds framework to student achievement by starting and ending with a student focus. Max explains:

Aside from ongoing professional development, our teachers engage in ongoing conversations about their students. We have developed a system of identifying students who would benefit from extra support and using that list to drive our work with teachers. A student might come onto Wasatch Academy's "all kinds of minds radar," in a number of ways. For example, if a student comes to our school with educational testing that indicates a need for academic support, he or she would be placed on the list. Another way a student might receive this extra scrutiny is if he or she has received an academic intervention at Wasatch Academy. Identifying struggling students alone, however, will not fuel the actual change we hope to see in the classroom. The fun part is in connecting theory to practice.

At Wasatch Academy, teachers of struggling students benefit from additional student-specific support. Max visits each teacher and reviews a list of "radar students," prompting the teacher to prepare and/or reflect on what might be done to support the students in the specific subject. Then he visits each classroom several times throughout the year, observing both students' learning-related behaviors as well as teachers' instructional delivery methods. Max explains:

> It is of critical importance that a trusted and knowledge-able administrator visits teachers regularly and with a clearly defined student focus. Ideally, I come into a classroom with a focus on intervention/accommodation for specific students. The specificity keeps me on track in terms of identifying actionable items for the student or teacher. Very often, larger issues surrounding teaching and learning emerge during my talks with teachers. A very rewarding and challenging job!

ONGOING PROFESSIONAL DEVELOPMENT SESSIONS AT WASATCH ACADEMY

The goal? Offer manageable doses of "non-jargony," practical classroom applications with construct mini-lessons. Lasting from fifteen to thirty minutes, the basic lesson plan format includes
- Review and preview (connects prior knowledge and activates learners' minds for new material)
- Non-jargon construct instruction (reviews construct in a user-friendly way, increasing chances for integration of new strategies)
- Activity (deepens personal relationship with information)
- Contextualizing and connecting to practice
- Closure and frontloading future sessions

These stories tell of schools that began the transformation to learner-centric educational environments by taking deliberate, actionable steps. The examples illustrate the four elements identified as key to integrating the All Kinds of Minds approach into today's schools. Teachers showed us how pedagogy can be reframed; those examples barely touched on the exciting developments in this area with technology. The new roles, work, and focus of teachers and administrators comes to light as well as the beginning steps to align school practices with beliefs about educational care of all students. Most important, these learning leaders and faculty continue this work year after year.

Revisiting School Practices and Policies

Learning leaders have also begun to examine K–12 school practices and policies through the lens of the All Kinds of Minds approach. They are also rethinking ways to deliberately promote benchmarks of postsecondary success more expansive than the current singular focus on equating adult success with college graduation. These issues can become thorny, but transformation to a learner-centered school with a goal of success for all can get stymied if such issues are not confronted. We have to look at policies to see if they have inadvertently created harmful practices that are counter to working on successful learning plans. There are two guidelines to use when revisiting practices and policies to ensure they support success for all learners.

First, do no harm.

Consider the struggling student from Chapter Five who was suspended from the basketball team because of failing grades. This is a real case from the students whom All Kinds of Minds worked with in its initial years of clinical experience.[15] The unintended outcome of this case was a de facto school practice that punished a learner for his weaknesses by banishing the use of his strengths. An alternative would be a compromise such as negotiating with the student, coach, and teachers that he may attend afternoon "practice" three times a week instead of every afternoon, with the other two sessions devoted to work on strategies to address the academic breakdowns.

This approach also requires that a school define new notions of student accountability. Learning profile weaknesses are never an excuse to avoid expectations. Understanding the complete profile of strengths and weaknesses permits schools to enact a "payback" policy. If students are allowed to do less of something at which they are weak, they have increased accountability to perform and contribute in areas in which they are strong. This balance needs to be an explicit part of learning plans for struggling learners receiving accommodations and interventions. In the long run, this can prevent students from feeling like second-class citizens in school and life. Schools can have a goal that all students are highly productive, but they do not all need to be turning out the same products.[16] Among the educational practices and policies that merit examination are labeling of students with dysfunctions, testing and assessments, grade retention, timing and pacing of learning (from the amount of time allocated to learning through course scheduling to the required time to graduate) and the demeaning way alternatives to college preparation tracks are often used with struggling students—most notably the persistent use of tracking "ability"-based students. Such policies need to be examined against what we know about how learning unfolds in all its variations, because researchers are now providing emerging evidence concerning their unintended, yet harmful effects.

Second, support success above all else.

Some school policies have been shown to boost achievement and the likelihood of adult success. One example is to establish a practice that every student becomes an expert in one domain. This is where early identification of affinities is essential and can become the basis of a one-page learning plan that is reviewed and refined annually by the student, parents, and teachers. Such expertise, kindled in the elementary years, forms the foundation of intellectual work that becomes scholarship. For example, an elementary student with an interest in sharks could be expected to

- Read all the relevant articles in the school library
- Learn how to find and sort through pertinent information about sharks on the internet
- Complete two science projects (one of which might involve developing a Web site) that convey key characteristics of sharks
- Write a fictional story about a shark for younger children
- Communicate with professionals at SeaWorld or other aquariums about jobs that involve working with sharks
- Engage in an online mentor relationship with a graduate student in marine biology about current research on sharks
- Write a blog linked to Discovery Channel's annual television production about sharks

The point of leveraging a student's interest in sharks is to expand the affinity to the wide world of scholarship, allowing the student to develop skills of inquiry that will serve the next great passion he discovers in his life. This kind of expertise kindles intellectual self-esteem: it helps us all feel smart, which is a critical strategy for those struggling students whose experiences with learning and school have led them to believe otherwise.

Learning leaders need to reexamine the definition of school success that dictates that "every student graduate college ready." We've all met plenty of successful adults who never attended college, particularly those in performing arts, culinary arts, technology innovation, carpentry, and other work that requires manual expertise. However, these successful adults were diligent in becoming their own kind of scholars of their work, spending dedicated time to gain the knowledge and skills necessary to succeed in their endeavors. These paths often involve both formal and informal postsecondary learning with apprenticeships with masters in the field, specific course learning, and on-the-job training. Anne Lewis, former editor for the *Kappan*, writes on national issues in education policy. She notes that there's a message many disengaged students and those who try to educate them aren't hearing from our policymakers—a message that they need to hear: "There is a good economic life for those who graduate from high school with some connection to careers immediately after high school."[17]

> " Learning leaders need to reexamine the definition of school success that dictates that 'every student graduate college ready.' "

In our quest to prepare our students well—and as the college-educated people who lead the current education reform discussions—we either disregard these promising alternative routes provided by career and technical education or we treat the students who chose them as lesser goods. Learning leaders must change this conversation and celebrate some of the exemplary examples of these students in the same manner that we celebrate the valedictorian.

Confronting Current Challenges in Practice While Creating Stories of Optimism

We have fewer stories of success than we would hope to have because learning leaders have to do this work while they cut against the grain of existing practice and policy. We have to remember two huge challenges when leaders begin to move to learner-centric schools.

First off, schools and our current educational approach are not structurally designed to look at children as individuals. We have to put them into groups (not meeting annual yearly progress [AYP], succeeding, struggling, special education, ELL, and so on) because that is the way our current system is set up to manage them. Grouping students, no matter how it is done, is the result of how we currently view what and how students are doing within this school system structure (passing a spelling test, failing at math). We are not currently equipped with the knowledge or tools to discover who these students are as learners or what their individual needs are and what their promise could reveal. This system and approach generates many interventions for schools that still look at groups of kids and address the symptoms of what they are not doing well rather than the interventions that look at individuals and address deeper, more specific causes (this currently is considered an expensive intervention approach reserved for identified special needs).

Second, children who aren't succeeding are viewed as lacking something internal (motivation, intelligence) or external (supportive parents, early learning opportunities, social well-being, and so on). Our current interventions focus on making up for those things. Many of these interventions have value, because there are plenty of kids who need to have these gaps (especially the external ones) addressed, but those interventions don't come close to solving the compelling problem that way too many students aren't succeeding despite those interventional efforts.

Bottom line: we want all children to succeed, but schools currently have a fixed approach and need to turn to interventions after the fact—when a child is struggling. We put the failure on the kids (they lack things) and the teachers (they can't teach those kids) for not being successful within this current system.

So what can a school leader do working within this system? She or he can't fundamentally restructure the grades or scheduling of school, and she or he usually can't implement frame-breaking change in required curriculum and assessments administration. But she can begin to change the conversation in the community to a learner-centric approach and take small steps to show "proof of concept" that when teachers understand learning in a much deeper way, more students can find success in school.

Parents and members of the community are receiving mixed and conflicting messages about what counts as success in school. A parent usually has one criterion for the result of their child's K–12 school experience: Is he or she on track to be a happy and productive adult? Policymakers, media, and schools answer with academic indicators: get good grades, pass state tests at a proficient level, graduate from high school in a school that makes AYP, go to college. We could add other predictable indicators of adult success that involve social-emotional growth to a comprehensive assessment of students, and we could focus on the role of schooling as one of discovering your passions and strengths and how to shape a life around that. We certainly could encourage parents or their children, particularly those who have not found great success on those academic indicators, to consider paths to success that require commitments to lifelong learning but do not require traditional postsecondary education.

Matthew Crawford, author of *Shop Class as Soulcraft*, is one of several thought leaders challenging the educational imperative of turning everyone into a "knowledge worker." He argues to restore the honor of manual trades as a life worth choosing, where work provides both the cognitive challenges of careful thinking with the intrinsic satisfaction of working with one's hands.[18] The point is not to discourage students from attending college but to present options for those students for whom college is not the path that will nurture their talents. We want learning opportunities for students that can embrace all their gifts, providing our communities with more productive citizens and adults. This is what the argument of choice in education should be about. Learning leaders can help parents and community members broaden their point of view about what constitutes school and learning success and help more students find a place on the graduation podium.

How powerful, then, is a lens that allows educators throughout a school to begin to look at students differently—to get insight into each of them and their individual brains within the context of what educators are already doing in their classrooms. How powerful, then, is the idea of developing capacity within a school faculty that shifts the focus from trying to make up for something lacking for a student—or a group of students—toward discovering the hidden learning strengths and affinities and building student achievement around this notion of asset management, not just deficit remediation. Learning leaders can take the approach in this book, use current initiatives, and broaden the professional expertise within that school so that more students are successful learners.

That is the story of this book and of the educators who have begun this journey. Each school and teacher represented has taken a first step toward creating a learner-centered environment for their students. Through a series of small wins, they are meeting the learning needs of all kinds of minds and influencing the future of education.

What will your story be? Where will your journey lead? What steps will you take as the learning leader in your school?

> "What will your story be? Where will your journey lead? What steps will you take as the learning leader in your school?"

Turn the page, and let us help you begin.

We invite you to take that first step by deciding on the best course of action for your school. Exhibit 8.1 provides a template to guide your thinking and planning as you create your school for all kinds of minds.

Exhibit 8.1 Sample Planning Template: Creating Schools for All Kinds of Minds

Long-Term Goal(s):	Small Win Strategy #1: School staff participates in All Kinds of Minds program, focusing initially on curriculum mapping team members at each grade level
• Differentiate instruction for students based on the All Kinds of Minds approach to teaching and learning	**Small Win Strategy #2:** Curriculum mapping team develops and implements one differentiated, thematic unit using neurodevelopmental variation as a criteria for differentiation
	Small Win Strategy #3: Development of grade-level appropriate learning about learning lessons for students
• Members of the school community (educators, students, parents) make decisions about student learning based on an understanding of learning variation	**Small Win Strategy #4:** Development and delivery of parent program, focusing initially on families involved in the tiers of Response to Intervention

Small Win Strategy #1:

School staff participates in All Kinds of Minds training program and ongoing study, focusing initially on curriculum mapping team members at each grade level

Planned Work, Activities, and Tasks *(practices and policies, infrastructure, technology, staff buy-in, marketing, role of teachers, professional development, and so on)*	Resources Needed *(budget, materials, time, partnerships, and so on)*	Timeline	Person(s) Responsible	Evidence of Success
All Staff Meeting presentation: Overview of initiative goals and multiyear implementation plan	Time— Principal conversations and presentation preparation Partnerships— All Kinds of Minds information and planning assistance	February– March 15, 3:00 PM meeting	Principal	Follow-up conversations indicate interest and willingness to pursue initiative

Exhibit 8.1 Sample Planning Template: Creating Schools for All Kinds of Minds (Continued)

Identify staff members for curriculum mapping process and training	Time— Principal Time— Administrative support	March 15–April 30	Principal	Teachers representing all grade levels self select to participate
School staff participates in a three-day All Kinds of Minds program	Time—School staff release time Budget— Program costs	Week of August 18	Principal	• Participant survey results • Observe use of neurodevelopmental language in team meetings • Evidence of neurodevelopmental ideas in beginning curriculum mapping

Note: A customizable template is available on the All Kinds of Minds Web site (www.allkinds ofminds.org).

APPENDIX A

Glossary of Key Terms

Academic subskills The specific tasks or abilities (such as punctuation, letter formation, and vocabulary use) that are required to perform broader, more complex tasks (such as written expression).

Accommodation A strategy designed to bypass an area of weakness so that the student can continue to perform or achieve certain learning objectives (e.g., having a student who struggles with reading decoding listen to a book on tape so that he can learn important information).

Active working memory A function in the memory construct that refers to the brain's ability to mentally juggle information while using it. Active working memory can be thought of as the brain's workspace.

Affinity A topic (e.g., whales) that a person pursues with a passionate interest or skill and activity (e.g., cooking) that a person loves to do, even if he or she is not particularly good at it.

Applied reasoning   A function in the higher-order cognition construct that refers to thinking in a systematic way in order to solve problems that do not have a readily apparent solution.

Asset   A valuable or useful element of a learner's profile that is typically associated with a strength or interest.

Attention   A construct in the All Kinds of Minds neurodevelopmental framework that refers to maintaining mental energy for learning and work, absorbing and filtering incoming information, and overseeing the quality of academic output.

Brainstorming and creativity   A function in the higher-order cognition construct that refers to generating original ideas or perspectives. Brainstorming and creativity includes thinking in innovative ways with regard to expressing ideas, resolving dilemmas, and overcoming obstacles.

Complex decision making   A function in the higher-order cognition construct that refers to applying stepwise approaches to resolving complicated questions or challenges.

Conceptualization   A function in the higher-order cognition construct that refers to integrating sets of features that form categories of ideas (e.g., "cooperation" and "social activism") or things (e.g., "fruits" and "invertebrates").

Discourse production   A function in the language construct (expressive language) that refers to the ability to communicate information in a cohesive chain of sentences.

Evaluative thinking   A function in the higher-order cognition construct that refers to critical thinking or appraising ideas, products, points of view, and opportunities.

Expressive language   A function in the language construct that refers to the output side that encompasses communicating and producing ideas orally and in writing.

Fine motor function   A function in the neuromotor function construct that refers to control over small movements (e.g., keyboarding, drawing).

Graphomotor function   A function in the neuromotor function construct that refers to motor abilities for handwriting.

Gross motor function   A function in the neuromotor function construct that refers to control over large movements (e.g., dance, play, athletics).

Higher-order cognition   A construct in the All Kinds of Minds neurodevelopmental framework that refers to complex and sophisticated thinking. Higher-order cognition includes comprehending concepts, generating original ideas, and using logical approaches to address complex problems.

Intervention   A strategy designed to improve an area of weakness (e.g., teaching word attack skills to a student struggling with reading decoding).

Language   A construct in the All Kinds of Minds neurodevelopmental framework that refers to understanding and using words. Language includes understanding incoming oral and written information, as well as communicating ideas orally and in writing.

Learning phenomena   All of the evidence educators have at their disposal that provides clues about learners' strengths and weaknesses, including students' behaviors, comments, questions, and work samples. (Also referred to as "observable phenomena.")

Long-term memory   A function in the memory construct that includes two processes: storage of information and retrieval of information.

Long-term memory access   A function in the memory construct that refers to the retrieval of information, experiences, and skills.

Long-term memory consolidation   A function in the memory construct that refers to the storage of information, experiences, and skills.

Memory   A construct in the All Kinds of Minds neurodevelopmental framework that refers to remembering information. Memory includes briefly recording new information, mentally juggling information while using it to complete a task, and storing and then recalling information at a later time.

Mental energy controls   A function in the attention construct that refers to regulating the initiation and maintenance of cognitive energy flow for learning, work, and behavioral control.

Metacognition   Often referred to as "thinking about thinking," metacognition includes one's knowledge about learning, as well as insight into one's own learning profile.

Neurodevelopmental construct   A set of related mental abilities, such as memory, that affects learning.

Neurodevelopmental framework   An organizing structure that helps educators understand learning and learners. A framework can be thought of as a set of file folders; the All Kinds of Minds neurodevelopmental framework is composed of eight file folders called constructs. These constructs are based on a synthesis of research about how the brain functions and how brain functions affect student learning and performance.

Neurodevelopmental function   A specific, relatively narrow mental ability, such as long-term memory, that is a component of a neurodevelopmental construct, such as memory.

Neurodevelopmental lens   Use of a neurodevelopmental framework and phenomena to interpret information about every student's unique learning profile. This perspective informs instructional decision making.

Neurodevelopmental profile   A balance sheet of learning strengths and weaknesses, also referred to as a "learning profile."

Neuromotor function   A construct in the All Kinds of Minds neurodevelopmental framework that refers to controlling movements. Neuromotor function include using large muscles in a coordinated manner, controlling finger and hand movements, or coordinating muscles needed for handwriting.

Observable phenomena   All of the evidence educators have at their disposal that provides clues about learners' strengths and weaknesses. Such clues include students' behaviors, comments, questions, and work samples. (Also referred to as "learning phenomena.")

Processing controls   A function in the attention construct that refers to regulating incoming information. Processing controls include determining the relative importance of available inputs, absorbing information with appropriate intensity, and maintaining focus for sufficient stretches of time.

Production controls   A function in the attention construct that refers to regulating the quality of academic output and behavioral control. Production controls include impulse and rate control, previewing and planning, and self-monitoring.

Receptive language   A function in the language construct that refers to the input side that encompasses the processing and understanding of oral and written information.

Saliency determination   A function in the attention construct (processing controls) that refers to the ability to discriminate between important and unimportant information.

Schools Attuned   All Kinds of Minds' five-day comprehensive course in which participants learn about the eight neurodevelopmental constructs and explore how to use this knowledge to pinpoint and address learning breakdowns.

Social cognition   A construct in the All Kinds of Minds neurodevelopmental framework that refers to making and keeping friends. Social cognition includes knowing what to talk about, when, with whom, and for how long, working and playing with others in a cooperative manner, and nurturing positive relationships with influential people.

Spatial ordering   A construct in the All Kinds of Minds neurodevelopmental framework that refers to visual thinking. Spatial ordering includes understanding information that is presented visually, generating products that are visual, and organizing materials and spaces.

Strength   A neurodevelopmental function that is operating reliably or with a high level of efficiency or sophistication. Strengths include solid or advanced academic skills, as well as talents and abilities that fall outside of traditional school areas (e.g., music).

Temporal-sequential ordering A construct in the All Kinds of Minds neurodevelopmental framework that refers to keeping track of time and order. Temporal sequential ordering includes understanding the order of steps, events or other sequences, generating products arranged in a meaningful order, and organizing time and schedules.

Twenty-first-century skills The skills, knowledge, and expertise students should master to succeed in work and life in the twenty-first century (e.g., lifelong learning, innovation, critical thinking, technology, global awareness, multimedia literacy, financial literacy, initiative, self-direction, and collaboration).

Weakness A neurodevelopmental construct or function that is not operating reliably or with a sufficient level of efficiency or sophistication, to the extent that academic skill development is affected.

APPENDIX B

All Kinds of Minds Schools of Distinction

Launched in 2009, the Schools of Distinction award recognizes schools that have embraced the All Kinds of Minds philosophy at a schoolwide level and have made a commitment to providing faculty with professional development based on the science of learning. These schools, which include a diverse group of public, charter, and private schools from around the world, showcase ways to integrate knowledge about learning and its variations into schoolwide goals and efforts to serve all learners.

To qualify, at least 50 percent of a school's faculty members must have participated in an All Kinds of Minds course, and the school must articulate how the All Kinds of Minds approach and course content are being implemented throughout the school.

The following pages contain brief profiles of some of the schools that have achieved this designation:

- The Academies for Educational Excellence, Tampa, Florida
- The British School of Bern, Bern, Switzerland
- Forsyth Country Day School, Lewisville, North Carolina

- Fort Worth Academy, Fort Worth, Texas
- Public School 23, The New Children's School, Bronx, New York
- Taft Middle School, Oklahoma City, Oklahoma

For a full list of current All Kinds of Minds' Schools of Distinction, visit www.allkindsofminds.org.

The Academies for Educational Excellence, Tampa, Florida

www.theacademies.us

A public charter school, the Academies for Educational Excellence serves 350 students identified with severe learning disabilities. Encompassing four small schools (elementary, intermediate, and high schools, as well as a postsecondary transitional school focused on developing work skills), the Academies seeks to employ "innovative instructional design to develop the gifts of a diverse population who frequently arrive at our doors already discouraged."

The Academies has broadly embraced the All Kinds of Minds approach, and 80–100 percent of the educators in each school, along with most school administrators, have participated in All Kinds of Minds professional development programs. "Having this training has united our faculty even further in our mission and belief in students as learners with endless potential," says Geri Henry, Speech Language Pathologist. "I also now have a specific language to back up and support our school philosophy."

The All Kinds of Minds neurodevelopmental framework is foundational to all educational strategies that educators employ at the Academies. When developing lesson plans, educators consider and specify the neurodevelopmental implications of what they will be asking students to do. In addition, teachers and diagnostic staff collaborate to develop an extensive learning profile and management plan for each student, which they use to identify and build on student strengths rather than focus only on identified disabilities.

Administrators at the Academies credit this focus for allowing them to foster success among diverse and complex learners. With a less than 1 percent dropout rate and a 100 percent promotion rate, the Academies has been asked by educators at other charter schools to provide them with training on ways to more effectively serve exceptional children.

The British School of Bern, Bern, Switzerland

www.britishschool.ch

The British School of Bern is a small international day school that serves 100 students ages three to twelve years who come from a variety of nationalities and cultures. After sending a single faculty member to attend a Schools Attuned to All Kinds of Minds course, head teacher Enid Potts realized she'd found an approach that closely fit her own views on learning variation; in 2005 she participated in the course.

Enid then recruited more of the school's teachers to attend a Schools Attuned course in Geneva. With more than half the faculty now trained, the team routinely integrates the approach into lesson planning, teaching, and assessment. While they draw on their learning profile knowledge to target particular interventions for students who are struggling, faculty members agree that the practice of considering how individual students learn benefits all their students.

The school has also used the approach as a way to directly engage students and parents in supporting learning. Older students participate in activities and lessons that introduce them to neurodevelopmental terms, encourage them to explore their own learning strengths and weaknesses, and to be respectful of those of others. In an effort to facilitate and build collaboration between teachers and parents, the school also offers workshops for parents to introduce them to the All Kinds of Minds philosophy and vocabulary and to equip them with ideas on how they can better support student learning outside of the classroom.

Enid and her staff credit their work with All Kinds of Minds for fostering their development as professional educators. "The initial course gave us input, inspiration and insight into re-evaluating our own methodologies of teaching," Enid notes. "Moreover, it gave us practical support in developing and maintaining relationships with students and parents."

Forsyth Country Day School, Lewisville, North Carolina

www.fcds.org

In 2002, three teachers from Forsyth Country Day School (FCDS), a private K–12 school in Lewisville, North Carolina, attended a Schools Attuned to All Kinds of Minds course. Excited about the prospect of using the All Kinds of Minds approach to address students whose learning challenges were occasionally puzzling, they eagerly met with FCDS headmaster, Henry Battle, to share their discovery. Henry had recently led the school's efforts to open its Johnson Academic Center as part of his agenda to build the school's focus on individualizing instruction to meet the needs of every one of its 948 students. He immediately saw the fit between his school goals and the All Kinds of Minds philosophy.

Henry and the faculty decided to work toward having all faculty members participate in a Schools Attuned course and to require all new hires to complete the training within three years. They also began the application process for FCDS to become one of a limited number of Professional Development Providers selected by All Kinds of Minds to deliver its courses regionally. The three lead teachers planned and lead monthly information sessions to engage parents and other community members in conversations about the neurodevelopmental constructs and their implications for better understanding students.

The staff continue to find new ways to implement the All Kinds of Minds approach into their instruction. For example, Forsyth's curriculum maps are all aligned with the neurodevelopmental constructs in that teachers apply a neurodevelopmental lens to the concept and content of what they teach, how they teach it (the strategies and activities they employ), and the skills students are expected to master. In addition, all faculty members are required to reflect on their work with the program in their yearly evaluations. Through these practices, they continue to deepen their comfort level with neurodevelopmental content and terminology. Henry says that the Schools Attuned program has made a substantial impact on the school, "in terms of the way we reach students, the way we communicate with parents, and frankly, the way we attract families."

Fort Worth Academy, Fort Worth, Texas

www.fwacademy.org

Fort Worth Academy is a private, independent school serving 245 students in grades K–8. Dedicated to providing a "collaborative environment of academic challenge and individual attention so students prosper as learners and citizens," Fort Worth Academy offers an accelerated curriculum and classes that are limited to fifteen students.

Since 2001, participation in the Schools Attuned to All Kinds of Minds course has been a condition of employment for teachers. Head of School Bill Broderick and one of his associate heads serve as members of All Kinds of Minds' national faculty, and the school hosts most of the All Kinds of Minds courses offered in northern Texas each summer.

"Every decision made at Fort Worth Academy is student-centered and based on the following question: 'What is best for *this* child at *this* time?'" Bill notes. "Going through Schools Attuned gives our teachers a sense of compassion and understanding for all students, which is central to our school values, and the confidence that there really are tools out there to help them work with those students with more complex learning needs."

Understanding of the neurodevelopmental framework drove the school's decision to become a one-to-one laptop school in 2007.

Bill explains that he and the faculty view technology as an essential supplement to their efforts to accommodate and intervene with students struggling with learning breakdowns. "Kids who struggle with graphomotor issues can take notes on the computer tablet, which translates their handwriting into computer text. For kids who struggle with organization, the laptops autosave documents so they don't lose things and provide other tools to keep them organized. With technology, these issues are no longer barriers to learning—and success—for these students in the classroom."

Public School 23, The New Children's School, Bronx, New York

http://ps23bronx.org

P.S. 23 serves more than 500 students in grades pre-K through 2 in a largely Hispanic area of the Bronx. The school has been listed in *New York City's Best Public Elementary Schools: A Parent's Guide.*

Since 2004, more than twenty teachers and administrators at the school have participated in a Schools Attuned course. Initially attracted to All Kinds of Minds as a way to help them better support their high proportion of special education students, both general education and out-of-classroom specialists at P.S. 23 agree that the training provided them with a framework and tools to look at students differently.

Teacher Rebecca Odessey notes, "Looking at how children approach learning, how they organize their tasks, and how they strategize to accomplish tasks and problem-solve gives us as educators an important lens to look through so we may better support our students. Endless possibilities are inherent in the process, as we unpack children's strengths and support their potential, to help them move beyond where we currently assess them to be."

The school's Inquiry Team has employed the All Kinds of Minds training to hone in on a cluster of students held over in first grade, some who had been held back several times. Using the Attuning a

Student protocol, the team generated learning profiles for each of the students in the group. The profiles provided the team with a basis for collaboration around reading-focused management strategies, including a creative intervention that leveraged a student's affinity for Hannah Montana song lyrics. The team's approach proved successful, all of the students were promoted to second grade, and many began performing above grade level in their classes.

Taft Middle School, Oklahoma City, Oklahoma

www.okcps.k12.ok.us/ms/Taft/

Taft Middle School, a public school in inner-city Oklahoma City, serves some 850 students in grades 6 through 8, more than 90 percent of whom are eligible for free or reduced-price lunches. In 2006, Principal Lisa Johnson told her staff she wanted to find and implement a schoolwide program to help them address the needs of the school's low-performing students.

Taft math teacher and 2009 Oklahoma Teacher of the Year Heather Sparks recalls, "The first program we tried didn't take root; we just didn't see a real connection with the learning issues we were seeing in our kids, many of whom come from very challenging situations."

The following summer, with support from a state grant, a cohort of Taft teachers participated in the Schools Attuned to All Kinds of Minds course, and during the next two years the rest of the school's seventy-plus faculty members took the course.

Faculty members credit the training for giving them a common language they now use when sharing observations and ideas about individual students, as well as tools that facilitate their ability to collaborate around student interventions, both across subject areas and as students move from grade to grade. With the assistance of Title I dollars, faculty at each grade level have taken on roles as "profile advisors" to coordinate and serve as resources on the development of learning management plans for students identified as needing help.

Lisa, the principal, notes, "Prior to implementing Schools Attuned as a schoolwide model, our intervention strategy was inconsistent and varied from teacher to teacher. Furthermore, intervention plans were often limited in scope and did not include strategies specifically tied to the root of the student's difficulties. The training gave us a great diagnostic tool, as well as practices that can be used by teachers, students, and families to help students be successful at school and at home."

APPENDIX C

The Effects of the Schools Attuned Program:
A Snapshot of Research Results

All Kinds of Minds (AKOM) has established four research activities to distinguish the programs offered by the Institute:

1. Establishing and updating a knowledge base for all AKOM program content and design grounded in findings from scientific, clinical and educational research,
2. Disseminating this knowledge base through programs, products, and communications developed by the institute,
3. Stimulating and supporting a growing body of evidence (outcomes research) about the effects of AKOM programs that provides an increasingly clear and complete understanding of our program impact, the strengths and weaknesses alike, and
4. Evaluating the quality of our programs to guide further design and delivery to maximize potential for positive effects.

Research Results

Following is a snapshot of outcomes research conducted from 2000 to 2007 on the effects of AKOM's Schools Attuned program. This program consisted of forty-five hours of facilitator-led instruction, use of a proprietary observational tool and process called "Attuning a Student," and online follow-up support resources. These studies looked at effects of the program on teacher practice and behaviors, on indicators and measures of student success and school practices and policies.

Results for Students: Predictors of Academic Success

- *More positive attitudes about school.* 91 percent of teachers in the UMASS (University of Massachusetts) study and 100 percent of teachers in the New York City Project reported improved student attitudes. WestEd study Schools Attuned educators reported improvements in students' attitudes toward school that would enhance long-term positive outcomes for students.
- *Increased confidence in abilities and self-understanding.* 84 percent of Schools Attuned students in the Oklahoma study reported increases in their confidence and self-understanding. 91 percent of teachers in the UMASS study attributed improved student self-confidence to Schools Attuned.
- *Increased engagement in learning.* Students of Schools Attuned-trained teachers in the Westat study had significantly higher engagement scores than those of their peers and showed significant growth in participation during class.
- *Improved behavior in class.* 74 percent of teachers in the New York City Department of Education study reported increased time on-task among students. Schools in Texas and New Jersey elementary studies reported 30–45 percent decreases in disciplinary referrals due to Schools Attuned.

Results for Students: Academic Skills, Test Scores, and Grades

- Schools Attuned teachers in the Westat study reported statistically significant gains for students in reading/language arts, mathematics, and critical thinking.
- Third- to sixth-grade Schools Attuned students in the Fort Worth District study showed statistically significant higher gains than non–Schools Attuned students on reading and math standardized test scores.
- 79 percent of teachers surveyed in the UMASS study reported small positive effects on student course grades and standardized test scores due to Schools Attuned.
- Course grade improvements were documented for students in the North Carolina study in reading (59 percent improvement), language arts (57 percent improvement), and mathematics (47 percent improvement).

Results for Teachers: Finding Pathways to Student Success

- *Better understanding of students as learners.* 80-100 percent of teachers across the New York City Department of Education, Montecito School District, and Park Tudor School studies reported increased understanding of their students due to Schools Attuned.
- *Greater efficacy to work with diverse learners.* Schools Attuned–trained teachers in the Westat study scored above comparison teachers on self-efficacy for instructional strategies (+.18) and classroom management (+.10). In classroom observations, WestEd study researchers rated Schools Attuned teachers as using significantly more instructional tools for working with diverse learners than non–Schools Attuned teachers.
- *Improved use of strategies to overcome barriers to student learning.* 80-91 percent of teachers in the New York City Department of Education and New York Jewish Day School studies reported increases in their ability to create educational plans and select strategies to improve academic achievement of their students.

Schools Attuned–trained teachers in the WestEd study were statistically significantly more likely than non–Schools Attuned teachers to initiate assistance or help to students, provide clear expectations to students, encourage active participation from all, and better manage disruptions in the classroom.

Results for Schools: In-School Practices, Teacher Collaboration, and Alliances with Families

- *Improved schoolwide collaboration.* 75 percent of teachers in the Westat study reported using Schools Attuned to collaborate with colleagues on student learning. Schools Attuned training provided schools in the WestEd study with a common language and a way to describe children that all staff members understood, and improved teachers' communication and collaboration around student learning.

- *Improved use of special education resources.* 98 percent of teachers in the Sulphur Springs District study reported that Schools Attuned has made them more willing to teach students with learning disabilities and learning needs. Results in this same study showed a 78 percent decrease in pull-out services (when students leave their classrooms to get assistance from a special education teacher), and a special education placement accuracy increase from 63 percent to 97 percent, meaning that special education assessments were being directed more accurately to the students who need special services most. 50–72 percent decreases in special education referrals were seen across other schools in Texas, California, New Jersey, and Ohio.

- *Stronger alliances between schools and families.* 87 percent of teachers in the UMASS study reported improved parent-teacher relationships through the use of Schools Attuned. Schools Attuned teachers in the WestEd study had statistically significantly higher ratings for parent and community involvement than non–Schools Attuned teachers, including collaboration with parents around strategies to use at home.

What Does This Mean?

These twenty-three studies, combined with the program evaluation annually conducted by All Kinds of Minds, establish an accumulated body of evidence that creates a compelling story of the impact of the Schools Attuned program. Bottom line: the evidence shows that, when implemented, this program has positive effects on teacher, student, and school practice outcomes.

Comprehensive materials about these research studies are available at www.allkindsofminds.org.

References

Ashmore, B. A. (2005). *Schools Attuned: A report of classroom implementation based on teacher self-reporting.* Austin: Texas Business & Education Coalition.

Ashmore, B. A., & Holcombe, L. W. (2007). *Investigational study of Schools Attuned-trained teachers and their students in Ft. Worth Independent School District.* Dallas: University of Texas at Dallas.

Bontempi, E., & Nash, S. S. (2002). *Oklahoma Schools Attuned 2002 program evaluation.* Norman, OK: Education Evaluation Associates. Retrieved February 8, 2007, from www.beyondutopia.net/akom/results.

Combs, J. P., & Jackson, S. H. (2006). *Program evaluation report for Project STYLE (Students and Teachers Yearning to Learn Effectively).* Sulphur Springs, TX: Sulphur Springs Independent School District.

Crandell, S. (2005). *Schools Attuned training: Teachers' survey.* Santa Barbara, CA: Orfalea Family Foundation.

Dyson, A. L. (2007). *Exploring teacher change in response to a professional development program.* Unpublished doctoral dissertation, University of North Carolina, Chapel Hill, NC.

Fiore, T. A., Wilaby, M., & Munk, T. (2006). *A research study to measure the impact of Schools Attuned on special education.* Durham, NC: WESTAT.

Gates, G. S. (2002). *Evaluation report: Project STYLE.* Sulphur Springs, TX: Sulphur Springs Independent School District.

Harman, A. E. (2006). *A better way of doing business: Embracing student strengths to improve teaching and learning. An initial evaluation of the Schools Attuned Program in the New York City public school system.* Chapel Hill, NC: All Kinds of Minds.

Hendrickson, L. (2005). *Schools Attuned opinion survey summary report.* Lafayette: Indiana Design Consortium.

Lightfoot, A. (2007). *A portraiture study of the Student Success Program at P.S. 246.* Chapel Hill, NC: All Kinds of Minds.

O'Sullivan, R. (2001). *Schools Attuned: Effects on educators and students*. Chapel Hill, NC: O'Sullivan and Associates, Evaluation, Assessment, & Policy Connections.

O'Sullivan, R. (2002). *North Carolina Schools Attuned: 2001 outcome information*. Chapel Hill, NC: O'Sullivan & Associates.

Ort, S. W. (2003). *Schools Attuned program evaluation 2003: The report card study*. Chapel Hill, NC: All Kinds of Minds.

Pack, G. (2002). *Schools Attuned Jewish Day School evaluation report*. Chapel Hill, NC: All Kinds of Minds and Nash Foundation.

Sireci, S. G., & Keller, L. A. (2007). *Evaluating the effects of Schools Attuned on teaching practices and student achievement*. Amherst: University of Massachusetts Amherst Center for Educational Assessment.

Tushnet, N. C., Herpin, S. A., McCormick, T., et al. (2007). *Schools Attuned and mentor applications of Schools Attuned: Final study report*. San Francisco: WestEd.

Wolfe, A. (2004). *Comprehensive school reform grant evaluation (Cycle 1) Scio Central School*. Olean, NY: Cattaraugus-Allegany BOCES.

Various authors. (2003–2007). *Action research on special education outcomes in California, Ohio, New Jersey, and Texas schools*.

Programs from All Kinds of Minds

All Kinds of Minds currently offers the following professional development programs geared toward helping educators create a constructive learning environment for all students.

Understanding Learning and Learners

A 1-Day "Overview" Workshop

This program introduces the All Kinds of Minds approach to helping educators understand how students learn and how this knowledge can help teachers more effectively manage diverse learning needs among their students. Perfect for school leaders and educators who want to understand our concepts at a "basic level." Participants take away a few next-day activities to use in their classrooms.

Teaching All Kinds of Minds

The Most Popular Program

This three-day course illustrates how strengths and weaknesses within various areas of brain function affect student performance and provides next-day activities and tools for classroom implementation. Case studies and hands-on activities demonstrate how to observe and identify students' learning profiles as well as how to select strategies for classroom use. Participants also become more aware of their own learning profile, and how their profile influences their efficacy with different learners. Appropriate for grades K–12; curriculum is suited to mixed grade-level groupings. This course is ideal for a broad range of educators interested in differentiating their instruction to reach the greatest number of learners.

Schools Attuned to All Kinds of Minds

The Most In-Depth and Content-Rich Program

This three-day course explores in depth the eight neurodevelopmental constructs and addresses how to use this knowledge to pinpoint and address learning breakdowns. A must for "learning leaders" who want to gain knowledge to lead or build a "learning expertise" team within their school. Two different tracks address implementation at the elementary and secondary school levels.

Tools for Learning Success

Graduates of either the three-day course or the classic five-day course can also select from more than a dozen modules included in the new Tools for Learning Success catalog. Designed to help educators and schools deepen and implement their knowledge about the science of learning and its applications, these modules address such topics as lesson analysis and parent engagement in student learning.

For more information about these and other All Kinds of Minds programs, visit www.allkindsofminds.org.

APPENDIX E

All Kinds of Minds Web Site Resources

Visit All Kinds of Minds online at www.allkindsofminds.org, where you'll find the following resources:

- *Discussion guide.* Download this free guide to use individually as you read this book or as part of a shared professional learning experience.
- *Learning Leadership in Action.* Download any of the professional development activities and templates that are located at the conclusion of the chapters.
- *Classroom materials and activities.* Download materials that are reproducible for your classroom and work with individual students.
- *Information about the All Kinds of Minds research base.* Information includes details regarding research related to All Kinds of Minds program content, program design, and program impact.
- *Parent Toolkit.* This is a collection of resources designed to give parents, caregivers, and educators a better understanding of

learning processes, insights into difficulties, and strategies for responding to difficulties.

- *Resources for continued learning and advocacy.*
  - Monthly e-mail *newsletters*
  - *Articles* related to the All Kinds of Minds approach
  - *Case studies* exploring students' neurodevelopmental profiles and suggested strategies
  - Information about *education policy* that relates to the mission of All Kinds of Minds
  - *LearningBase,* an extensive collection of resources that explores skills that students typically must master, the neurodevelopmental factors that may influence a student's success, common obstacles, and helpful tips
  - *Podcasts* and associated materials

NOTES

INTRODUCTION

1. Vergano, D. "New 'Science of Learning' Could Reinvent Teaching Techniques." *USA Today*, July 22, 2009.

2. Levine, A. "Waiting for the Transformation." *Education Week*, Feb. 25, 2009, pp. 35 and 48.

CHAPTER 1

1. KnowledgeWorks Foundation and Institute for the Future. *2020 Forecast: Creating the Future of Learning*, 2008.

2. Harvey, J., and Housman, N. *Crisis or Possibility: Conversations About the American High School*. Washington, DC: Institute of Educational Leadership, Inc., 2004, p. 12.

3. National Association of Secondary School Principals and the Education Alliance. *Breaking Ranks II: Strategies for Leading High School Reform (Executive Summary)*. Reston, VA: National Association of Secondary School Principals and the Education Alliance, 2004, p. 2.

4. Harvey and Housman, 2004.

5. As early as 1994, the Education Commission of the States and the Charles Dana Foundation convened more than 100 scientists, scholars, and education association leaders on bringing together neuroscience and education. A year later, the nonprofit organization All Kinds of Minds was incorporated to bring neurodevelopmental research to educators, clinicians, and parents to promote better understanding of learning variation. Since the 1980s, scholars such as John Branford and colleagues at National Academy of Sciences, Howard Gardner, Michael Gurian, David Rose, Robert Sternberg, Mel Levine, and Daniel Willingham and

practitioners such as Eric Jensen, Judy Willis, Pat Wolfe, and Renate Nummela Caine and Geoffry Caine, have written and presented about the value of findings from brain research for better understanding of learning and what constitutes intelligence. A new journal called *Mind, Brain, and Education* has emerged out of Harvard University. Yet adoption of insights and findings is still done in an ad hoc manner, and the full benefits of such new research have yet to find the way to the classrooms that could use this information the most. Teacher preparation requirements rarely stipulate that acquiring expertise in this science of learning is essential to becoming a teacher.

6. KnowledgeWorks Foundation, 2008.

7. Coutu, D. "The Science of Thinking Smarter." *Harvard Business Review,* May 2008.

8. Berns, G. *Iconoclast: A Neuroscientist Reveals How to Think Differently.* Boston: Harvard Business School Publishing Corporation, 2008.

9. Pink, D. "Get Ready for the New Age of Individualized Education." *Reason: Free Minds and Free Markets,* October 2001. Retrieved from: www.reason.com/news/show/28174.html.

10. Christensen, C., Horn, M., and Johnson, C. *Disrupting Class: How Disruptive Innovation Will Change the Way the World Learns.* New York: McGraw-Hill, 2008, p. xii.

11. Friedman, T. *The World Is Flat: A Brief History of the Twenty-First Century.* New York: Farrar, Straus and Giroux, 2005.

12. Finn, C. Jr. "Lessons Learned: A Self-Styled Troublemaker Shares Wisdom Gleaned from 57 Years in Education." *Education Week,* Feb. 27, 2008, p. 28.

13. Reeves, D. *The Learning Leader: How to Focus School Improvement for Better Results.* Alexandria, VA: Association for Supervision and Curriculum Development (ASCD), 2006.

14. Hargreaves, A., and Fink, D. *Sustainable Leadership.* San Francisco, CA: Jossey Bass, 2006, p. 40.

15. Delors, J., and others. *Learning: The Treasure Within. Report to the UNESCO of the International Commission on Education for the 21st Century.* Paris: UNESCO, 1996. This report describes four fundamental types of learning, which throughout a persons life, will be the pillars of knowledge. They are consistent with other reports referenced that indicate that "traditional demands for education that are essentially quantitative and knowledge based are no longer appropriate and that each individual must be equipped to seize learning opportunities and adapt to a changing, complex and interdependent world" p. 85.

16. Hargreaves and Fink, pp. 40–43.

17. Hargreaves and Fink, pp. 40–43. Reprinted with permission of John Wiley & Sons, Inc.

18. Council of Chief State School Officers. *Educational Leadership Policy Standards: ISLLC 2008.* Washington, DC: Council of Chief State School Officers, 2008

19. National Association of Independent Schools. *NAIS Opinion Leaders Survey: Forecasting Independent Education to 2025.* Washington DC: National Association of Independent Schools, 2005.

20. National Association of Independent Schools, p. 17.

21. Levine, A. "Waiting for the Transformation." *Education Week*, Feb. 25, 2009, pp. 35 and 48.

22. KnowledgeWorks Foundation and Institute for the Future.

23. Weick, K. "Small Wins: Redefining the Scale of Social Problems." *American Psychologist*, 1984, *39*(2), 40–49.

24. Nelson, G. "Partnerships and the Preparation of Effective Science Teachers." Presentation at the National Comprehensive Center for Teacher Quality. What Works Conference, Washington, DC, Nov. 11, 2008.

CHAPTER 2

1. Vergano, D. "New 'Science of Learning' Could Reinvent Teaching Techniques." *USA Today*, July 22, 2009.

2. Gardner, H. *Intelligence Reframed: Multiple Intelligences for the 21st Century*. New York: Basic Books, 1999.

3. Sternberg, R. J. *Beyond IQ: A Triarchic Theory of Human Intelligence*. New York: Cambridge University, 1985.

4. Flanagan, D. P., McGrew, K. S., and Ortiz, S. *The Wechsler Intelligence Scales and Gf-Gc Theory: A Contemporary Approach to Interpretation*. Needham Heights, MA: Allyn and Bacon, 2000.

5. Rose, D. H., and Meyer, A. *Teaching Every Student in the Digital Age*. Alexandria, VA: ASCD, 2002.

6. Bransford, J. D., Brown, A. L., and Cocking, R. R. "Mind and Brain." In *The Jossey-Bass Reader on the Brain and Learning*. San Francisco: Wiley, 2008, 89–108.

7. *Mind, Brain, and Education* is the title of a new peer-reviewed journal, published beginning in 2007. It is also the title of one of Harvard's graduate program options in the School of Education. The recently formed International Mind, Brain and Education Society (www.imbes.org) aims to create a new field of researchers and educators collaborating on integrating those aspects into research and practice.

8. Fischer, K. W., Bernstein, J. H., and Immordino-Yang, M. H. *Mind, Brain, and Education in Reading Disorders*. New York: Cambridge University Press, 2007.

9. Christensen, C., Horn, M., and Johnson, C. *Disrupting Class: How Disruptive Innovation Will Change the Way the World Learns*. New York: McGraw-Hill, 2008, p. 10.

10. In his book *Why Don't Students Like School? A Cognitive Scientist Answers Questions About How the Mind Works and What It Means for the Classroom* (Jossey-Bass, 2009), Daniel Willingham argues that no one has found consistent evidence supporting a theory of learning or cognitive styles (p. 113). We respect his viewpoint and contributions to the field of cognitive science and classroom practice and find much in common with the recommendations and nine principles in his book. We point out that the intent of using a neurodevelopmental framework is not to assign a label or type of learning style using this terminology to students. Rather it is a way of organizing research findings from the brain, mind, and learning to contribute to helping teachers know how best to target and differentiate instructional strategies for struggling students.

11. Coyne, P., and others. "Applying Universal Design for Learning in the Classroom." In D. H. Rose and A. Meyer (Eds.), *A Practical Reader in Universal Design for Learning.* Cambridge, MA: Harvard Education, 2006, 1-13.

12. Christensen, Horn, and Johnson, 2008, p. 10.

13. Riccio, C. A., and Hynd, G. W. "Contributions of Neuropsychology to Our Understanding of Developmental Reading Problems." *School Psychology Review,* 1995, *24,* 415-425.

14. Imbo, I., and Vandierendonck, A. "The Development of Strategy Use in Elementary School Children: Working Memory and Individual Differences." *Journal of Experimental Child Psychology,* 2007, *96,* 284-309.

15. Taub, G., McGrew, K., and Keith, T. "Improvements in Interval Time Tracking and Effects on Reading Achievement." *Psychology in the Schools,* 2007, *44,* 849-863.

16. Brauer, J., and Friederici, A. "Functional Neural Networks of Semantic and Syntactic Processes in the Developing Brain." *Journal of Cognitive Neuroscience,* 2007, *19,* 609-1623.

17. Berends, I., and Reitsma, P. "Orthographic Analysis of Words During Fluency Training Promotes Reading of New Similar Words." *Journal of Research in Reading,* 2007, *30,* 129-139.

18. van Garderen, D. "Spatial Visualization, Visual Imagery, and Mathematical Problem Solving of Students with Varying Abilities." *Journal of Learning Disabilities,* 2006, *39,* 496-506.

19. Rosen, P., Milich, R., and Harris, M. "Victims of Their Own Cognitions: Implicit Social Cognitions, Emotional Distress, and Peer Victimization." *Journal of Applied Developmental Psychology,* 2007, *28,* 211-226.

20. Tenenbaum, H., Alfieri, L., Brooks, P., and Dunne, G. "The Effects of Explanatory Conversation on Children's Emotion Understanding." *British Journal of Developmental Psychology,* 2008, *26,* 249-263.

21. Stecker, P. M., Fuchs, L. S., and Fuchs, D. "Using Curriculum-Based Measurement to Improve Student Achievement: Review of Research." *Psychology in the Schools,* 2005, *42,* 795-819.

22. Lyon, G. R., and others. "Rethinking Learning Disabilities." In C. E. Finn, A. J. Rotherham, and C. R. Hokanson (Eds.), *Rethinking Special Education for a New Century.* Washington, DC: Thomas B. Fordham Foundation and the Progressive Policy Institute, 2001.

23. Gibb, G. S., and Wilder, L. K. "Using Functional Analysis to Improve Reading Instruction for Students with Learning Disabilities and Emotional/Behavioral Disorders." *Preventing School Failure,* 2002, *46,* 152-157.

24. Raskind, M. H., Goldberg, R. J., Higgins, F. L., and Herman, K. L. "Patterns of Change and Predictors of Success in Individuals with Learning Disabilities: Results from a Twenty-Year Longitudinal Study." *Learning Disabilities Research and Practice,* 1999, *14,* 35-49.

25. Werner, E. E., and Smith, R. S. *Overcoming the Odds: High Risk Children from Birth to Adulthood.* New York: Cornell University Press, 1992.

26. Brooks, R., and Goldstein, S. *Raising Resilient Children: Fostering Strength, Hope, and, Optimism in Your Child.* New York: McGraw-Hill, 2001.

27. Seligman, M.E.P., and Csikszentmihalyi, M. "Positive Psychology: An Introduction." *American Psychologist,* 2000, *55,* 5–14.

28. Pohlman, C. *Revealing Minds: Assessing to Understand and Support Struggling Learners.* San Francisco: Jossey-Bass, 2008.

29. Brooks and Goldstein, 2001.

30. Kolic-Vehovec, S., and Bajsanski, I. "Metacognitive Strategies and Reading Comprehension in Elementary-School Students." *European Journal of Psychology of Education,* 2006, *21,* 439–451.

31. Garrett, A., Mazzocco, M., and Baker, L. "Development of the Metacognitive Skills of Prediction and Evaluation in Children with or Without Math Disability." *Learning Disabilities Research and Practice,* 2006, *21,* 77–88.

32. Raskind, Goldberg, Higgins, and Herman, 1999.

33. Raskind, Goldberg, Higgins, and Herman, 1999.

34. Brooks, R., and Goldstein, S. *The Power of Resilience: Achieving Balance, Confidence, and Personal Strength in Your Life.* New York: McGraw-Hill, 2004.

35. Werner, E. E., and Smith, R. S. *Journeys from Childhood to the Midlife: Risk, Resilience, and Recovery.* New York: Cornell University Press, 2001.

CHAPTER 3

1. Levine, M. D. *Developmental Variation and Learning Disorders* (2nd ed.). Cambridge, MA: Educators Publishing Service, 1998. And Levine, M. D. *A Mind at a Time.* New York: Simon and Schuster, 2002.

2. Posner, M. I., and Rothbart, M. K. *Educating the Human Brain.* Washington, DC: American Psychological Association, 2007.

3. Luria, A. R. *The Working Brain: An Introduction to Neuropsychology* (B. Haigh, Trans.). New York: Basic Books, 1973.

4. Levine, 1998.

5. Cohen, N. J. *Language Impairment and Psychopathology in Infants, Children, and Adolescents.* Thousand Oaks, CA: Sage, 2001.

6. Evans, J. J., Floyd, R. G., McGrew, K. S., and Leforgee, M. H. "The Relations Between Measures of Cattell-Horn-Carroll (CHC) Cognitive Abilities and Reading Achievement During Childhood and Adolescence." *School Psychology Review,* 2001, *31,* 246–262.

7. Ashbaker, M. H., and Swanson, H. L. "Short-Term Memory and Working Memory Operations and Their Contributions to Reading in Adolescents with and Without Learning Disabilities." *Learning Disabilities Research and Practice,* 1996, *11,* 206–213.

8. Denckla, M. B. "Biological Correlates of Learning and Attention: What Is Relevant to Learning Disability and Attention-Deficit Hyperactivity Disorder?" *Developmental and Behavioral Pediatrics,* 1996, *17,* 114–119.

9. Prutting, C. A., and Kirchner, D. M. "A Clinical Appraisal of the Pragmatic Aspects of Language." *Journal of Speech and Hearing Disorders,* 1987, *52,* 105–119.

10. Prutting and Kirchner, 1987.

11. Cohen, 2001.

12. Prutting and Kirchner, 1987.

13. Blake, R. and Shiffrar, M. "Perception of Human Motion." *Annual Review of Psychology,* 2007, *58,* 47–73.

14. Pohlman, C. *Revealing Minds: Assessing to Understand and Support Struggling Learners.* San Francisco: Jossey-Bass, 2008.

15. Brooks, R., and Goldstein, S. *Raising Resilient Children: Fostering Strength, Hope, and, Optimism in Your Child.* New York: McGraw-Hill, 2001.

16. Gardner, H. *Intelligence Reframed: Multiple Intelligences for the Twenty-First Century.* New York: Basic Books, 1999.

17. Gardner, 1999.

18. Carroll, J. B. *Human Cognitive Abilities: A Survey of Factor Analytic Studies.* New York: Cambridge University Press, 1993.

19. Flanagan, D. P., McGrew, K. S., and Ortiz, S. *The Wechsler Intelligence Scales and Gf-Gc Theory: A Contemporary Approach to Interpretation.* Needham Heights, MA: Allyn and Bacon, 2000.

20. Luria, 1973.

21. Das, J. P., Naglieri, J. A., and Kirby, J. R. *Assessment of Cognitive Processes: The PASS Theory of Intelligence.* Needham Heights, MA: Allyn and Bacon, 1994.

22. Rose, D. H., and Meyer, A. *Teaching Every Student in the Digital Age.* Alexandria, VA: ASCD, 2002.

23. Brandeis, D., and others. "Multicenter P300 Brain Mapping of Impaired Attention to Cues in Hyperkinetic Children." *Journal of the American Academy of Child and Adolescent Psychiatry,* 2002, *41,* 990–998.

24. Calhoun, S. L., and Mayes, S. D. "Processing Speed in Children with Clinical Disorders." *Psychology in the Schools,* 2005, *42,* 333–343.

25. Leech, R., Aydelott, J., Symons, G., Carnevale, J., and Dick, F. "The Development of Sentence Interpretation: Effects of Perceptual, Attentional and Semantic Interference." *Developmental Science,* 2007, *10,* 794–813.

26. Savage, R., Cornish, K., Manly, T., and Hollis, C. "Cognitive Processes in Children's Reading and Attention: The Role of Working Memory, Divided Attention, and Response Inhibition." *British Journal of Psychology,* 2006, *97,* 365–385.

27. Blakemore, S. "Brain Development During Adolescence." *Education Review,* 2007, *20,* 82–90.

28. Glaser, C., and Brunstein, J. C. "Improving Fourth-Grade Students' Composition Skills: Effects of Strategy Instruction and Self-Regulation Procedures." *Journal of Educational Psychology,* 2007, *99,* 297–310.

29. Araz, G., and Sungur, S. "The Interplay Between Cognitive and Motivational Variables in a Problem-Based Learning Environment." *Learning and Individual Differences,* 2007, *17,* 291–297.

30. Paik, S., Cho, B., and Go, Y. "Korean 4 to 11 Year-Old Student Conceptions of Heat and Temperature." *Journal of Research in Science Teaching,* 2007, *44,* 284–302.

31. Amsterlaw, J. "Children's Beliefs about Everyday Reasoning." *Child Development,* 2006, *77,* 443–464.

32. Katzir, T., and others. "Reading Fluency: The Whole Is More Than the Parts." *Annals of Dyslexia,* 2006, *56,* 51–82.

33. Nagy, W., Berninger, V., and Abbott, R. "Contributions of Morphology Beyond Phonology to Literacy Outcomes of Upper Elementary and Middle-School Students." *Journal of Educational Psychology,* 2006, *98,* 134–147.

34. Booth, J., Bebko, G., Burmana, D., and Bitan, T. "Children with Reading Disorder Show Modality Independent Brain Abnormalities During Semantic Tasks." *Neuropsychologia,* 2007, *45,* 775–783.

35. Johnson, D. J. "Relationships Between Oral and Written Language." *School Psychology Review,* 1993, *22,* 595–609.

36. Saddler, B., Asaro, K., and Behforooz, B. "The Effects of Peer-Assisted Sentence-Combining Practice on Four Young Writers with Learning Disabilities." *Learning Disabilities: A Contemporary Journal,* 2008, *6,* 17–31.

37. Windfuhr, K. L., and Snowling, M. J. "The Relationship Between Paired Associate Learning and Phonological Skills in Normally Developing Readers." *Journal of Experimental Child Psychology,* 2001, *80,* 160–173.

38. Woodward, J. "Developing Automaticity in Multiplication Facts: Integrating Strategy Instruction with Timed Practice Drills." *Learning Disability Quarterly,* 2006, *29,* 269–289.

39. Riggs, K., McTaggart, J., Simpson, A., and Freeman, R. "Changes in the Capacity of Visual Working Memory in 5- to 10-year-olds." *Journal of Experimental Child Psychology,* 2006, *95,* 18–26.

40. Ackerman, P., Beier, M., and Boyle, M. "Working Memory and Intelligence: The Same or Different Constructs?" *Psychological Bulletin,* 2005, *131,* 30–60.

41. Graham, S., Struck, M., Santoro, J., and Berninger, V. W. "Dimensions of Good and Poor Handwriting Legibility in First and Second Graders: Motor Programs, Visual-Spatial Arrangement, and Letter Formation Parameter Setting." *Developmental Neuropsychology,* 2006, *29,* 43–60.

42. Rosenblum, S., Dvorkin, A. Y., and Weiss, P.L. "Automatic Segmentation as a Tool for Examining the Handwriting Process of Children with Dysgraphic and Proficient Handwriting." *Human Movement Science,* 2006, *25,* 608–621.

43. van Mier, H. "Developmental Differences in Drawing Performance of the Dominant and Non-Dominant Hand in Right-Handed Boys and Girls." *Human Movement Science,* 2006, *25,* 657–677.

44. Contreras-Vidal, J. "Development of Forward Models for Hand Localization and Movement Control in 6- to 10-year-old Children." *Human Movement Science,* 2006, *25,* 634–645.

45. Williams, J., Thomas, P., Maruff, P., Wilson, P. "The Link Between Motor Impairment Level and Motor Imagery Ability in Children with Developmental Coordination Disorder." *Human Movement Science,* 2008, *27,* 270–285.

46. Bar-Haim, Y., and Bart, O. "Motor Function and Social Participation in Kindergarten Children." *Social Development,* 2006, *15,* 296–310.

47. Holtgraves, T. M., and Kashima, Y. "Language, Meaning, and Social Cognition." *Personality and Social Psychology Review*, 2008, *12*, 73–94.

48. Sandstrom, M. J, and Herlan, R. "Threatened Egotism or Confirmed Inadequacy? How Children's Perceptions of Social Status Influence Aggressive Behavior Toward Peers." *Journal of Social and Clinical Psychology*, 2007, *26*, 240–267.

49. van Garderen, D. "Spatial Visualization, Visual Imagery, and Mathematical Problem Solving of Students with Varying Abilities." *Journal of Learning Disabilities*, 2006, *39*, 496–506.

50. Mammarella, I., and others. "Evidence for a Double Dissociation Between Spatial-Simultaneous and Spatial-Sequential Working Memory in Visuospatial (Nonverbal) Learning Disabled Children." *Brain and Cognition*, 2006, *62*, 58–67.

51. Stanford, M. S., and Barratt, E. S. "Verbal Skills, Finger Tapping, and Cognitive Tempo Define a Second-Order Factor of Temporal Information Processing." *Brain and Cognition*, 1996, *31*, 35–45.

52. Parmentier, F.B.R., Andres, P., Elford, G., and Jones, D. M. "Organization of Visio-Spatial Serial Memory: Interaction of Temporal Order with Spatial and Temporal Grouping." *Psychological Research*, 2006, *70*, 200–217.

53. Claus, B., and Kelter, S. "Comprehending Narratives Containing Flashback: Evidence for Temporally Organized Representations." *Journal of Experimental Psychology*, 2006, *32*, 1031–1044.

54. Alexander, J., and others. "Relations Between Intelligence and the Development of Metaconceptual Knowledge." *Metacognition Learning*, 2006, *1*, 51–67.

55. Kolic-Vehovec, S., and Bajsanski, I. "Metacognitive Strategies and Reading Comprehension in Elementary-School Students." *European Journal of Psychology of Education*, 2006, *21*, 439–451.

CHAPTER 4

1. Reeves, D. *The Learning Leader: How to Focus School Improvement for Better Results.* Alexandria, VA: ASCD, 2006, p 14.

2. Earl, L. *Assessment as Learning: Using Classroom Assessment to Maximize Student Learning.* Thousand Oaks, CA: Corwin Press, 2003.

3. Marzano, R. "Setting the Record Straight on High Yield Strategies," *Kappan*, Sept. 2009, *91*(1), 30–37.

4. City, E., Elmore, R., Fiarman, S., and Tetel, L. *Instructional Rounds in Education: A Network Approach to Improving Teaching and Learning.* Cambridge, MA: Harvard Education Press, 2009.

5. Olsen, K. *Wounded by School: Recapturing the Joy in Learning and Standing Up to Old School Culture.* New York: Teachers College Press, 2009, p. 15.

CHAPTER 5

1. Partnership for 21st Century Skills. *The Intellectual and Policy Foundations of the 21st Century Skills Framework.* Tucson, AZ, 2007. Retrieved from www.21stcenturyskills .org/route21/images/stories/epapers/skills_foundations_final.pdf.

Chapter 6

1. Hall, C. W., and others. "Perception of Nonverbal Social Cues by Regular Education, ADHD, ADHD/LD Students." *Psychology in the Schools,* 1999, *36,* 505–514.

2. Loeber, R. "Development and Risk Factors of Juvenile Antisocial Behavior and Delinquency." *Clinical Psychology Review,* 1990, *10,* 1–41.

3. Hartley, E. T., Bray, M. A., and Kehle, T. J. "Self-Modeling as an Intervention to Increase Classroom Participation." *Psychology in the Schools,* 1998, *35,* 363–372.

4. Vallance, D. D., Cummings, R L., and Humphries, T. "Mediators of the Risk for Problem Behavior in Children with Language Learning Disabilities." *Journal of Learning Disabilities,* 1998, *31,* 160–171.

5. McCabe, P. C. "Social and Behavioral Correlates of Preschoolers with Specific Language Impairment." *Psychology in the Schools,* 2005, *42,* 373–387.

6. Berninger, V. W., and others. "Tier 1 and Tier 2 Early Intervention for Handwriting and Composing." *Journal of School Psychology,* 2006, *44,* 3–30.

7. Dodge, K. "Social Cognition and Children's Aggressive Behavior." *Child Development,* 1980, *51,* 162–170.

8. de Castro, B. O., and others. "Hostile Attribution of Intent and Aggressive Behavior: A Meta-Analysis." *Child Development,* 2002, *73,* 916–934.

9. Rosen, P., Milich, R., and Harris, M. "Victims of Their Own Cognitions: Implicit Social Cognitions, Emotional Distress, and Peer Victimization." *Journal of Applied Developmental Psychology,* 2007, *28,* 211–226.

10. Sandstrom, M. J, and Herlan, R. "Threatened Egotism or Confirmed Inadequacy? How Children's Perceptions of Social Status Influence Aggressive Behavior Toward Peers." *Journal of Social and Clinical Psychology,* 2007, *26,* 240–267.

11. Bauminger, N., Edelsztein, H. S., and Morash, J. "Social Information Processing and Emotional Understanding in Children with LD." *Journal of Learning Disabilities,* 2005, *38,* 45–61.

12. Elias, M. J. "The Connection Between Social-Emotional Learning and Learning Disabilities: Implications for Intervention." *Learning Disability Quarterly,* 2004, *27,* 53–63.

13. Eslinger, P. J. "Conceptualizing, Describing, and Measuring Components of Executive Function: A Summary." In G. R. Lyon and N. A. Krasnegor (Eds.), *Attention, Memory, and Executive Function* (pp. 367–395). Baltimore: Brookes, 1996.

14. Kravetz, S., Faust, M., and Lipshitz, S. "LD, Interpersonal Understanding, and Social Behavior in the Classroom." *Journal of Learning Disabilities,* 1999, *32,* 248–255.

15. Eslinger, 1996.

16. Eslinger, 1996.

17. Logan, L. *Are We Teaching Potential Entrepreneurs in the Best Way to Enhance their Career Success?* London: Cass Business School, City University, 2007.

CHAPTER 7

1. The National Commission on Writing. *Writing and School Reform*. (NCW publication No. 060301855). New York: The National Commission on Writing, 2006. Retrieved from http://www.writingcommission.org/prod_downloads/writing-com/writing-school-reform-natl-comm-writing.pdf.

2. Chute, E. "New Slant on Writing Encourages Participation." *Pittsburgh Post-Gazette*, Feb. 23, 2009.

3. Levine, M. *The Myth of Laziness*. New York: Simon and Schuster, 2002, p. 7.

4. Reeves, D. *The Learning Leader: How to Focus School Improvement for Better Results*. Alexandria, VA: ASCD, 2006.

5. King, S. *On Writing: A Memoir of the Craft*. New York: Pocket Books, 2002.

6. Reeves, 2006.

7. Tucha, O., Mecklinger, L., Walitza, S., and Lange, K. W. "Attention and Movement Execution During Handwriting." *Human Movement Science*, 2006, *25*, 536–552.

8. Altemeir, L., Jones, J., Abbott, R. D., and Berninger, V. W. "Executive Functions in Becoming Writing Readers and Reading Writers: Note Taking and Report Writing in Third and Fifth Graders." *Developmental Neuropsychology*, 2006, *29*, 161–173.

9. Saddler, B. "Increasing Story-Writing Ability through Self-Regulated Strategy Development: Effects on Young Writers with Learning Disabilities." *Learning Disability Quarterly*, 2006, *29*, 291–305.

10. Johnson, D. J. "Relationships Between Oral and Written Language. *School Psychology Review*, 1993, *22*, 595.

11. Beers, S. F., and Nagy, W. E. "Syntactic Complexity as a Predictor of Adolescent Writing Quality: Which Measures? Which Genre?" *Reading and Writing*, 2007, *22*, 185–200.

12. Olive, T., Kellogg, R. T., and Piolat, A. "Verbal, Visual, and Spatial Working Memory Demands During Text Composition." *Applied Psycholinguistics*, 2008, *29*, 669–687.

13. Olive, T. "Working Memory in Writing: Empirical Evidence from the Dual-Task Technique." *European Psychologist*, 2004, *9*, 32–42.

14. Chartrel, E., and Vinter, A. "The Impact of Spatio-Temporal Constraints on Cursive Letter Handwriting in Children." *Learning and Instruction*, 2008, *18*, 537–547.

15. Berninger, V. W., and others. "Tier 1 And Tier 2 Early Intervention for Handwriting and Composing." *Journal of School Psychology*, 2006, *44*, 3–30.

16. Berninger, V. W., and others. "Early Development of Language by Hand: Composing, Reading, Listening, and Speaking Connections; Three Letter-Writing Modes; and Fast Mapping in Spelling." *Developmental Neuropsychology*, 2006, *29*, 61–92.

17. Goetz, E. T., and others. "The Role of Imagery in the Production of Written Definitions." *Reading Psychology*, 2007, *28*, 241–256.

18. Vallecorsa, A., and DeBettencourt, L. U. "Using a Mapping Procedure to Teach Reading and Writing Skills to Middle Grade Students with Learning Disabilities." *Education and Treatment of Children*, 1997, *20*, 173–188.

19. Baker, W. P., and others. "Writing-To-Learn in the Inquiry-Science Classroom: Effective Strategies from Middle School Science and Writing Teachers." *Clearing House: A Journal of Educational Strategies, Issues and Ideas,* 2008, *81,* 105–108.

20. Midgette, E., Haria, P., MacArthur, C. "The Effects of Content and Audience Awareness Goals for Revision on the Persuasive Essays of Fifth- and Eighth-grade Students." *Reading and Writing,* Feb. 2008, *21*(1–2), 131–151.

21. Olive, Kellogg, and Piolat, 2008.

22. Espin, C., Shin, J., and Deno, S. L. "Identifying Indicators of Written Expression Proficiency for Middle School Students." *Journal of Special Education,* 2000, *34,* 140–153.

23. Troia, G. A., Graham, S., and Harris, K. R. "Teaching Students with Learning Disabilities to Mindfully Plan when Writing." *Exceptional Children,* 1999, *65,* 235–252.

24. Berninger V., and others. "Tier 3 Specialized Writing Instruction for Students with Dyslexia." *Reading and Writing,* Feb. 2008, *21*(1–2), 95–129.

25. Greenwald, E., Persky, H., Campbell, J and Mazzeo, J. *National Assessment of Educational Progress: 1998 Report Card for the Nation and States.* Washington DC: US Department of Education, 1999.

26. Midgette, E., Haria, P., and MacArthur, C., 2008.

27. Online course taught at DePaul University, 2007. Syllabus and course notes by Dr. Carol Wren. Retrieved from: http://condor.depaul.edu/~cwren/courses/other/outmn44/ch10writ.htm.

28. Writing Study Group of the NCTE Executive Committee. *NCTE Beliefs About the Teaching of Writing.* Urbana, IL: National Council of Teachers of English, 2004. Retrieved from: www.ncte.org/positions/statements/writingbeliefs.

29. Duncan, A. "Every Child, Every School." PowerPoint presentation to Chicago Public Schools, Chicago, IL, Sept. 2006.

30. Texas Education Agency. *Texas Assessment of Knowledge and Skills (TAKS) Grade 7 Written Composition Scoring Guide.* Austin: Texas Education Agency, 2006.

CHAPTER 8

1. Levine, M. *A Mind at a Time.* New York: Simon and Schuster, 2002, p. 307.

2. Throughout this book we have referred to the contributions to new ideas for schools and education in a student-centric world from Clayton Christenson and colleagues, Chester Finn, Jr., Tom Friedman, the KnowledgeWorks Foundation, Mel Levine, John Medina, and the Center for Applied Special Technology (CAST). We add George Lucas and his foundation which produces Edutopia (www.edutopia.org), a resource describing schools and teaching that are based on a student-centric approach.

3. Medina, J. *Brain Rules: 12 Principles for Surviving and Thriving at Work, Home and School.* Seattle: Pear Press, 2008, p.67.

4. Friedman, T. *The World Is Flat: A Brief History of the Twenty-First Century.* New York: Farrar, Straus and Giroux, 2005, p. 237.

5. The Partnership for 21st Century Skills (www.21stcenturyskills.org) has developed a framework for 21st century learning that is a basis for many state initiatives. It includes standards, assessment, curriculum and instruction and professional development suggestions.

6. Christensen, C., Johnson, C., and Horn, M. *Disrupting Class: How Disruptive Innovation Will Change the Way the World Learns.* New York: McGraw-Hill, 2008, p. 227.

7. Christensen, Johnson, and Horn, 2008, pp. 207–218. The authors argue for a new concept of school choice, one that is based on finding a school environment that best matches the way a student learns with his or her affinities.

8. More information on how to bring UDL principles to classrooms can be found at www.cast.org.

9. Educators can find examples of cutting-edge use of technology for learning, technology use in schools, and ideas from the leading experts by visiting the following Web sites: www.thefutureofeducation.com, www.marcprensky.com, www.edutopia.com, and the Second Life wiki http://sleducationwikispaces.com.

10. Levine, 2002, pp. 316–317.

11. Levine, M., Swartz, C., and Wakely, M. *The Mind That's Mine: A Program to Help Young Learners Learn About Learning.* New York: Educators Publishing Service, 1997.

12. Levine, M. "The Essential Cognitive Backpack." *Educational Leadership,* 2007, 64(7), 16–22.

13. Levine, 2007.

14. Craig Pohlman describes a comprehensive approach to assessing struggling learners in his book, *Revealing Minds: Assessing to Understand and Support Struggling Learners.* San Francisco: Jossey-Bass, 2008.

15. All Kinds of Minds operated clinical assessment centers in New York and North Carolina until 2007, where more than 5,000 families received in-depth assessments of their child's learning profile. Many of these cases have informed the development of the All Kinds of Minds approach detailed in this book.

16. Levine, 2002, p. 320.

17. Lewis, A. "Washington Commentary: Educating More Americans Requires Broader View of Learning." *Kappan,* 2009, 90(9), 619–620.

18. Crawford, M. *Shop Class as Soulcraft: An Inquiry into the Value of Work.* New York: Penguin, 2009.

INDEX

Page references followed by *fig* indicate an illustrated figure; followed by *t* indicate a table; followed by *e* indicate an exhibit.